THE SECRET GOSPEL

OF THE

VIRGIN MARY

www.edaf.net

MADRID — MÉXICO — BUENOS AIRES — SANTIAGO

2025

Table of contents

Introduction

In 1884, a specialist in ancient manuscripts surprised the world by uncovering a priceless piece of archaeology. It was not an ancient vase or a Greek sculpture, but a manuscript. J.F. Gamurrini had found, in the library of Santa Maria of Arezzo (Italy), a file that contained the almost complete travelogues to the homeland of Jesus: The *Itinerarium*. It was a compilation of the impressions that a nun had experienced at the end of the fourth century when she decided to defy all danger and embarked on the adventure of visiting the Holy Land. That woman, born in the still Roman Hispania, put down in writing what she saw and felt, with the intention, as she says, of not depriving her sisters of the community —whom she calls "Soul friends"— of the joys and spiritual gifts she received during her visit to the holy places.

The *Itinerarium* discovered by Gamurrini in the abbey of Arezzo was a copy made in the abbey of Montecassino, the heart of the Benedictine world and a source of knowledge and intellectual production throughout the Middle Ages. The Benedictine monks had reproduced that book as they had done with so many others, because that was part of their daily work; from Montecassino, as from other Benedictine abbeys, manuscript books were then "exported" to cathedrals and palaces, copied in series in the Scriptorium while a monk read aloud the original. One of these copies reached Arezzo and was discovered there by Gamurrini.

The *Itinerarium* of the Hispanic nun Egeria (or Eteria or Echeria, as others know her), as discovered in 1884, was incomplete. The beginning and the last part were missing. In addition, there were also some missing pages inside, although these gaps have been filled in by specialists by turning to other sources of information that provide data on the situation of Israel at the time, especially the *Liber de locis sanctis* of Peter Deacon, written in the eleventh century.

But of course, the copy that came out of Montecassino was complete. Just as the copy that was used as the original in that important abbey was complete. The vagaries of history, the looting and plundering of monasteries by ambitious and unscrupulous people, have destroyed countless works of art linked, in their origin, to the faith. The case of *Itinerarium* was one more. In fact, it would have disappeared forever if one of the hundreds of copies that were in circulation in the West during the Middle Ages had not been saved, almost miraculously, in Santa Maria de Arezzo. However, Montecasino was not the only place to conserve the writings left by the nun Egeria. She lived in a monastery located in the Hispanic Gallaecia, whose capital was Bracara Augusta at that time (late fourth century), but which had a remarkable density of important cities, heirs of past splendors (the current Astorga, Leon and Lugo, to name just a few). At the time of the journey to Israel, a certain peace reigned in all of the empire. Theodosius, Hispanic like Egeria, had just died (395) and had left the territory, relatively pacified, divided between his two sons. Honorius had the West and his brother Arcadius the East, including Palestine. The pilgrimages, interrupted for many years by the continuous struggles and by the repression against the Christians undertaken by the apostate emperor Julian, flourished. Egeria embarked on one of them.

Even if the *Itinerarium* had been lost, the name of Egeria would not have disappeared, because her work attracted attention almost immediately. The Galician monk Valerius, in the middle of the 7th century, speaks of her in a letter "*Ad fratres Bergidensis*" —addressed to a monastery, now gone as well, located in El Bierzo. Both the language used by Egeria, her idioms when writing in Latin, and Valerius' text, confirm the Hispanic origin of this singular nun. This data also confirm her high social and economic position, which greatly enabled her to travel, since it was not safe, unless one had enough money and influence to receive protection in the numerous stopovers that a fourth century pilgrim was forced to make to travel from the northwest of Spain to the other end of the Mediterranean.

Egeria set out and returned. She took notes along the way, like a modern tourist, and at the end of her journey she wrote down her impressions, which she entrusted to her sisters in the community, as well as to her superiors and to those who had made her experience possible thanks to their alms. The *Itinerarium* began to circulate and would have been destined for great "editorial" success had it not been for an unfortunate circumstance. In 407, very soon after Egeria arrived in her homeland and with only a few copies of her original manuscript circulating around the world, the Vandals, Suevi and Alans entered Spain and razed it to the ground. While the Visigoths established themselves in Italy as allies and protectors of the emperor, the other Gothic tribes alternated plundering with working as mercenaries.

In that unstable context, the monastery of Egeria was destroyed. We know nothing of her personal end, nor of her companions in the community. The Suevi settled in the ancient province of Gallaecia and kept the present Portuguese city of Braga as their capital. The Vandals, on the other hand, left the Peninsula —they had remained mainly in Andalusia— and went on to ravage Africa (429), destroying, among others, the city of Hippo, of which St. Augustine was bishop at the time. The gap left by the Vandals in Spain was soon filled by the Visigoths, who were already established in southern France and had a prosperous capital in Toulouse.

With so many comings and goings, not only was the monastery of Egeria destroyed, just as so many rural villas, prosperous villages and some cities were razed to the ground, but her work disappeared, as well. Miraculously some of the few copies were saved, one of which finally found its way to Montecassino.

This is how it would have ended had it not been for a very recent discovery of which this book aims to report. In the set of disasters and wars that Spain has suffered, the anticlerical policy of some of its politicians is framed. One of them, Juan Álvarez Mendizábal, ordered, for the greater glory of the royal coffers, to "disentail" the capital "invested", for centuries according to him, by the people in convents and monasteries. The disentailment (1835 and 1836) was nothing more than a fine way to justify a gigantic robbery, a monumental larceny that did not even achieve its objectives, since the rich were the ones who kept at low prices the auctioned goods from the monasteries, while the poor, for the most part, did not even get the crumbs.

In addition, as everything was put up for sale at the same time, it was settled at a bargain price, with which the royal treasury's problems were not solved either. What did happen, however, was that the cultural heritage collapsed and today we still see hundreds of ruins throughout the Spanish geography, silent witnesses of what were once flourishing monasteries, centers of spirituality as well as culture and even support for the rural economy.

In one of those plunders, an old Benedictine monastery, Obona, located in the Asturian council of Tineo, disappeared. The Benedictine monks took notice of that fertile and elevated valley and who, during the 11th century, evangelized the area and helped its rough inhabitants to improve their standard of living. The twin monasteries of Obona and Bárcena were key in that operation. Both fell victim to Mendizábal's useless plundering. Both churches passed to the archdiocese of Oviedo, but not their lands or part of their cultural and artistic treasures.

Most of Obona's possessions were acquired by a wealthy Asturian family that had made its first savings with the import of coffee from Cuba and the installation of a roasting factory. The library of the monastery turned out to be a delight for that *indiano*, who moved it almost in its entirety to his house in Oviedo, without even knowing what he was taking, almost like someone who buys books by weight, or for its covers and not for its content.

Those works spent years in the darkness of the attics, although everyone in the family knew that they contained great treasures, and there was talk, every time the inheritance had to be divided, of valuable treasures that no one knew how to specify. Finally, in one of these ocasions, a fragment of the initial treasure, cut and distributed over time as if it were pieces of cloth or bank account numbers, came into the hands of a friend of mine, an enlightened priest of the archdiocese of Oviedo, fond of reading and dusting manuscripts, almost as much as to the fidelity to the Pope and to the legitimate outlines of the Roman liturgy.

One day, a few months ago, I received a call from him. He had already spoken to me on countless occasions about the legacy he had received in his inheritance from an uncle of his, a direct descendant of the family that benefited from Mendizábal's outrage. To him, as a clergyman, they had been kind enough to entrust some of the books from the monastery of Obona as inheritance compensation. He would browse through them little by little and some of them he gave to the archdiocesan funds, while he kept for himself the ones he was most excited about, among them an illuminated copy of the ancient pious that was written for the first time around the valley of Liébana.

My friend, whom we will call don Ignacio, was nervous when he contacted me. He knew of my interest in ancient and medieval history and my professional contacts with publishing companies. Although Oviedo is not exactly a short distance from Madrid, he urgently requested my presence in the Asturian capital. He could come, but he did not want to move the "treasure" that, as he told me, he had just discovered.

What he showed me did not disappoint me at all. It is true that the land of Oviedo contains even greater treasures —there is more and more data that identify the shroud kept in the holy chamber of its cathedral with the cloth that was used to shroud the face of Christ, but what Don Ignacio had could be considered a discovery comparable to the famous Qumran manuscripts, the scrolls of the ancient Essenes who lived by the Dead Sea, and perhaps even more important than them.

It was, as you might have guessed, a copy of the *Itinerarium* by the nun Egeria. A very old copy, perhaps from the early years of the 7th century. Possibly fourth or fifth generation of those first ones that were made and that were taken to some monastery of the Hispanic-Roman Gallaecia, passing later, along with other precious books, vicissitudes and dangers, until, after the reconquest undertaken by the mythical Don Pelayo, some copy was deposited in the Benedictine monasteries that flourished in the new Christian kingdom and from there, around the tenth century, it passed to Obona, always in Asturian lands.

Don Ignacio was aware of the adventure of the nun Egeria and her *Itinerarium*. He realized, therefore, that the possession of the ancient book was an extraordinary treasure. However, he wanted to compare it with the one of Arezzo because he had read that the latter was missing two chapters, while his was complete. I contacted the Italian embassy in Spain and the Spanish delegation of the neighboring country. Thanks to their good offices we were able to obtain, at no small cost, a microfilmed copy of the text found in Italy, which we compared to the one from Obona. The differences were minimal, just the logical ones of the successive copies, with the usual transcription errors made by medieval copyists. It was then that we decided to translate the two chapters that were preserved in the Asturian text and that had been destroyed in the Arezzo text.

Since I do not know Latin and Don Ignacio felt overwhelmed by the importance of the undertaking, even in secret and without making the discovery known to anyone, we entrusted the first chapter to experts from the National Library in Madrid and the last chapter to specialists from the National Museum of Archaeology. We did not put them in contact with each other, nor did we tell them where the material whose translation we were requesting came from.

In the first case everything went as expected. It was a pious introduction in which Egeria explained the reasons for her trip and thanked the help received from donors and protectors. There was only one quote that we found puzzling and she was alluding, almost apologetically, to the contribution that she was going to make in the last chapter of her work, for she was not sure that it was something rightfull, of an orthodox work instead of a text coming from a heretical deviation. She said nothing more and left the reader and the Church authorities to judge for themselves, reiterating her apologies if she had not acted correctly in incorporating that text, which was not hers, into the work as a whole.

When we received the report from the experts of the Museum of Archaeology, my friend and I thought we were going to die of a heart attack. The emotion of a believer was mixed with the nerves of an antique enthusiast who has in his hands, by chance, a work as majestic as it was unknown until then. Already the title put us off our game. It was *the apocryphal Gospel of the Virgin Mary*. A text to which some of the primitive fathers of the Church had made reference, but of which there was no certainty that it had even existed. Naturally, when Egeria picked it up, already translated into Latin, from the hands of a Greek monk who was a companion of St. Jerome (who lived in Bethlehem at the time Egeria was there, since he lived in the birthplace of Jesus between the years 387 and 420), she was shocked, but she was afraid that it was a heretical text, given the confusion that surrounded the Dalmatian saint, in full fight in those years against the Pelagian heresy, but who had had to flee from Rome after the death of Pope Damasus, himself accused by Rufinus of fidelity to the Origenist heresy.

Egeria explains her fears in her introduction to the Marian apocryphal. She clearly states that she does not believe in its authenticity and that, although the monk who gave her the copy assured her that it was an authentic and orthodox text, she could not affirm it to be true. In any case, the Hispanic nun does not hesitate to assure that she had found it very pious and of great spiritual benefit, which is why, after much hesitation, she dared to include it as an appendix to her *Itinerarium*.

It is possible that this doubt of Egeria's spread to the monks of Santa Maria in Arezzo. It is possible that the absence of both chapters in the text preserved in the library was not accidental. Perhaps some zealous defender of orthodoxy may have thought that the memories of the Virgin Mary diminished the divinity of Christ, because they show the human side of her Son.

Perhaps someone feared, in the harshest period of the Inquisition, that the inclusion of an apocrypha in his library might arouse suspicions of collusion with the hated heresies. It is even possible that it was a severe inquisitor who ordered the two missing chapters of the Italian copy of *Itinerarium* to be separated and burned. In any case, the complete text is now preserved in Spain and the best thing to do is to read what has remained hidden for centuries.

This is, according to a pious tradition, the secret *Gospel of the Virgin Mary*, her memoirs, narrated to St. John the Evangelist on many of those afternoons when both were resting from their respective labors in the Greek city of Ephesus. Let the reader judge on its spiritual value and let themselves be penetrated by the tenderness with which an elderly mother speaks of herself, of her son and of the adventure that God, one spring day, had set in motion.

I was fifteen years old

I was once fifteen years old.

I had just become a woman a few months ago.

I remember, despite the fact that so much time and so many things had happened, the tenderness of my mother, Anne, and the gentle firmness of my father, Joachim.

That very day was Saturday. As always, my father had gone to the synagogue to listen to the reading of a Torah text and the explanation given by the rabbi. My mother and I also used to go and we stood very close and attentive behind the lattice that separates men and women. That day, however, we had not been able to be there, so we waited for Joachim to return to tell us what he had heard.

The sun was setting, and the Sabbath was ending when my father reminded us of the text that had been read in the synagogue. It was from the prophet Isaiah, one of my favorites. With a solemn voice and singing more than reciting, Joachim said:

> "How beautiful upon the mountains are the feet of the messenger who proclaims peace, who brings good tidings, who announces salvation, who says to Zion, 'Your God reigns! One voice! Your watchmen lift up their voices, with one shout of joy, because with their own eyes they see the return of Yahweh to Zion. Break forth together in shouts of joy, you, solitudes of Jerusalem, for Yahweh has comforted his people, he has ransomed Jerusalem'".

After this, my father explained to us what the rabbi of our town, Asaph son of Korah, had said. He was a kind man, now very old, but always caring with everyone, especially with the children, so I always listened to him with pleasure and would have my cousins interrupt their games when he passed by us in the street to go to his side to kiss the fringe of his mantle.

Joachim told my mother and me that Asaph had been worried that morning. The news coming from the cities where there were Roman troops were not good; there was talk of tumults and some rabbis had said that the arrival of the Messiah might be near, as could be deduced from a certain prophecy that referred to his birth in the city of David, Bethlehem. Asaph, calm as he was, did not want any alarms among his listeners, among other things, as he himself had recalled that morning, because similar news had been coming since the Romans occupied Israel and even before, under the domination of the Syrians of Antiochus. However, my father remarked to us that on that occasion our rabbi's voice seemed more uneasy than usual and that his calls for calm were less convincing.

There was something brewing and people like Asaph, like my father and my mother, sensed it, without knowing exactly what it was. That is why the rabbi had chosen the text of Isaiah, to give us, the inhabitants of our village, a message of peace and hope. If the Messiah was about to come, as some said, we should be calm, because his coming would be that of the Prince of peace. Any other attitude was, at bottom, a distrust of the Almighty, in whose hands our lives are always in.

Anne, my mother, and I were passionate about these things. We listened to Joachim pressed close to each other, in the firelight of our home, on a beautiful and gently cool late-Nisan night. We both firmly believed in what the Torah and the other holy books taught, and Anne had taken great care to teach me what faith in Yahweh meant, the love and respect we owed Him, and the need to faithfully observe the Covenant He had sealed with our people. That is why we were not surprised by anything that might happen, convinced as we were that, at a single gesture of God, not even the mighty Roman legions would be able to confront the Messiah when he appeared on earth. We awaited his arrival and prayed every day that it would happen as soon as possible, but never before the appointed time, the moment when the will of the Almighty would have foreseen it.

I, more than my mother, because I was only fifteen years old, liked to dream about the Messiah. So did my peers, and we would talk about him whenever we met, especially at the village fountain or when we went to wash in the stream. But I ardently wished that this Messiah would be a messenger of peace and God's love, the two sentiments that my parents were always instilling in me, while almost all my friends enjoyed talking about palaces and big parties. It was even worse with my cousins, with whom I had to confront on more than one occasion because it seemed that the Messiah they longed for was nothing more than a military leader. When I spoke to them about the spiritual qualities that would adorn his soul, they would mock me and pull my braids, telling me that I was still a child incapable of understanding what was good for the people of Israel and asked me if I believed that a kindly Messiah would be able to expel the Romans from our homeland.

That spring Saturday night, my mother and I were listening very attentively to Joachim, who was telling us about Rabbi Asaph's preaching. Everything was going well and was developing according to the mood of my revered rabbi and my parents, until Joachim said something that surprised my mother and me. He said that at one point in his exhortation, Asaph seemed to become mute. He had been reading the text of Isaiah paragraph by paragraph and then explaining it, until suddenly, as he read what was written, he turned pale, closed the book, sat down and burst into tears.

Several men of the town, among them my cousin Joseph, to whom my parents had betrothed me, and my own father, approached him, but failed to get a word out of him. The assembly broke up and did not cease to talk about the matter, intrigued by what Asaph might have read. Since none of us had a book of Isaiah in our house, it was not possible to consult the text that had so impressed our good rabbi, so it was decided to go to a man from Cana who lived in our town and who had not gone to the synagogue that morning because he was in bed with a fever. He was an expert in the knowledge of the Holy Scriptures and recited whole passages from memory, besides being a friend of my family.

My father, aware of the intrigue he was giving to his story, paused and looked at us attentively. We were both dumbfounded. I don't say scared because Anne, my mother, has such faith in God that I doubt that anything could disturb her spirits. But we were frankly interested. So, Joachim, after a moment of silence that increased the expectation, told us that they arrived at Adonijah's house, closed his eyes and began to mumble in a low voice until he reached the point in the story where the rabbi had interrupted. Thereafter, already in a loud voice, he added: "Who has believed our message? And to whom was the arm of Yahweh revealed? He grew up as a shoot before him, as a root out of a dry ground. He had no appearance nor presence; we saw him, and he had no countenance that we could esteem. He was despised and rejected by men, a man of sorrows and acquainted with griefs, as one whose face is hidden from view, despised, and we esteemed him not: yet our griefs he bore, and our sorrows he endured! We esteemed him stricken, smitten of God, and afflicted. He was wounded for our transgressions, he was bruised for our iniquities, he was crushed for our iniquities. He endured the chastisement that brings us peace, and with his bruises we have been healed. All we like sheep have gone astray, we have turned everyone to his own way, and Yahweh has laid on him the guilt of us all. He was oppressed, and he humbled himself and opened not his mouth. He was led like a lamb to the slaughter, and like a sheep that is dumb before those who shear it, he did not open his mouth".

Of course, my father had been able to remember that long paragraph before us because he had heard and meditated on it many times, and it was enough for him to hear Adonijah begin reciting it, so that he could recite it softly, accompanying him.

Joachim also told us that some of those who had gone to consult Adonijah did not want to believe what he said, because that would mean that the Messiah announced by the prophet Isaiah was not a king Messiah, a Messiah deliverer from the Roman yoke, and that it could even be understood that he had been betrayed by the chosen people themselves, which was in every way absurd and impossible.

Thus, divided and confused, they all left the Canaanite's house, even more worried than when they had entered.

My father and Joseph, my dear cousin and now almost husband, returned together, walking up the hill to our house, where Joseph left my father not without first asking him to greet me on his behalf, which always made me blush. The fact is that they both agreed in recognizing that Adonijah had not mistaken the text and that, possibly, the Lord Almighty had sent some sign to our rabbi Asaph that had surprised him to the point of making him mute.

"We are in great times, times of God. We should not be afraid because the Lord never abandons his people, but we should pray intensely so that his divine will may be done at every moment".

This is what my father said, ending the story and then telling us that it was time to go to bed. I obeyed him immediately and went to help my mother with the last chores around the house and then went to my room.

I could not sleep. Outside the crickets were chirping. The moon was beautiful, and its light filtered through the sackcloth that covered the window of my room. There was hardly any air flowing and I was calm, strangely calm, because in spite of what my father had told us, I did not feel anxious. Still, I could not sleep.

So, I began to pray. Something inside me told me that the Lord was waiting for a word from me. I gave it to Him right away and told Him that if He wanted to send a Messiah who was not going to be like most people expected, that it was all the same to me. I did not want His will to suit my desires, but I aspired to be the one to suit His. I also told him that I was very sorry that the Messiah was going to be sacrificed for our sins, like one of those lambs that are killed on the night of the Passover, when we remember the deed that signified the origin of our people, the action of God against the first-born of the Egyptians.

I could not understand how the coming of the Messiah would end in failure. The arguments of my friends, my cousins and my elders, with the exception of my parents, seemed to me to be full of reason. It seemed logical to me that God would intervene on our behalf, as He had done in the past, in the time of the Judges or the Kings, and that He would raise up a powerful leader who would restore freedom and greatness to our homeland. But, like my parents, I had no illusion of recreating myself in the images of war and violence, of blood and desolation that would necessarily accompany that liberation, no matter how victorious it might be. Moreover, and things were now getting more complicated, it seemed rare and even strange to me that the Messiah who was to come would have to suffer on behalf of everyone, being innocent and us the guilty ones.

But I felt very strongly that the Lord expected something from me that night, so I said yes to everything. I told Him that for me things should only be done according to his will and not according to my calculations and predictions. Therefore, if He, Yahweh, had decided that this was how events should unfold, this was how I accepted them and, as on previous occasions, I offered to help in whatever way I could, knowing that what I could do was very little, young as I was and about to get married.

And that's when it happened.

I had done no more than pronounce my last yes when the little room filled with light. I was still kneeling, in my poor nightclothes that I had pulled up above my knees so as not to wear them out, when he appeared.

I have to say that I wasn't frightened. Well, I was, but it was a different kind of fear.

And there he was. Beautiful and bright, sweet, full of peace. Not for a moment did I think he might be an envoy of the Evil One, because the peace that emanated from him was only of that caliber that God gives; besides, caught a glimpse of that peace before when I prayed and spent the free hours of Friday afternoons among the olive trees or in my room. That peace, God's peace, found a deep echo in myself. His peace embraced my peace, as if nothing else had ever existed within me but divine harmony, a peace similar to that which emanated from this messenger of the Lord.

For I am referring, naturally, to the angel Gabriel.

Not only was he beautiful and full of peace, but he spoke. If he had been quiet, maybe I would began playing with him, so great was my attunement to his soul and my calmness. But when he began to speak, I did get a little scared. And not because his voice was unpleasant, but because what he said left me perplexed.

"Rejoice, full of grace, the Lord is with you", were his first words.

Clearly, it was scary. What did he mean by "full of grace"? Weren't we all under the effect of the original sin, as we were taught in the synagogue? Wouldn't this be an invitation to arrogance, and would I have been deceived by his apparent spirituality?

He immediately noticed and tried to reassure me: "Do not be afraid, Mary, for you have found favor with God; you will conceive in your womb and bear a son, and you shall call His name Jesus. He will be great and will be called the Son of the Most High, and the Lord God will give Him the throne of his father David; He will reign over the house of Jacob forever and ever, and His kingdom will have no end".

In truth, these were not very reassuring words. There was the "do not be afraid", but what came next was very serious and worrying. However, because I was used to saying yes to whatever God asked me, and with the intimate certainty that he was His messenger, I didn't even think about the mess I was getting into, nor about the consequences of the fact that I was already, in some way, married or at least engaged to Joseph. I was about to say yes when that sixth sense that we women have led me to ask a question, a kind of test to make sure if it was really the Lord Almighty who was sending that messenger. So I said, "How will this happen, since I have no knowledge of man?"

It was not unimportant. For me it was fundamental. In fact, either that point was resolved by making it clear that I would not be forced into anything unbecoming of an honest young woman, or I could be sure that what I was being offered was not from God. God cannot contradict God. God could not have been sowing in my soul all my life a need for purity and consecration and then lead me in ways that were quite the opposite. And since the previous thing was his doing, if the new thing also came from his hand, it would necessarily have to be in harmony with that.

The angel Gabriel was able to dispel all my doubts. "The Holy Spirit will come upon you", he said, "and the power of the Most High will overshadow you; therefore, He who is to be born will be holy and will be called the Son of God". That put everything in its place. I continued to maintain my virginity and my cleanliness of soul and body, without having to go through situations that were repugnant not only to me, but to any honest girl. My parents had often told me never to accept that the end justifies the means, even though that was such a common motto, especially when it came to making lucrative business deals or when they wanted to justify violence against the Romans. The end was, in this case, the best, or at least it was being presented to me: to let nothing less than the Messiah be born. But I wanted to make sure that also the means, the way in which this end was to take place, was the right one. Deep down, if this had not been the case, I would have known at once that God was not behind the matter. The Lord does not contradict Himself; He is not a "yes" today and a "no" tomorrow. He is always a great, noble and permanent "yes". Besides, the situation was not so different from the one I had been pondering just before God's envoy filled my small room with his light. The people of Israel, my people, wanted a deliverer at all costs, and it seemed to my parents and me that in that "at all costs" there was something that did not quite match the divine goodness. We too wanted the Messiah to come and free us from the foreign yoke, but not at any price, not at the price of hatred, war and violence.

But I was still thinking these thoughts when the angel spoke again. Perhaps he thought that I still had doubts. The fact is that he added:

> "See, Elizabeth, your relative, also has conceived a son in her old age, and this is already the sixth month for her who was called barren, for nothing is impossible with God".

He would not have needed that argument because I had already made up my mind. So, to prevent him from suspecting my willingness to accept what God was asking of me, I hurried to tell him what my heart had been crying out from the first moment, a kind of matrimonial consent, a "yes, I do" that came out of me with such force that I was even frightened because I was not used to such impetus.

"Behold the handmaid of the Lord", I said to him.

"Let it be done to me according to your word".

Then Gabriel left. He smiled at me and left. Well, I also felt like a kiss on my hand. Like a brush of goldfinch wings, soft and sweet. But the best thing was his smile. During the whole time of our meeting, it was as if he had been nervous, even more than me; his attitude was that of expectation, that of one who fears that his request might be rejected and stakes his life on it. Later I understood that it was not only him, but the whole of creation that was waiting for my lips on that spring night. All waiting for an insignificant one like me, a fifteen-year-old girl, who had just embraced womanhood, to give permission to the Almighty to inaugurate a new creation, an alliance, a definitive and eternal love story with his people in which all men would fit.

The fact is that I said yes. I told the messenger to take the message to his Lord. I did not think too much about the concrete words. Those were the ones that came out of my soul at that moment. You know how these things are; if you had time, you would compose a beautiful prayer and even commission a rabbi or a man of letters, but suddenly, a poor village girl like me could only think of using the simple and vulgar language to which she was accustomed, without adornment or elaboration. That's why

I said "handmaid", but I was not a "handmaid". My parents were free, and we had the dignity and desire for freedom that have always characterized our people, untamed among the untamed and very zealous of their traditions. Moreover, I was and am absolutely against slavery, even though some of the people had slaves at home and others said that without their existence nothing could work from the economic point of view. As I said, in my house we never liked the idea of bad means for good ends, just as we were not too convinced by the "lesser evil" that others used to talk about, usually to justify something unjustifiable.

However, when it came to expressing my consent, I mentioned the slave. It may seem silly, even a contradiction in terms, given that I was against slavery. But I don't regret it either, despite having spent so many years and having meditated significantly upon it. Not only did it come out suddenly, without thinking, but if I had to repeat what I said then, I would say it again.

I want to be the Lord's handmaid. Only the Lord's, that's for sure. But of Him, with all my strength. To be his slave does not mean to have no dignity or lack of freedom, but to place my freedom at his service and entrust my dignity to his care. He knows how to take care of me much more than I do and, if not, there are so many who presume to be free and then are slaves to wine or even worse things. I live by Him and for Him. It is something I have chosen, no one has imposed it on me, as was seen when He asked my permission so that the Messiah could be born. But, from the freedom I have, I say to Him: here I am, I am your handmaid, you can do with me what you want, I abandon myself to you, use me for your purposes and I only ask that you take care of me; I am the work of your hands and I desire nothing more than to be a mirror that reflects your glory and your prestige.

I am the handmaid of the Lord. I am his bride. I am the mother of his Son. But this is another story, dear John, which I will tell you tomorrow.

CHAPTER 2

The day after

As you can understand, John, I could hardly sleep that night. And the thing is, I wasn't nervous. You see, it is as if I had known everything long before it happened, but without being aware of it. My body and soul had always been waiting for that moment and that tenant, unknowingly to me, but they knew it. That's why everything was so normal. And because it was so normal, I was surprised and worried.

I spent the night, almost until dawn, curled up in bed and praying. My prayer was not full of words, but of silences full of sensations, of questions, of affections.

Physically I did not notice anything, so I came to doubt that everything had been a dream, a fantastic apparition that I had built myself. But I soon discarded that idea. I did not notice anything, but something was inside me and I knew it without the slightest doubt. It was something new, alive, wonderful. But what was it? Or rather, who was it? What kind of Messiah was he who came to be born in a lost village in Galilee, instead of seeking the capital, Jerusalem? Who in his right mind would have chosen a poor girl, the daughter of a craftsman, as his mother, instead of seeking the protection of a powerful family? Was it not Moses himself who, born poor, was raised and educated in the palace of Pharaoh? Would the same thing happen to me, would they snatch this son from me to take him to the house of some great person to be educated there? Would I be only a temporary mother, just a wet nurse, instead of being able to enjoy the company of this creature whom I already loved passionately?

That's how I spent the night, dear John, I had so many questions to ask the father of my child! Because what I was aware of from the first moment was that I was on the way to becoming a mother and that the father had not been a man. I don't know how it happened, and I still don't understand it today, but it was enough for me to hear something that all of us believers accept, that "nothing is impossible for God". That is why it was not very difficult for me to accept that God could beget the Messiah in me without the intervention of a man. And all this made Him, the Almighty, the father of my child, making me, in a way, His wife. Furthemore, the son I was already carrying in my womb, what was He in relation to God? Could He be called his son? But how could a human being be the son of God? How could the people of Israel, who did not allow sculptures or paintings representing God to be made, accept a Messiah who was also the Son of the Most High? And as if this sea of doubts were small, there were hundreds of other things. For example, was my son going to be a warrior or a peacemaker? Was He going to stain his hands with blood and wield victorious swords, or was He going to be a holy man who would lead the people along paths of inner renewal, of conversion, of mercy?

Well, I have to say that I immediately knew the answer to this last question. As soon as it arose in me, I felt a reaction inside me, as if coming from that tiny life that was already stirring in my womb. No, He would not be a warrior messiah. Violence would never tarnish his gaze. Neither with the best of intentions, nor with the noblest of causes, would He bring destruction to men and peoples.

But this certainty, which made me happy, also made me afraid: what would my cousins, my countrymen, the entire people of Israel who, with a few exceptions like my parents and a few others, were expecting a victorious leader, a military leader, say? What would have happened that night, after the reading of the passage from Isaiah by Asaph and his significant silence, with the rejection by the majority of the prophet's words written below, would it not be what would happen to my son if He tried to preach peace and not war? Could it be the case that the Messiah would be rejected by the people if He did not bring the message that the people were eager to hear? But even more, as some had suggested, could the Messiah be despised and even killed, like the meek lamb led to the slaughter, and not only by the pagans but by the chosen people themselves?

Understand me, John. I thought I was going crazy. It was all too complicated for me, I was only fifteen years old and had barely left my village to visit some of the neighboring towns. Since I didn't understand anything, I just let my heart, my intuition, provide me with a glimmer of light anid the confusion in wich, when the angel left, I found myself in.

Because, in addition, I had my own personal problem. You know, dear boy, how strict the laws of our people are, especially compared to those of these Greek lands. Once, when I was about eight years old, a girl from Nazareth had been stoned to death. She was betrothed to Tobias, a cobbler of the village, but she had fallen in love with another boy of the village, a certain Jacob son of Yair. They did the wrong thing, and she became pregnant. The news was a terrible scandal and in Nazareth there was no talk of anything else. The future husband felt outraged and demanded reparation. The girl's parents, Michal was the poor girl's name, like Saul's daughter, offered all their money to Tobias. He only had to say that he had had relations with Michal, which was not at all good, but carried with it no punishment. But the cobbler refused even though the offer was very tempting. The affair had transcended, everyone knew about it because the foolish Jacob had talked about it with his friends in the middle of a drunken binge, so Tobias publicly repudiated Michal and she received the punishment of adulteresses and was stoned to death. They took all the girls of the town to see the terrible spectacle, and also all the young boys. All except me, and not because I was a girl, but because my father opposed it, since he was against that kind of measures, even if they were recommended by law and endorsed by the utility of punishment.

So, I knew what could happen to me. My case had nothing to do with poor Michal's, but who would believe that? When the angel left, I began to realize the consequences of what I had done. Those consequences were nothing less than a child. A child that was going to be seen by everyone, following a nine month pregnancy, both impossible to hide. What would people think? What would Joseph think, how would he react? Would he disown me, like Tobias did with Michal? And, in that case, what would become of me and my child?

How could I tell them about the angel? How could I tell my sweet mother that I was pregnant and that it was God himself who had come into my womb? No matter how much confidence my parents had in me, how could they fall for such a story? And my dear father, with whom I had never had any displeasure and who was so proud of me, what would he think? Would the men of the village laugh at him when they saw his daughter disgraced, pregnant by a stranger whose name they didn't even know?

You have to understand well all this that I am telling you, John, because otherwise, no one will ever be able to understand what my acceptance of God's will meant. It is very easy to say "yes" to the Lord, but it is not so easy to put it into practice, especially at times like this. Later, when things were settled, especially when my son Jesus was performing miracles and everyone was applauding him, some women envied me and praised my good fortune for being the mother of the Messiah. It is true that all the girls of Israel dreamed of it, but not in that way, not at that price. I was aware that I was risking my life, and the life of my son. I was aware that I had placed in God's hands my own honor, my reputation, my future, and also that of my own. And I did not know how I could find a way out of that mess.

I did not know it, but then the grace of the Most High came to the aid of my weakness. The same one who had covered me with his shadow, came to reassure me. I felt his hand, gentle as well as powerful, caressing my hair and saying to me again, as the angel had said to me before: "Do not be afraid, my beloved, my dove, trust in me. I am the Almighty and for me nothing is impossible. Has it not been possible for you to be pregnant without losing your virginity? Do not worry, therefore, and be confident. Look at the lilies of the field and the singing birds, not a single petal nor a single feather falls from them without my knowledge and consent, and do you not think that I care for you more than all the flowers of the world and all the nightingales? Do you think that I have placed my Son in your womb so that now He may die stoned to death by a law that you unjustly attribute to me? Do you think that I have been waiting for millennia for this moment so that some louts may destroy Him with stones and hatred? Fear not, my beloved, my dove. He and you, you and He, are in my charge and the power of hell will not prevail".

That was how I fell asleep. In his arms, cradled by the sweetness of the Lord, certain that I was in his hands. I received no lights to enlighten my intelligence. I saw no solutions and understood nothing at all. I only knew that, if God was behind the matter, everything would be all right and that all I had to do was to let myself go. I remembered a phrase from Isaiah that my father used to repeat because it was his favorite motto: "In trust is your strength". My strength lay in trusting the power of God and His love. In trust in God's power and in his love was my strength. I put myself in his hands and fell asleep. It was almost daylight.

It was just a nap. My mother came into my room soon after. With her everlasting smile she sat by my bedside and woke me up, teasing me and calling me a sleepyhead.

I opened my eyes, sat up, threw my arms around her neck and, unable to help myself, burst into tears. I needed so much to get it off my chest! I was calm, I believed in God without the slightest doubt, but I had to go through the ordeal of telling my parents, and it was no small matter.

I was crying with no little anguish and at the same time with a surprising peace. My mother kissed my cheeks, stroked my hair and asked me if I had had a bad dream, if I was in pain, if I had had a bad night.

I thought I was dying when I had to start talking. The words refused to come out. My mouth was completely dry. I had to clear my throat several times and finally I told her, looking down at the bed sheets instead of directing my gaze into her eyes. "I'm going to be a mother". Then I fell silent.

The silence lasted a long time. It seemed like an eternity to me. It was certainly several minutes. My mother was next to me. She was still holding my hand in hers, so I could know what was going through her heart, the caliber of the disappointment I had given her, the disappointment she felt, the immense pain that was breaking her holy soul. And yet she knew nothing of who the father was.

After a while, she grabbed my chin with her hand and made me look at her face. Her eyes were full of tears, just like mine. We looked at each other for a long time and then she hugged me. I don't know how long we stayed like that. We were both crying uncontrollably. I for one thing and she for another, but both for the same thing.

When we calmed down, she asked me about Joseph. She didn't want to know when it had been, or how. She only asked me when I was going to move in with Joseph, because she assumed he was the father.

So, I told her everything.

The surprising thing was that she believed me and breathed a sigh of relief. Actually, I had no reason to be surprised, since my mother was a woman of God and, beyond my words and the truthfulness of what I was saying, incredible as it may seem, the Lord was also working in her. I even offered to prove to her that I had not lost my virginity, to which she flatly refused, because, she told me, that would be not accepting my word.

"I believe you, my child", said Anne. "I believe you because the story you tell is too incredible for it to have the slightest chance of it being accepted, if you were to invent it. Moreover, I believe you, because I have never had any reason to doubt you. You have been an exemplary girl. You have never given neither your father nor me any displeasure, and to doubt you, however difficult it may be to accept your word, would be an offense that you do not deserve. If I did not believe you, I would be breaking something pure and clean, the trust you deserve. But the Lord has also told me some things. For many years. I have had the impression, since you were born, that you were more his than your father's and mine. I do not mean to say that there was anything strange about your birth;

you were the fruit of a genuine love between Joachim and me. What I am saying is that, both to your father and to me, and to many others in the town, it always seemed to us that the same muddy waters did not cross your forehead as those of all the others, including the holiest of our town. You were always God's and you were so by nature as much as by intensity. I have talked with Joachim a lot about you. We had the impression that the Lord wanted you for Himself in a different way than He calls us to union with Him, but we did not know how or when. We were even very hesitant to commit you to anyone, until we thought of your cousin, Joseph, who seems to be made of the same dough as you, even if he does not live up to the strange gift that you have been given. But even so, on more than a few occasions we wondered how you would react to married life, to the commitments that a woman must fulfill to her husband. Still, we decided to go ahead, waiting for God to somehow manifest his will if it was different from what we were planning. And now this has happened. It has nothing to do with what we could have imagined, but I am sure that it is the work of his hands, so all will be well".

"Who will tell Dad?" I asked my mother.

"Leave it to me. It would be too violent for you, though you may rest easy about your father. He has nothing to do with the common man, and that of sullied honor does not enter into his schemes. Furthermore, in your case, there is not only no offense, but privilege. My child, I do not know if you realize, because I imagine that everything has happened so fast that you must be deeply upset, but you are going to be the mother of the Messiah and that is the greatest honor to which a Jewish woman can aspire".

My mother threw her arms around my neck again. We were no longer crying. She gently ran her hand repeatedly through my hair, while she said, softly and tenderly, "my child, my child". Then she got up and left to look for my father.

Our house was small, like all the others in the village. But it was cozy and, above all, very clean. But, because of its smallness, from my room I could hear the conversation between Joachim and Anne.

"Joachim, my dear", my mother began to tell him, "the Lord has taken notice of us, he has looked at our humility and has granted us an extraordinary gift. Stop working for a moment and listen to me. I'm a little nervous and I don't want to complicate things any more than they already are.

My father put down the basket in which he was mixing some grain with straw to feed to our little donkey. He looked attentively at my mother and impressed, let out a deep sigh and sat down. He must have sensed something right away, because he pulled a handkerchief from his sash and wiped away the sweat that had suddenly begun to appear on his forehead. He asked my mother for some fresh water and, with the clay bowl in his hand, waited for Anne to tell him what was so extraordinary that he did not know whether to fear or long for.

"Our daughter is pregnant", my mother began. "But be calm and don't be distressed. The girl is fine, and, above all, she has done nothing wrong and has not committed any fault. Incredible as it may seem to you, there is no man involved, not even Joseph. If you doubt it, we can prove to you that she is still a virgin. She says, and I believe her, that tonight an angel of the Lord appeared to her and asked her to accept to be the mother of the Messiah. Remember what the prophecies say, what we have talked about so many times and even what you told us last night. The Lord wants to save his people, and we, his unworthy and last servants, have been the lucky ones. So, don't give me any nonsense about honors and dishonors, because what we have to do is to pray to thank God and calm that girl who is a bundle of nerves". As my mother spoke, Joachim had risen from his stool, nervous and anxious, and sat back down. When Anne finished, he was silent for a few minutes, first looking at the dirt floor of our house and then looking into my mother's eyes. Finally, with words that almost didn't come out of his mouth, he said to her:

> "Dear Anne, if I did not know you so well and did not love you
> so much, I would have been angry with you at this hour. Why do
> you think that I am going to give you a hard time, woman? Do

you think that I am like the father of that girl who was the first to push his daughter out of the village, throwing her into the bad life that she now leads there, in Capernaum? Do you think that only you, as a woman, and as a mother, love our daughter and understand her? She, our daughter Mary, is the joy of my soul, the happiness of my life and the hope of my future. But I know, as you know, that she is not ours and that since her birth she belongs to God. What you are telling me is indeed hard to accept. Maybe no one in town will believe it. But you and I know it is true. And we don't need to have it certified to us even by an angel from heaven; in fact, it would have been an offense to us if the Lord had thought that we were not going to believe our daughter and that we needed some extraordinary demonstration. I know her well enough, as you know her, to be sure, absolutely sure, that she is incapable of telling a lie and of offending God by violating the sixth commandment of the law of Moses".

My father and mother embraced each other and together, they got down on their knees. "O Lord Almighty", I heard my father chant in that tone of voice of his with which he loved to repeat the psalms on Sabbath evenings, "to you I lift up my eyes, you who dwell in heaven; look upon them, as upon the eyes of the handmaid in the hand of her mistress, so our eyes upon Yahweh our God, until he has mercy on us". When he had finished reciting the old psalm that King David wrote, Joachim continued praying, now already with words of his own. "Eloi, Lord blessed forever, faithful to your promises, I lift up my eyes to you so that you may free them from all doubt and remove from them the smallest shadow of per-plexity. Help me to accept your will, to submit to your plans. Look upon my fragility and give me the strength to live up to the mission that, as the father of my daughter, you have just entrusted to me. Give me wisdom to discern the right path. Help my little one, who has always been at your service; do not put on her back more weight than she can bear and, if you need someone to carry it, use me and relieve her. We, Lord, do not aspire to greatness beyond our capacity. Although everyone wishes to count the Messiah among the members of their household, we have never dared even to think of it. We have only asked you for one thing throughout our lives, to be able to be useful to you, to be able to be of service to you, even in the humblest and smallest place. Now, Eloi, you have noticed us, so we are in your hands. Do not let what you have sown in my daughter's womb be spoiled, nor let your redemptive plans be twisted. But do not give us glories or honors that we do not want; help us only to fulfill your will and not to twist your plans with our clumsiness".

Having said this, he bent down and put his forehead on the floor. My mother did the same and the two of them stayed like that for a long time, in silence. I watched, surprised and full of gratitude, from my room, with the curtain half drawn.

I must have made some noise because they both lifted their faces off the ground at the same time and looked over to where I was. I did not hide. They got up and came to me. First was my father. He hugged me and kissed my cheeks three times and then, with a gesture that made me freeze he knelt down in front of me and kissed my hand. I pulled him up, almost indignant. But he put his hand on my mouth and gently cut off my reproaches. Then my mother did the same. At the end, the three of us melted into a long embrace and I had the feeling that the hardest part was over and that, indeed, the Lord can do everything, even make my parents understand and accept the wonderful story that had begun to grow in my womb.

Then, as we calmed down, we began to discuss how to behave next. My mother remembered that the angel had told me that Elizabeth, our first cousin, who lived in the south, in Ain Karem, near Jerusalem, was pregnant. It was unbelievable and almost as difficult to accept as it was to accept my own, because she was older than my mother and had never been able to have children. Therefore, a visit to Elizabeth was necessary, to help her, since she was already six months pregnant, and also to ask for advice —she was married to Zechariah, a priest of small rank but with influence in high clerical circles— and even to put some land in the middle, while waiting to see how things would develop in the village. My parents would take it upon themselves to talk to Joseph. None of us were unaware of the delicacy of the situation, for if Joseph reacted badly and I found myself in the village, my fate would be sealed. It was therefore a matter of saving me from danger and also of saving the son I was carrying in my womb and who was the hope of our people.

We decided, therefore, that I would leave Nazareth that very afternoon and head south to our cousin's house. The journey was long and very arduous, and even dangerous. But from Cana there were frequent caravans leaving for Jerusalem, and perhaps a relative or acquaintance could be found who would accompany me to Ain Karem.

My father went to see Adonijah, our friend, just twenty-four hours after he had been at his house to consult him about the text of Isaiah. He wanted to ask him to recommend a place in Cana where I could stay and a travel expert who could vouch for my safety, since he could not accompany me all the way. There were no difficulties. Adonijah told us about his brother Manasseh, who was very rich even though he was younger than he was. He was a merchant and had married a girl of a very good family, who had brought a splendid dowry to the marriage. At Manasseh's house, he assured Joachim, I could wait until a caravan left for Jerusalem, with someone trustworthy to take me to the very door of the house of Elizabeth, my aunt.

My father took me to the house of Manasseh, in Cana. This small town is not far from our town, although, being more in the valley, it is better connected, because the road that connects the coast with the lake of Gennesaret passes through it. In its fields are cultivated beautiful bunches of grapes, which give fame to its wine, the best, they say, of all Israel. And its wheat, oats and barley crops are also generous, feeding numerous herds.

Joachim was silent most of the way. He was not, usually, too expressive. He became easily distracted and began to pray, muttering psalms and paragraphs of the Holy Scriptures under his breath, or unburdening his restless heart to the Lord. With me, things had returned to normal, as if nothing had happened. My father and mother had decided this by mutual agreement, both of them understanding that it could be bad for me to be treated as if I had suddenly become the mistress of the house. I was still their daughter, even though I carried the greatest of all treasures in my womb.

However, my father refused to let me go on foot and forced me to ride on the donkey. This was so strange, not only because of the customs of our village, but also because I was a strong little girl and he was not an elderly man, but he was older. So, I begged him that, in order not to attract attention, I would agree to go on the back of our donkey but only when we had left the houses of our village behind us, to change again when we were in sight of Cana.

Along the way, and while he held the reins and I let myself be led by the cavalry, from time to time he would turn his gaze to me and address me some of those kind and loving words that had woven our father-daughter intimacy. He called me, as he had always done, "little girl". It was not that I was short in stature, but that he had grown accustomed to calling me that since I was a child and, deep down, for him I had not yet grown up. So, he would turn to me and say, with incredible tenderness: "How is my little girl, how are you doing, are you dizzy? Or he would ask me to tell him things about God, not about what had happened that night, but about how I saw things and what I thought the Lord would think about this or that.

This is how the journey passed, which was not very long, in a sweet intimacy. It was a delightful and unrepeatable journey, almost a farewell between father and daughter, a daughter who was leaving as a girl, with storm clouds over her head, and who would return as a woman, to leave her father's house for good, if she could return.

Manasseh welcomed us magnificently. His brother had already let him know we were coming and had arranged two rooms in his beautiful house, one in the women's area for me and one in the men's area for my father. Since it was already late, he offered us water to wash ourselves and then introduced us to his young wife and two children, still very young. I had dinner with the women and Joachim had dinner with the men, so I said goodbye to my father until the next day.

Before going to bed I was talking with Leah, Manasseh's wife. She was ten years older than me. She had no parents and had inherited a large fortune, which she had shared with her only brother. Her marriage was going well, as was her husband's business, which she had helped to favor with what she had contributed to the marriage. Since no one knew anything about what had happened to me, and the visit to my relative Elizabeth was very normal due to her pregnancy, no one was surprised by my trip and the conversation proceeded normally. Leah was very kind to me and after a while she took me to my room and left me by myself.

That night I slept straight through. I woke up at dawn, wide awake and as if nothing had happened. The maids were already bustling around the house and I let them pamper me when they offered me warm milk and bread for the first meal of the day. Earlier, as soon as I woke up, I had prayed to thank God for his protection and to renew my willingness to do his will at all times, always counting on his strength to carry it out.

I was having breakfast when Leah appeared with her little boy in her arms. He was sick and had spent a very bad night. His face was full of pimples and he was crying incessantly. The young mother was frightened. It was said that there was an epidemic in the village, and, in fact, three children had died in the past few days after showing symptoms like those of Manasseh's son. I did not know what to do. They had been so good to me that I wanted to reciprocate in some way, but I did not understand medicine, not even the old remedies that some women successfully applied with herbs and plasters. But I did know how to pray. So, I proposed to Leah to kneel down and ask the Lord to help her child and that, in any case, His will be done for him. The mother looked at me in surprise, but after a moment's hesitation she agreed. She knelt down next to me, with the little one in her arms who wouldn't stop crying and waited silently for me to do something. For my part, I had no idea what to say. If my father had been there, I was sure he would have recited some old psalm or a passage from a prophet, but I didn't dare to do so, lest I make a mistake. For a few minutes we were silent me, a little nervous and Leah rocking the child and waiting. Then I raised my voice and begged, in simple words, the Almighty to help that child, if it was His will, and to help his parents to accept His plans at all times. When I had finished my poor prayer, I kissed the little one on the forehead.

And that's when it happened. Levi, that was the boy's name, suddenly calmed down. He smiled, opened his little eyes wide and snuggled up against his mother. Then he fell asleep right away. The pimples started to disappear instantly. Leah looked at me and understood that my prayer had been heard because the child had a calm breathing, as he had not had since his rashes had appeared. She left the child, gently so that he would not wake up, in the hands of a maid and gave me a big hug, showering me with words of gratitude.

I was stunned. Not because I doubted in the least that prayers were of any use or that God was listening to me. On many occasions I had seen how my supplications were answered almost immediately, to the point that I had decided to ask only for important things, because I had the impression that the Lord was always waiting for me to ask Him for anything in order to grant it, and I did not want to take advantage of Him. But nothing like this had ever happened to me, as far as the seriousness of the case was concerned. Anyway, I didn't have much time to meditate on it. Leah took me by the hand all over the house and explained to one and all what had happened. Manasseh, her husband, and then Joachim, my father, appeared and congratulated me on the healing of the little boy. I remember that my father looked at me very seriously and I had the impression that, if me had not been in the presence of so many, he would have knelt down again before me as he had done the day before. But he said nothing. He only turned to Manasseh to recommend him once again to watch over me and prepared everything for his return to Nazareth.

I watched him leave along the road lined with olive trees. I had the impression of having placed a heavy burden on his shoulders, that of having to explain to everyone —even Joseph— that his daughter had become pregnant before he had definitively regularized his marriage. It was one of the hardest moments of those years. I sighed deeply as I watched my father leave and asked the Almighty to help him. I knew that one must be faithful to God even before men and, as the Torah teaches, I knew that the commandment to love one's family is the fourth, while the commandment to love God is the first. But I could not stop suffering thinking about Joachim and also about Anne, about the ordeal they were going through because of me, so I begged God to be kind to them and to help them find a graceful and honorable way out.

A new life began for me from that moment on. I was alone, with no one of my own by my side, and I was very young. But I had within me a strength more powerful than that of an army; the strength that any woman gets from knowing that she is the bearer of a child in her womb. I had to fight to bring my son forward and I knew that I was in God's hands, in the best hands.

Then I went into Manasseh's house. Leah, with little Levi in her arms, was waiting for me. She had preferred to stay inside to leave my father and me alone to say our goodbyes. She knew nothing of what was happening, but she sensed that I was suffering. As soon as he saw me, the boy reached out his hands towards me and I picked him up. That child was living by the grace of God, thanks to what I had somehow managed to do for him. I understood that this was a symbol, the symbol of what my life and that of my son should be: to renounce having nothing of my own, so that I could belong to everyone and take care of everyone; to renounce my life, in order to distribute it among others; to renounce even my own, so that everyone could consider me as theirs. And I said yes to God again. I said it with a kiss to little Levi, with a smile to his mother, and with a furtive tear that slipped into my eyes because I could not stop thinking about my father's hunched back.

CHAPTER 3

Joseph, a surprised bridegroom

What I am going to tell you today, John, I did not know until much later. I had been at my cousin Elizabeth's house for a month and everything was going as smoothly as possible when I received a message from my father. I have zealously guarded it all these years, among my meager belongings. Take it. You will sense from it how difficult everything turned out to be, although I did not know the details until my return to Nazareth, which, by the way, I was not able to carry out until much later than my family wished.

"Shalom, dear daughter. May the Lord continue to protect you and show you always, as He has done so far, His face.

We, your mother and I, are well, waiting and longing for your return. Without you, our house is empty and only the certainty that everything that happens is willed by Yahweh is of comfort to us. I hope you are well too, as you let us know when you arrived at Elizabeth's house, whom I ask you to greet on our behalf and whom I thank for her hospitality.

I am writing to let you know that you can come back whenever you want. Everything went as smoothly as possible, although it was not easy at first. I will tell you everything in detail when you return, but I can only tell you that for a moment you were on the verge of being repudiated. The Lord had to intervene and He did it in such a way that Joseph not only has not made any more difficulties, but he is waiting for you with open arms and considers himself fortunate to welcome you and your son into his home.

Come soon, daughter. Your mother and I need you by our side. We have suffered so much that only your presence can comfort us now. We want to take care of you and also, forgive me for saying so, to serve you. We can't wait to hold you in our arms again.

I have already spoken to Manasseh and soon a caravan of his will return, which left two weeks ago for Jerusalem. Ask Zechariah to accompany you to the crossroads and never make the journey alone.

Take care of yourself, light of our eyes. May the Lord fill you always with his peace. Greetings from your mother and from me".

Joachim

My father told me, when I was finally able to return home, that, indeed, when he said goodbye to me in Cana, the world came crashing down on him. In front of me he had pretended to be strong, putting on a good face to bad weather so as not to worry me. But when he was left alone and had barely turned his back on me, he burst into tears, grief-stricken.

How was he now going to explain to his friends and neighbors that his daughter, his little girl, was expecting a child without having married? Even if it was not the first time it had happened, and as long as Joseph agreed to recognize the child as his own, it was still the talk of the town's women that Mary had not known how to wait a few months before consummating the marriage with her fiancé. The thing was legal, certainly, but it was the custom that the betrothed did not have relations until they cohabited, after the second and definitive phase of the marriage.

For my father, my name was sacred. That my fame and my honesty could be questioned by people was something that revolted him. He had always been proud of me, because I was not like the other girls, I did not participate in the mischief that the other children sometimes did, and I did not flirt, as my friends sometimes did, with the young men of the village. And now all that pride was coming crashing down on him.

He could already hear the ironic comments of the women of Nazareth: "Look, look, look, as good as Mary seemed, so holy. She looked like butter wouldn't melt in her mouth, yet there she is, pregnant. That will teach you to trust still waters". He trembled at the thought of the men's questions. "How are you, Joachim, how is your girl doing? My, my, young people nowadays. As soon as you let your guard down, they make you a grandfather".

Suddenly, he told me, he noticed something strange. The sun had been rising and was almost reaching its zenith. Spring was showing itself, as in the previous days, in all its splendor. But it was not these outward signs of hope that cheered him. It was something outside of him and at the same time within him. It was not an apparition, but a divine presence. A presence that my father noticed at once, accustomed as he was to intimacy with God.

Joachim, as I have already said, was a religious man. Religious in the best sense of the word. He did not belong to the sect of the Pharisees, nor to any other of the sects or associations that so proliferated among our people. Rather, he was an anawin, one of those of whom Isaiah had prophesied when he said that there would be a remnant in Israel from which the Messiah would be born. The "remnant", the small portion of true Israelites to which my father belonged, was characterized by seeking the spirit of the Law and not obsessing over the letter. His relationship with the Lord was a relationship of the heart rather than of meticulous precepts scrupulously fulfilled, without meaning to say that he infringed them; he simply gave them their just value, no more and no less.

My father did not need spectacular apparitions. He was used to dealing with God, to speaking with Him from respect but also from intimacy. So, immediately, God used the channel He had permanently open with him and explained to him and they explained to each other.

"What a mess I have gotten you into". God began to say to my father. "Dear Joachim, I know that you are troubled and that it seems to you that the burden I have placed on your shoulders is beyond your strength.

But this is not true. If I can't ask this of you, who am I going to ask? Aren't you the one who for so many years has told me that I could count on you, even without asking your permission? Or is it that all that we have built together during this time was nothing more than a game, an appearance that was worthwhile as long as your availability was not put to the test? As for the rest, Joachim, you should feel very, very happy about the fact that in your house the Messiah is going to be born. Isn't that, perhaps, the dream of every good Jew? Wouldn't all your friends, whose judgment you now fear, envy you if they knew what has happened?"

"Almighty Lord", answered my father, "your name is everlasting, and your mercy goes on from age to age and from generation to generation. Forgive this servant of yours if he has felt, at any time, like he has been tested beyond his strength. It is true that I am distressed, but do not think that my pulse trembles or my decision wavers. You have done well to act in my house without asking my permission, for my house is yours and I am your servant and you my Lord. You have already asked my daughter's permission and she, who is the one who should have decided, gave it to you. So, I have nothing more to say. On the contrary, I know that I am being the object of great honor for having noticed my littleness and for having granted me the immense fortune that it is my humble house that gives a renewal to the stump of the house of Israel. But, Lord, do not be surprised that I am afraid. I am not afraid for myself, nor for the trouble I have to go through when it comes to telling things. I have it for her, for Mary, and I have it for the child she carries in her womb. What will Joseph do? What will become of them if he, as is most likely, rejects her as his wife? It is true that, acting quickly, I have succeeded in getting her to safety, and before long she will be far away. But, if she cannot return to Nazareth, she must always live far from home, as an outcast, without resources since we are poor".

"Joachim, Joachim", said the Lord, is your belief in me so little? "Do you doubt that I, who has built the Universe and at whose word the waters of the Red Sea were opened, am not able to solve such a simple thing? You have confidence in me and do not fear. It is in trust, never forget it, that your strength lies. Leave it to me and be attentive to act as I tell you, even though at times it may seem to you that the abyss opens before your feet".

And so, he arrived in Nazareth. The morning was ending, and it would soon be time for lunch. My father set out for home, walking slowly up the hill, tired as he was and trying not to attract attention. He found my mother alone, as was to be expected, since with my absence the family was reduced to the two of them. Anne threw herself around his neck and asked him for news. Joachim filled her in on everything, including the miracle that had occurred after my prayer, as well as the very comforting conversation he had had with the Lord during the trip. Anne, for her part, told him that Joseph had walked by the house that very morning and that he had been surprised that Mary had left so hastily for Ain Karem, without even saying goodbye to him. He wanted to know how long I would be gone because he was already looking forward to finalizing the details of the wedding. He was so in love, my mother said, that it broke one's heart to think of the blow he was about to receive.

My father swallowed hard at this news, but he did not abandon the decision he had made: to trust in God and not to doubt at any moment that everything was in His hands and that, therefore, everything would be all right. He agreed with Anne that that same afternoon he would go to see Joseph and that to him, before anyone else, things had to be explained. Afterwards, they ate and while my mother was arranging things around the house, Joachim went to rest for a while.

The sun was already setting when Joachim asked permission to enter Joseph's house. It was a house very similar to mine, and it was not far from it. Joseph lived alone; his parents had died a few years before and he had only one sister who lived in another part of town. There, in his house, he had his carpenter's workshop, which was really a bit of everything, because he was a craftsman who could build a door, shoe a horse or repair a plow if necessary. Joseph invited him in and kindly offered him water for his hands and the best stool for him to sit on. He immediately understood that something serious was going on, which was not difficult to guess in view of my father's worried countenance. He went straight to the point.

"Joseph, as you know, Mary is on her way to Ain Karem, next to Jerusalem. We have a cousin there, Elizabeth, whom you may know, married to Zechariah. She is older, about the age of Anne, my wife. Until now she had had no children, and we all thought her barren and pitied her for her terrible misfortune. But the Lord has had mercy on her and on her husband's house. She is six months pregnant and Mary has gone to accompany her until the moment of delivery. But this is not what I have come to tell you", my father paused, took a deep breath, and launched into a confession that looked incredible and had all the makings of a bad ending.

"What I want to tell you, Joseph, is that Mary is pregnant. We know it wasn't you and we can assure you that she is completely innocent and that she loves you. I can tell you no more. The thing is not public. Her pregnancy is very recent and now it is up to you to decide what you want to be done".

According to what my father told me Joseph burst into tears. He was certainly in love with me. And I was in love with him. We had gotten along very easily and, in our case, the marriage arranged by our families had been a complete success. He was a good man to say the least. He was religious, in the style of my father and mother, without fuss or affectations. God-fearing and faithful to his precepts, but not to discover the traps of the law and do the minimum with a clear conscience, but to adjust his life to the will of the Lord with normality and joy.

When he calmed down, without my father daring to say anything to him or even put his hand on his shoulder, for fear of an abrupt reaction, Joseph raised his eyes. He looked at my father and asked for explanations. What had happened, had it been a rape? Was I in love with some boy in the village? And, above all, how was it possible that I, whom he and everyone in the village considered incapable of committing even a minor offense, could have committed such a blunder? My father refused to explain. He only reiterated that I was innocent of what had happened, that there was no man involved and that it had not been a rape. Understanding how difficult the situation was, he did not want to take things to the extreme, but insisted strongly that, beyond appearances, I was a worthy person and that no one had anything to reproach me for.

Joseph was astonished at what he was hearing. What do you mean there was no man involved? And then, how had the pregnancy occurred? And if I was innocent, who had raped me? In short, too many questions that had no other answer than the truth of what had happened, but that my father was reluctant to tell because it would have sounded like a hoax, an incredible excuse. Joachim trusted in God and had decided to leave the explanations in His hands, because He, God, was the one who had triggered everything.

When Joseph had calmed down a little, hot flashes still showing in his eyes, he assured my father that he would not denounce me. He would repudiate me before the rabbi, but he would do it secretly, without demanding for me the punishment that falls on adulteresses and to which he was entitled so that his honor would not be sullied. However, he demanded that I should never return to the village and asked my father that neither my pregnancy nor the birth of my child should be made public when it occurred. He hoped that the news would reach Nazareth after a few months, when perhaps he would have married some other girl from the village.

My father thanked him for his generosity. As harsh as what he had said was, Joachim knew that Joseph had behaved as very few men in Nazareth would have behaved. He had just spared my life. My sentence had already been passed: I was an outcast among my own kind and would have to live a wandering life, without a husband, with a fatherless child, helped only by Joachim and Anne as long as they could help me, and then condemned to who knows what kind of slavery. But, for the time being, I was given a break.

Joachim did not embrace Joseph, nor did he give him the two kisses of peace with which they always greeted each other when they met and said goodbye. He was sorry to have made that good boy suffer, whom he truly loved like a son. He understood his pain and did not reproach him for his attitude, although all the time he had been waiting for a miracle. But the miracle had not happened. He left the house with his head down and with a heart somewhere between anguished and relieved. Inside he left a young man completely sunk and his life broken. It was already night in Nazareth. A terrible night for Joachim, Anne and Joseph, no matter how much the moon insisted on painting the streets and roofs of the village white.

Months later, when everything had been resolved, Joseph told me what had happened after my father left. He got down on his knees. He put his head in his hands and cried for hours. He couldn't hate or despise me, but at the same time he couldn't get over his surprise at what had happened. He could not stop thinking about me, nor modify the affection he felt. Then he began to curse himself for his stupid pride, which had led him to reject me, although the way he did it saved my life. Why did he have to reject me? Why couldn't he live with me and accept the child I was expecting as his own? What ridiculous habits prevented him from ignoring what had happened and going ahead with the plans that had already been made? And yet he could not behave as if nothing had happened. It was beyond his strength. His love for me, the pain that was destroying him on the inside at the thought that we could no longer share life together, was not strong enough to accept me with the child of a stranger, of someone who didn't even know who I was because my father hadn't wanted to tell him.

He spent a long time like this. It was already late into he night when he went to bed. As usually happens when one has cried, he fell asleep at once. But he woke up immediately. Someone was in the room. He sat up startled and frightened. For a moment he thought it was a nightmare, a bad dream, perhaps the result of his remorse. But no, there he was, with a dim light coming out of him, illuminating the whole room.

"He looked at me calmly and quietly", Joseph explained when he told me what had happened; he seemed to be waiting, full of tranquility, for me to calm down. Calmer, with the impression that he was not going to do me any harm but keeping as far away from him as I could, I asked him who he was and what he wanted from me: "Joseph, son of David, I am an angel of the Lord, a messenger of good news. I come from him to convey to you a command from him. Do not be afraid to take Mary as your wife, for that which is begotten in her is of the Holy Spirit".

Joseph was stunned. If that creature was a man, it meant that Mary's affair was known, which complicated the situation even more. But if it was, as he said, an angel of God, then the mysterious words of his father-in-law, Joachim, were perfectly understandable. Something strange was behind it and the situation could be understood if it was a divine intervention that had been mediated by his fiancée, Mary. His heart began to leap with joy. It could all be a deception, but it could also be a way out of the dark tunnel in which Joachim's revelation had plunged him. And it seemed more like the latter than the former. So he asked him:

> "Why is all this? Why does God come into our lives and change people's plans without consulting them? What is behind such an intervention, so strange, so extraordinary? And, furthermore, how do I know that you are God's envoy?"

The angel was not long in explaining. He reminded him of some of the prophecies, particularly that of the prophet Isaiah: "Behold, the virgin shall conceive and bear a son, and shall call him Emmanuel"; he even spoke to him of the scene that had taken place in the synagogue last Sabbath. The hour had come for the appearance of the Messiah and his betrothed, Mary, had been the one chosen so that this birth could take place. It was she who had been asked for permission, as was fitting. And now he had to play his part so that all would be well and God's saving work could be accomplished.

"Mary will give birth to a son", concluded the angel, bringing the explanations to a close, "and you shall call his name Jesus, for He will save his people from their sins". As for the proof that he came from the

Most High and was a messenger of his, he said ironically: "You have been God's friend for so long and you still cannot distinguish what comes from Him by the peace it produces in the spirit? If you want, I can leave you some more convincing proof, but it would be preferable that you do not tempt the Almighty with your distrust and that you limit yourself to listen to your heart". Joseph bowed his head, ashamed, because, indeed, he knew without a doubt that he had been wrong to demand more proof than what his certainty gave him. Seeing him thus, the angel smiled and, silently, as he had done with me, left.

Joseph had no more doubts about what he should do. It was true that it could all be a trap, a suggestion, a dream. But he was sure that it was not. That apparition had been true, as true as the fact that he was now standing in his room, inside his locked house. Besides, everything fit. It fitted, above all, what was most important to him: the honesty of his fiancée, my honesty, dear John. He felt a deep pain: for a moment he had doubted me, and I had never given him any reason to do so. He understood that he should have accepted Joachim's word, even if what he was told was nonsense. He understood that the greatest proof of a person's honesty is that person's word when it comes to someone who is trustworthy, and that all other evidence put together can be completely false and purposely fabricated to deceive those who demand papers or a thousand witnesses.

He dressed quickly and went out into the street. It was already dawn, although the shadows still clung to the narrow streets of Nazareth. He arrived at my parents' house and knocked softly on the door so as not to wake up the whole neighborhood. As he waited, the first rooster crowed. His surprise was even greater when my father opened the door, fully dressed and smiling. He showed him in. My mother was inside, waiting for him.

The mystery was soon revealed, as they explained to him what had happened. Shortly after leaving his house, Joachim felt a great peace. He had done his part, he had swallowed the bitter pill, and now he was sure that everything would be all right, even though he had left behind him a desolate boy. He knew that God would act, and that the outcome would be the best possible.

When he arrived at our home he spoke with my mother and they realized that there was only one thing he could do: pray. God had to act, but He had to do it in a hurry, and they had to urge Him not to delay. They decided to stay up all night, praying, to beg the Lord to hasten the hour and to help Joseph understand that He was behind all that immense mess. Shortly before Joseph knocked at their door, they had both been certain that their plea had been heard. So, they got up, after thanking God, and decided to wait, because they were sure that Joseph would soon appear at their house to explain, as he had. They knew him, they knew of his immense goodness, and so they had no doubt that he would not let time pass before coming to reassure them.

The three embraced each other and burst into songs of praise to the Lord, who had deigned to look upon them to entrust them with the most precious task to which any member of the chosen people could aspire: to serve as a cradle for the birth of the Messiah.

Then they made plans. They had to give the news to the people of Mary's pregnancy, going through the trouble of accepting that Joseph was the father, but without giving too many explanations. Everything had to be prepared for the wedding so that the child would be born into a fully constituted family. And, above all, they had to let me know that I could come back whenever I wanted because everything had been taken care of. Immediately, my father wrote me the letter I told you about, John. But what they did not know was that I had encountered another gift from God when I arrived at Ain Karem and that I could not leave my cousin Elizabeth alone and return immediately to Nazareth, as was her wish.

CHAPTER 4

The exaltation
of the handmaid

I had arrived at Ain Karem after a heavy but very peaceful journey. The miraculous healing of little Levi, the son of Manasseh and Leah, had not only opened wide the hearts of that couple, but had surrounded me with an aura of mystery and respect before the servants. They all looked at me in a strange way, as if instead of being a young girl of fifteen I was someone very important. I allowed myself to be looked after and cared for, especially because I was a little frightened before such an extraordinary trip for me, who until recently had hardly left my village.

Not far from Jerusalem, at a crossroads as planned, Zechariah, my cousin's husband, was waiting for me with two servants to take me to his house. Zechariah could not speak; he had become mysteriously mute, coinciding with his wife's pregnancy. However, he let me understand his surprise at having learned of the forthcoming birth of his son, since they had been very careful not to let the news get out, as Elizabeth was already old, and they did not want to expose themselves to untimely curiosity. Anyway, through the servants I was able to find out some things, since the rumor was circulating that the conception of Elizabeth's son had been wonderful, although not as in my case, and that it was Zechariah's lack of faith that had caused his muteness as a punishment from God.

So, speaking to one by sign and to the others by word of mouth, and contemplating a mountainous landscape that seemed to me the most beautiful in the world, perhaps because it was so close to our beloved Jerusalem, we arrived at the valley where Zechariah and Elizabeth lived. She was not in the house at the time. The harvest, which in our land as you know is earlier than on this seashore, was about to begin, so she had left for a farm they had a short distance from their house to arrange stores, threshing floors and beds. As I was not too tired and was very eager to see my cousin, I left Zechariah at his house and accompanied by a young maid, went to look for Elizabeth.

It took me a while to climb the hill, but I finally got there. There she was, well into her gestation, much older than I remembered, but as energetic and determined as ever. I couldn't hold back a shout of greeting. "Elizabeth!", I said, "I've arrived". She turned her head. She knew I was on my way and yet she looked surprised. As soon as she saw me, she dropped everything and ran to me. She had shock painted on her face, as if something had just happened to her. She threw her arms around my neck and even, to my and everyone else's surprise, made an attempt to get down on her knees, which I managed to prevent with great effort.

"Blessed art thou among women", she said in such a loud voice that everyone interrupted their labors to look at us, "and blessed is the fruit of thy womb; and how is it possible that the mother of my Lord should come to me? For, as soon as the voice of thy greeting reached my ears, the baby in my womb leaped for joy; happy is she who has believed that the things spoken to her from the Lord would be fulfilled!".

I couldn't get over my astonishment. I hadn't even been pregnant for two weeks, almost as long as the trip had lasted. No one, except my parents, knew about it. It could have happened that, in the village, word had already spread, but it was almost impossible that the news had reached my cousins' house before I did. No, there was something else behind it. There was, once again, the hand of God.

And then, possessed by a mysterious force that spoke through me, that of the Spirit of God, I unburdened myself to her and let out all that

I carried inside and that I had meditated on so much along the way, so I exclaimed:

> "My soul glorifies the Lord, and my spirit rejoices in God my Savior. From now on all generations will call me blessed, for the Mighty One has done great things for me, holy is his name. His mercy extends to those who fear him, from generation to generation. He has performed mighty deeds with his arm; he has scattered those who are proud in their inmost thoughts. He has brought down rulers from their thrones but has lifted up the humble. He has showered the hungry with goods but has sent the rich away empty. He has helped his servant Israel, remembering to be merciful to Abraham and his descendants forever, just as he promised our ancestors".

We were both surprised. We were aware that the Lord had used us to proclaim a message, just as he had done in the past with judges and prophets. A message that, by telling it to each other, remained in the memory of both of us and was to be transmitted, through us, to all mankind.

I, above all, realized that I had said things that were beyond me. I repeat, John, I was only fifteen years old. Everything that was happening was too much for me and that is why I dedicated long hours to meditate calmly on events that overwhelmed me. And that greeting from my cousin, calling me "blessed" and alluding to my pregnancy, had left me surprised. As surprised as what I myself had answered her, since I had practically recited a psalm, a *tehillim* as we say in our Hebrew language. In reality, I tell you, we had both been instruments of the Holy Spirit, as in the old days the prophets had been.

As for the content of my words, I believe that something similar happened to the answer I gave to the angel Gabriel that blessed night when it all began. I am referring to the "handmaid" that I already told you about.

You see, John, neither my family nor myself were ever supporters of the sect of the Zealots, the *Qanna'im*, although we had a cousin, almost a brother, who went around with them in the mountains plotting attacks against the Roman patrols. I do not pretend to be a revolutionary because I have already told you that, long before all this began, influenced above all by my parents and by God himself, I was very opposed to wars and violence, including those whose purpose was the liberation of our people. In my soul there was no place for hatred; there never was, and I do not know whether it was by virtue or by grace.

I am telling you all this because I know that the words that Elizabeth said to me and those that I answered her have been circulating over the years and I do not want them to be misinterpreted. My cousin, inspired by the Spirit, had guessed not only my pregnancy, but also the way in which it had occurred. She revealed to me something that I myself was unaware of and that even now I prefer not to touch, because it embarrasses me: that I had always been full of God's grace. So it must have been, as you will understand, not out of honor to me but as homage to Him who was to occupy my house as His own and from whose flesh He was to be born. But, dear John, do not think that it is my merit. All is God's work, all is grace. I too have been saved by my Son, only He redeemed me first, preventing me from falling, and He redeemed the rest of you afterwards.

It has taken me a long time to understand this, but at last the light has dawned for me too.

As for what I replied to Elizabeth, the most important thing I want to make clear to you, dear boy, is that I am not in favor of any kind of violence. When I affirmed that God overthrows the powerful from the throne and exalts the humble, I was not instigating any kind of revolt, even though I would like that all the good that there is on earth was better distributed, and that neither one wasted, nor the others lacked. But, in reality, what the Lord inspired me was a proclamation of his greatness. The mighty and the proud are in the palaces, but not always all those who are there are so, and not all those who are outside cease to be so. Pride is the sin of the Evil One, the worst of sins, the sin that closes the door to the action of God. No sin is as pernicious as this one, and if I have received, I believe at least, a gift from the Most High, it is the ability to sense where pride is, so as to get away from it at once. This is what I wanted to tell my cousin, answering her greeting: that God alone is great, that it is He whom we should glorify and that if we are capable of doing marvelous things —like being the Mother of the Messiah, for example— it is his merit. We are, as my Son once said, useless servants and when we do things well, we have to conclude the day by saying that we have limited ourselves to fulfilling our duty, and nothing more.

But my stay in Ain Karem was not filled with heroic deeds, or moments of rapture and prophecy. No. Life went on normally. My cousin loved me very much and I helped her by being at her side and helping to organize things in the house, because she didn't want me to work either, since I was a guest and not a maid, and besides, what she needed most from me was company and conversation about God and His purposes.

Thus, those three months passed. During this time, I received my father's letter, of which I have already told you, and I knew that everything was going well in Nazareth. But in spite of the pleading of my people, I did not return in the first caravan from Manasseh. I was at ease in Ain Karem, my cousin needed me, and, above all, I was learning a great deal about something that for me had become the most important goal of my life: how to become not only a mother, but a teacher.

My cousin had not had any children. She was already old when the angel Gabriel, the blessed messenger who announced to me the conception of my son, appeared to Zechariah, Elizabeth's husband, to announce that his wife, despite her age and consummate sterility, was going to become pregnant. Zechariah did not believe it, and even demanded proof. You can't play games with God, either you are with Him or you immediately turn against Him. Perhaps what bothers Him the most, after the proud, are the lukewarm ones, those who are praying all their lives, but without giving their heart, without really going His way, calculating what are the minimums that must be given in order not to go to hell, to

Sheol. The fact is that Zechariah, who was a priest and of the prestigious guard of Abijah no less, did not believe the angel and asked for a test; he remained mute and remained so until the birth of the boy, the ill-fated and courageous John the Baptist.

But at that time, neither Elizabeth nor Zechariah, nor of course I, knew how the future would unfold. All I knew was that I had found in my elderly relative a bottomless well of wisdom.

As I was telling you, John, she had not had children, so she could not give me advice about baby food, illnesses and diapers. But she was a great woman. She had learned much from the "world" as befitted the wife of a distinguished priest, yet not even on her travels and worldly experiences entered her soul to extinguish the spark of the Lord, the union with Him. So, I decided that if Yahweh had sent me to Ain Karem, He had surely sent me so that I could learn something of the much that was known in that house. To learn in order to teach later, for as you well know, John, being a mother is much more than begetting a child; educating is more difficult, and I would almost say more important, than conceiving.

I spent one of the most beautiful periods my life with Elizabeth. I will never forget Ain Karem. From her house you could see the valley, populated by pine trees, pine trees like those that grow here in Ephesus and move to the sea in search of the kiss of the waves. Many afternoons, as long as she could, when the sun took pity on the men and it began to get a little cooler, we would sit on the terrace of her house and talk. Well, she would talk, because I would gaze at her almost spellbound, avidly drinking in the wisdom she poured out on me.

Elizabeth was from our Galilean land. Her marriage had made her famous, but that did not stop her from being a healthy woman of the people. She was not a passive woman, a kind of husband's maid, like most women of our land. Elizabeth was a good wife, docile and fulfilling of her duties, but she was aware that she had a life of her own, that God also wanted something from her. This allowed her to understand herself outside of her domestic duties, which she carried out because they were

God's will and not only because she had no other choice. She had reflected much on Yahweh's relationship with his people. As the wife of a priest, she knew all the tricks of the law. She knew, because she had heard it countless times at the dinners and meals that her husband's companions held in their home, the economic importance of the offerings of the faithful and she understood that, for a long time, money had become a kind of leprosy that was destroying worship and the true relationship with God. Galilean as she was, she felt at a disadvantage before the cultured people of the priestly circle of Jerusalem. But she had seen how much of the respectability of those priests, scribes and Pharisees, who stretched out their phylacteries and did not break the smallest precept of the law but who, at the same time, had a very hard heart, incapable of compassion for their neighbor, was pure facade. "They filter the mosquito —she told me one day— and swallow the camel". "They are very respectful —she added— with the precept of the Saturday (she always said *Sabbath*), but when it comes to helping others, if there is no business involved, they don't know you. The commandments, for them, are always a matter of doing the minimum. You have to do what is commanded, but everything that is not a strict obligation, as it is not mandatory, they do not fulfill it".

It was she who introduced me to the prophet Amos, so fearsome and so hard on the priests. "I detest, I despise your feasts, I do not like the smell of your solemn gatherings. If you offer me burnt offerings, I take no pleasure in your oblations", she recited to me, to teach me that there is a part in the sacred books in which Yahweh has spoken clearly against the hypocrisy of the external fulfillment of the precepts while keeping the heart hard.

But my cousin did not despise the law. On the contrary. She helped me to understand its importance, even better than my parents, because, as a priest's wife, she knew all the details of it well. But, like my family, she taught me to give everything its proper value. From her I learned that the heart of the law is the covenant and that the heart of the covenant is love and not business, barter, and the I give you something in exchange for something. I heard the word love many times from her lips, especially when she recited to me the prophet Hosea, who was her favorite: "When Israel was a child, I loved him, and out of Egypt I called my son", she would say, reminding me that God loves us even though we do not deserve it and that he is faithful to his love for us, despite our repeated betrayals.

She also taught me things about men.

She didn't know Joseph, so she didn't know what great luck awaited me. But she warned me that, in general, men tend to get lost in theories, to have extraordinary and grand ideals, but then forget the concrete details.

"They spend the day —she told me— arranging the world with friends, while it is the woman who has to solve the daily issues, without which life would be unsustainable. And this happens even among the best", she added, and gave me the example of her Zechariah. From her I learned that one can serve the Lord even in the kitchen and doing the humblest jobs around the house. That, if what matters is love, it is pleasing to the Lord to serve a good meal as much as to recite a *haggada*, a long psalm without making a mistake, a long passage from a prophet or even to keep a strict fast. And she taught me that there are times when the Lord prefers that we serve our neighbor a meal rather than recite a psalm, even if at other times it is prayer that should occupy our time.

"Men", she told me one day, "are, almost always, like children. They are always looking for the reward, for the word of praise that their mother used to say to them when they were little. They always want to find out why things happen, when in reality what matters is to know how to live once they have happened, because few are the important misfortunes that can be avoided. They do not know how to live with mystery and want to have everything clear in their head, as if it were big enough to contain God and all the things He has created. They love to make plans and feel satisfied when they have made them, even if they are useless. They are not afraid of war, for example. But they do not know much of the daily suffering, of the anguish that we women go through when they, husbands or sons, have gone off to fight, or of what it means to feel like spoils for the conquering army. That is why, dear Mary", she added, "you and I have a particularly important mission. We must educate our children so that, even though they are men, they may have something of our feminine soul. Try to ensure that your Jesus, the future Messiah, always has peace in his eyes. Teach Him to value the little things, to understand that God cares about the love that is put into what is done and not only what is done. Teach Him also to value women; to understand that we are not animals or donkeys; teach Him that we are good for much more than giving birth to children and that we can be as faithful or even more faithful than men, because men easily have their mouths full of promises that they forget when things go wrong. Finally, dear Mary, through your breasts will pass the wisdom that will instruct the world, that will save Israel, that will rescue the authentic message revealed by God to our people".

When Elizabeth gave birth, I was still with her for a few days. John was a beautiful child, not at all quiet, full of strength. One could guess what he would become later, a great prophet, the forerunner of the Messiah. His father broke off speaking the day he was asked about the name of the child and said things very different from what he used to proclaim. I remember a phrase that was completely in tune with the conversations between my cousin and me and which showed that the lesson God had given him had changed his soul and helped him to convert:

> "And you, child", he said, addressing his little son, to the astonishment of all, "will be called prophet of the Most High, because you will go before the Lord to prepare his ways, announcing to his people salvation, the forgiveness of their sins. By the tender mercy of our God —he added, looking at me— the sun that rises from on high will visit us, to enlighten those who live in darkness and in the shadow of death, to guide our steps on the path of peace".

That was my farewell. If Elizabeth had welcomed me into her home, calling me "blessed" and greeting the fruit I was carrying in my womb with the nickname "Lord", Zechariah, the priest, so scrupulous in his observance of the law, no longer seemed to be so concerned about respect for the *Sabbath*, but rather about the forgiveness of sins, the mercy of God, and, in tune with his wife's intuition, he had discovered that my son was going to be the one to pour out all these graces on the people, leading them, first of all, on the path of peace.

Shortly thereafter I was able to join a caravan from Manasseh, which was returning from Jerusalem to Cana. Thus, I left Ain Karem. Zechariah, Elizabeth and little John in his mother's arms, came out to see me off. I carried in my soul a treasure of wisdom. I had arrived as a frightened little girl and I was leaving as a woman who had opened her eyes to life and was beginning to sense the importance of the mission that awaited her. I was almost four months pregnant, although it was still easy for me to hide my pregnancy. Peace, as I tell you, and God's mercy, enveloped me. And these were the two messages I intended to pass on to my son when he was born, when I had the joy of holding Him in my arms.

Soon, however, I would have to travel south again, retracing my steps. But this story, dear John, I will tell you another day. Now I am tired and excited. These memories are sweet to me and put more than moisture in my eyes. Let me be with them now. I need to be alone with God to thank Him for what once was and still now continues to illuminate my soul with its memory.

CHAPTER 5

Back home again

The journey was a week-long prayer. Manasseh's servants treated me with the same respect as when I arrived. They knew nothing of my pregnancy because I successfully concealed it, although word had spread that my marriage to Joseph was near.

Undisturbed by anyone, I dedicated those long and tiring days to meditation. I took advantage of the calm to mentally review the things that in the preceding days I had been keeping in my heart, so as not to let pass in vain treasures that I sensed were very great but that, upon receiving them, far exceeded my immediate capacity of comprehension.

Moreover, since I could already feel the child within me, I began to do what all mothers do: talk to Him. You see, John, I already knew, by now, that he was the Messiah and, after having listened to Zechariah and Elizabeth, I was much more aware than at the beginning of the spiritual greatness of his mission. But I could not treat Him as if He were something other than my son. It was ridiculous for me to talk to Him as if I were talking to a great lord, a tribal chief or a very important priest. He was my son, and I could only speak to Him out of love. Don't think there was any disrespect in that.

It was simply that respect for Him, even though I did not know about His divine nature at the time, was surpassed by love, since love is the fullness of all feelings. So, on the one hand, I felt small before that littleness that I felt bubbling inside me; but on the other hand, I felt I was not his superior, but his mother, the one who had to take care of Him, the one who had to help Him and, more than anything else, the one who loved Him madly, intensely, infinitely.

My love for Him surprised me from the first moment I was aware of its intensity. I had never loved like that before. Not even to my parents, not even to Joseph, and I loved him very much. I had heard about the enormous love of mothers for their children, and since I had no other child than Jesus, I cannot compare. But the fact is that at first, when I noticed how much I loved him, I was a little afraid. Would God be jealous of that love? If He says that He should occupy first place in the heart of the believer, wouldn't I be relegating Him to second place by loving someone as much as I loved the one I already felt in my heart? And that was when I began to understand that my son was God. I began to sense it because I felt that God was not jealous at all; moreover, I noticed that there was not a God and my son, as if they were two different realities, but that love for my son was love for God, and this in a different way from the way we now know that one loves God when one loves one's neighbor.

But, in any case, a week is not enough time, and I was in these meditations when I arrived at Cana and there, I met my father, who was waiting for me at Manasseh's house and who, to spare me explanations that might be annoying, insisted that we should immediately start the trip to Nazareth, in spite of my tiredness, alleging that my mother was so impatient to see me that she could not bear even a delay of an hour.

Joachim immediately filled me in on everything. Well, first he scolded me for not having returned sooner and told me that I did not realize the mess I was in and the trouble I could put Joseph in if it was noticed that I was pregnant. I told him about my cousin Elizabeth's situation, about the enormous need she had for my presence with her and also about how important it had been for me to be in that house, which had become a real school for a young village girl like me. Moreover, I told him, without a tone of defiance but with firmness: "Dear father, we cannot be guided by exclusively human motives. Are we going to follow the criteria of prudence and selfishness? Father, if I had wanted to be prudent and stay out of trouble, I would have told the angel no, to find someone else. We have chosen to always be on God's side and if we abandon His way for an instant, that is when we will be lost. Our salvation lies in trusting in Him and in letting love be the light of our steps".

My father smiled. He looked at me, now calmer, and agreed with me. He had just noticed that I was no longer a child, that I was coming back more of a woman, more self-confident and also more aware of what I had to do. Besides, since he was a good man, he knew how to distinguish right where it was found, without being obsessed by his opinions just because they were his own. So, he told me to excuse him if he had been nervous, but that I should understand that everyone in the family was anxious to get things settled as soon as possible. The wedding, he added, would be immediate, the following week. It would be a good idea to take advantage of the fact that no one noticed my pregnancy to avoid gossip and bad feelings. "Now", he said to me finally, "it's your turn to talk to Joseph. Be calm, because God has intervened at the right time, but you should reassure him and give him explanations about how your wedding is going to be, because neither your mother nor I honestly know, and we have not been able to clarify it. The boy loves you very much and you can't imagine what he has suffered, although, as I said, he is much better now".

We arrived home in just few hours. It was almost dark, so we were able to cross the village without being seen. Anne was waiting for me, with the fire lit and the poor table in our home ready. She jumped as soon as she felt our footsteps prowling around the house and threw herself into my arms. At once she burst into tears, while she smothered me with kisses and asked me, in a broken voice, for my health and for the fruit of my womb.

For my part, I was very calm. I caressed my mother and, smiling, assured her that everything was fine. "Above all". I told her, "we must stay calm. Either we have faith in God or we will perish. There is no need to be nervous. If the Lord has begun this work among us, He will know how to bring it to a successful conclusion". Then, as we sat around the table and ate our olives, bread and cheese from my father's goats, I explained everything that had happened at Ain Karem and the traces of God that I had found in the house of Zechariah and Elizabeth.

The next morning, it was barely dawn, and Joseph was already at my house. That was what had been agreed with my parents. He could not get over his impatience and had to make an effort not to accompany Joachim to Cana to look for me. My parents left us alone and the two of us sat down, facing each other, with the table in between.

I was not blushing, I had nothing to be ashamed of, nor was I afraid. He already knew everything and had accepted it. The truth is that I would have liked him to have trusted me, as my parents had done but it was already an act of generosity on his part that he decided to repudiate me in secret instead of denouncing me publicly, although that decision made the angel's intervention necessary. In any case, we must take into account in his defense the implausibility of the story and also that he knew me much less well than Joachim and Anne.

In any case, there we both were, still engaged, imminent spouses. I was pregnant with the Holy Spirit and awaiting the Messiah, he did not know what to do or what role he should adopt for me and for my son. For a moment I waited, with my eyes on the table, a little out of politeness, since that was how we were taught to behave with men, and a little so as not to be the first to break the fire of explanations so as not to go beyond where it was convenient.

So, it was he who started. And he did it by hitting the nail on the head, like the good carpenter he was. "Forgive me", he said, "I should never have doubted you. I have offended you, even if it was unintentionally and even if I have as an excuse that your father did not want to give me any explanation when he told me. I should have believed the impossible. You deserve that I accept that donkeys fly before doubting your honesty. Deep down, I behaved like a scorned groom and like someone without faith, because I did not imagine that the one who could be behind it was Yahweh. And what's worse, when I decided to repudiate you, even if it was secretly, I did nothing but call myself a fool; something inside me was screaming at me that I was an imbecile for not accepting you, with the child included, since you were still the most valuable thing in my life, and I understood that by rejecting you I was condemning myself to the darkest sentence. But you know how ridiculous we men are and how we have been taught not to cry, not to show weaknesses, not to ask and also not to forgive. So, the angel had to intervene. Thank goodness he was good to me and didn't give me the punishment I deserved for having thought for a moment of rejecting you".

Having said this, he stretched his arm across the table and reached out his hand to me. He was waiting for a gesture from me, he was begging for it not only with his hand; his eyes were watery, and his gaze was that of someone pierced by pain and shame, waiting for a caress as a sign that he had been forgiven. I did not play hard to get. I shook his hand with mine —it was the first time we had touched— and I did even more, I brought it to my lips and kissed it tenderly.

"Joseph", I said to him, with a courage and with words that until recently I would have thought myself incapable of "I love you very much. I am going to be your wife, and I am going to be your wife out of my own free will. Perhaps now, more than before, I realize how much I love you. But I am not going to be a piece of furniture in your house, nor am I going to be a maid. I am going to be your wife. However, some things will be different between us than they are in other marriages. We will no longer have children, nor the normal relations between husband and wife. I want you to know that right now, when there is still time for you not to go through with it. This is a decision that I had already sensed before all this happened and that I did not know how I should explain it to you, or even if it was fair for me to demand it of you.

I always dreamed of being entirely God's, although when my parents proposed marriage to you I was not bothered by the idea, among other things because I was very fond of you and because I did not see how I could carry out this inner call to consecrate myself to the Lord, since in our religion there are no vestal virgins as there are among the Romans. I know that what I am asking of you is difficult to assume, but you and I are believers and, before anything and anyone else, we respect God, and we know what the first commandment of the Law establishes. "Therefore, dear Joseph, think carefully and realize that if the Lord could not ask this of us, you and me, who would He ask it from? As for doubting me". I continued, always with my hand in his, "the truth is that I would have liked it if the angel had not had to intervene, as it happened with my parents, who trusted me without God having to make extraordinary gestures; but it is also true that you knew me much less than they did, and furthermore, it was already a lot from you to accept separating from me without demanding public reparation. In short, what counts is that we have, you and I, you have to understand it well, the both of us, a great mission to fulfill. I am going to be the mother of the Messiah and you are going to be the father. No one, until God wills it, will know how the gestation of the one to be born has taken place. In the eyes of all, you will be his father as much as I will be his mother. Besides, in practice you will have the most important part of this paternity, because being a father, the same as being a mother, is not only to beget and conceive, we are not animals but people; we have to raise and educate our child and, in that task, Joseph, you cannot leave me alone".

Joseph behaved like what he was, like a man of God. While I was talking to him, he was very serene, and I noticed that it was hard for him to accept the fact that our relationship would not be the normal one between a husband and wife. But I also noticed that he accepted everything because he knew that it was God who was asking him to do so. As soon as I finished speaking, he got up, walked around the table and asked permission to kiss me on the forehead. I gave it to him, he embraced me and, in my ear, said to me: "My dove, my beloved, you have told me the most important thing, what I needed to hear and without which my soul would have been in pain all my life, even though I would have gone through everything out of love for God and for you. You have told me that you love me, that you will be my wife and that you are in love with me. Everything else is unnecessary for me. Love, I have understood these days, is not only a matter of physical connection. I will respect your virginity and I will offer you mine, so that they may be useful to the Lord. In our house there will be only love and in that love we will educate our son who, as you say, is also mine. For Him and for you I will fight like a lion and I assure you that there will be no father in Galilee more self-sacrificing than I when it comes to raising my family. That all this is what God wants is enough for me. That you also love me is the greatest gift I could hope for from the Most High and from life".

There was no more, John, I assure you. And that's how it always was. Gestures of tenderness between us, if there were any, because we were husband and wife. But never, absolutely never, was there anything else. I understand that it is difficult for the Greeks and Romans to understand this, as relaxed as their customs are. But anyone who does not understand that two people can live together, loving each other very much, and at the same time remain virgins, believes that man is only an animal, who eats when he is hungry and copulates when he feels like it. We, Joseph and I, put ourselves in God's hands, because we knew that the undertaking was arduous, and we never lacked His grace. Moreover, when our son was born, the house was filled with his presence and, I assure you, he charmed us in such a way that the sacred became daily and, truly, as my cousin Elizabeth had told me, we saw the Lord walking among the pots in the kitchen and among the timbers and nails in the carpenter's shop. Being at his side, watching him grow, feeling ourselves filled with his presence, who had the soul and even the body for anything else but to live for God and for him alone?

After that conversation between us, we called my parents. They came in and immediately smiled when they saw that we agreed on everything. Since Joseph was an orphan and the master of his own actions, he didn't have to do any explanation, so preparations were finalized so the wedding could take place within a week.

Everything went very well, following the strictest ritual established by Jewish law. The *migdanot*, what the groom gives to the bride's family, was given to my father with splendor and he immediately gave it to me so that I could bring it to the marriage in addition to the dowry. It was fifty shekels of silver and some clothes, the usual for a man of modest condition as Joseph was. For my part, I received from my parents as much money and much more in trousseau; things that Anne and I had woven for years, preparing my future home and now became the garments that were destined to welcome the Messiah. The set was not much, but to us, to Joseph and to me, it seemed wonderfull, especially when we saw each other at home, in his house, which from now on was also mine. The festivities, as was the custom in our town, lasted a week and we spent part of the money we had to pay for them, although my parents and other relatives helped us a lot. This expense made me sad, because it meant depriving the little one who was soon to be born and to whom I wanted to offer the best in the world. However, not to do so would have to draw attention to myself and make people talk, and that, dear John, would have much worse. So, from then on, I began to educate my child, and I told Him, feeling Him move inside me, that in order to love, it is sometimes necessary to break with everything, while at other times the best becomes the enemy of the good.

The wedding took place like all the others in the village. Accompanied by my family and my friends, I went to Joseph's house. They used less make up on me than on the others, but I couldn't help but let them apply blush on my cheeks, for the same reason I told you before. On the other hand, I liked the tiara of flowers with which they had adorned my hair better. As we walked through the streets from my parents' house to Joseph's, the shouting was enormous, but when we arrived, when he lifted my veil, took me by the hand and, before the rabbi, pronounced the ritual phrase: "Mary is my wife and I her husband, from this day forward", there was absolute silence. I could not help but feel a sense of duplicity. On the one hand, I was marrying that boy whom I truly loved, and on the other hand, I was renewing to God, inwardly, my first "yes", the one I had given to the angel Gabriel a few months before. I was God's wife and the future mother of the Messiah. I was also Joseph's wife. I was determined to be faithful to both commitments, but a shudder ran through my body because the difficulty of the challenge was not lost on me.

The truth is that it only lasted an instant. While all around me the cries of joy burst out again, those cries so typical that the women of our people make with their tongues, I told the Lord that I was not afraid at all. I was in His hands and I had no reason to doubt that He would know how to lead me through the labyrinth into which He Himself had introduced me. If anyone was trustworthy it was God, so any doubt in this respect was an unforgivable offense to His love and providence. Yet Joseph must have noticed something. With a quick gesture he wiped away a tear running down my cheek, squeezed my chin and whispered in my ear, "Don't be afraid. All will be well. God is with us and I will not live for anything else but to protect you. I feel like the luckiest man in the world to be able to do that. I will keep my promise to respect you, because I am in love with you and to be by your side, and to be able to help you and love you is already more than enough for me".

CHAPTER 6

The crooked lines

In our town, dear John, you know how people say, "God writes straight with crooked lines". I have seen that this is also known here in Ephesus, and perhaps it is the fruit of the common experience of all the people who live around this sea that the Romans call theirs. I can think of no better saying than that to describe what happened shortly after we were married.

It didn't take long for my pregnancy to be noticed. It did not take long for the tongues of the gossipy women to be untied. There was no danger, because we were married, and besides, in the eyes of the others it was only a symptom that Joseph had been too quick to take possession of his future wife. It was not the first time it had happened in Nazareth, nor would it be the last. The difference was that from us, from Joseph and me, something like that could not be expected.

The two of us, and also my parents, who were the ones in on the secret, were not too hurt to see rather dirty things being said about us. It was not that we liked it, far from it, but we were prepared to receive those remarks, and when we had given God our blessing, we had already counted on it. It is an advantage, dear John, to accept beforehand that there are going to be problems and to accept them. It prepares you to deal with them without sinking. I worry about those couples who get married believing that everything is going to be easy. Difficulties are inevitable and the best thing to do is to know that they are going to come and not be surprised when they do. What did you expect, should you tell the girl who discovers after the wedding that her husband has defects? Did you think you were marrying an angel? And, of course, the same should be said to him.

Therefore, for Joseph, Anne and Joachim, the scathing remarks did us less harm than expected because we were already counting on them. Whenever a neighbor said something to my mother when she went shopping, she did not get indignant or jump up angrily to defend my unjustly sullied honor, but inwardly offered it to the Lord and said a prayer that we all repeated: "For You, Lord". In this "for You" we found the strength to resist everything. The truth is that for them it was more difficult than for me, because as I was the main target of criticism, since Joseph was more likely to be congratulated by his friends, they were worse off than I was, since they would have liked to be the ones who suffered in order to spare me the difficulties. You know, in love it is always like that, the one who loves wants to replace the beloved in the problems. But both they and I were comforted by that "for You" that we repeated every time something hurt us. Yes, John, we grew a lot spiritually in those days thanks to all those remarks. Those were lessons that I was later able to teach my son. As I also taught Him to keep quiet when you were insulted, as the prophet said: "He was oppressed, and he humbled himself and did not open his mouth...". So, you see, John, from the womb my son was the patient servant announced by Isaiah. Conceived miraculously, in the purest and cleanest way that human beings could imagine, he had to listen, through his mother's ears, to slanders that undermined not only my honor but also his. That is why my silence, offered to God, was from the beginning the best school for what He later had to carry out on the cross. But those were not the only crooked lines through which the Lord wrote his plans straight. We had not been married long, I had just entered my eighth month and we were already preparing, my mother and I, to welcome the child to be born. The comments in the village had died down, as it always happens with these things, and our humble silence had made it possible for us to have no enemies, which would not have happened if we had responded with acrimony to the irony of the neighbors. So, all was going well when a Roman patrol arrived and assembled the men in the square by the synagogue. The writing was read in Latin, and then a scribe accompanying the soldiers translated it into Aramaic for us to hear. It was a surprise for everyone, but more so for Joseph and me.

It was an edict of the emperor Augustus, which, it was said, was valid for the whole empire and therefore also for Israel. It ordered every man to go with his family to register in his place of birth or in the place where his family originally came from. This was, politically, terrible, for it reminded us once again of our subjection to the Romans; in fact, there was no lack of riots and revolts among the Zealot guerrilla groups, who spoke of resurrecting the ancient rebellion of the Maccabees against the pretensions of Antiochus the Syrian. In reality, it was an economic measure, destined to have the people under control in order to be able to collect their taxes properly and so that no one would escape from them because they were not registered in the census. This was understood by everyone and for this reason the people felt hurt, because it affected their pockets more than their honor.

But for Joseph and me the problem was very different. Joseph was of the lineage of David. He was forced, therefore, to go to Bethlehem, which is south of Jerusalem. From Nazareth and in my condition, it was a week-long trip, similar to the one I had made when I was in the home of Zechariah and Elizabeth. We ran many risks in doing so, risks of miscarriage, because my pregnancy was very advanced and the trip was tiring, risks of suffering attacks and looting, not only by bandits but also by the Zealots, who immediately threatened to kill those who supported the edict of Augustus, accusing them of being idolaters and collaborators; risks, in short, because we did not know what we would find in Bethlehem, since there were many in Israel who had their origin in David, and, if they all went there, there would be no possibility of finding a place in the town.

However, we had to obey. Once again, we felt like a reed whipped by the wind. We looked at each other, our hands clasped and worry in our eyes. The baby was playing inside me and kept kicking me, which made me even more nervous because it reminded me of the imminence of his birth and the fragility of his and my condition. Besides, I was constantly fatigued, since it was my first delivery, and I had no experience on how to deal with that tiredness that took over me completely and left me almost useless from the early hours of the afternoon.

"What are we going to do, Mary", asked my husband. "If we don't go, we will have a lot of trouble with the Romans. If we set out, we will have to risk an attack by the Zealots and put you and our son in danger for the hard journey".

"Joseph". I replied as I smiled at him to reassure him, "it seems to me that we are going to have to get used to surprises. I've already had a few in these eight months and I'm sure this won't be the last. Don't forget what we have already talked about: only if we blindly believe in God and that He is behind everything, including the most incomprehensible things, will we be safe. If we doubt, if we get nervous and want to implement our plans at all costs, it is very likely that we will make a mistake. Don't you think that if God has taken the trouble to undertake this work, that of the birth of the Messiah, He will not allow it to be frustrated by an edict of the Roman emperor? Is He not much greater and more powerful than all the lords of the earth? Again, Joseph, I repeat to you the words of the prophet Isaiah, words we must never forget. 'In confidence is your strength'. So, let's get everything ready to leave as soon as possible".

It did not take us many days to do so. As we were not the only ones who had to travel, many caravans were organized throughout the country, so that the roads were crowded with people. It was an additional nuisance, but at the same time it was a measure of protection against bandits.

My husband prepared the donkey we had at home with great care and made me a kind of basket in which I could ride protected from the sun and in relative comfort. He, on the other hand, always marched on foot, next to me, carrying the bridle of the animal. Fortunately, he was so tame that he did not give us a single scare on the way. This time we did not stop at Ain Karem, so as not to take a detour and thus take less time to reach Bethlehem. We did not pass-through Jerusalem either, but went around it to avoid the huge crowds of people in the city, which made me tired just by seeing it from afar. We did stop, almost at the beginning of our trip, in Cana, at the home of Manasseh and Leah. They had attended our wedding and had given us a splendid gift that helped us a lot in the first steps of the marriage, with so many expenses. Now they welcomed us as warmly as ever and made it easy for us to travel to Jerusalem, for Manasseh had organized several caravans to lead through most of Israel the pilgrims who, like Joseph, had to comply with the edict. Leah showed me little Levi, who had grown a good deal during that time, and made him kiss me, at the same time asking me to continue praying for him, because she did not want him to be healthy only in body, but also in spirit. As we left their house, they gave us several shekels, as they always did, which Joseph refused to accept and which I had to take so as not to snub them. I did not feel bad about accepting them, because, dear John, there is nothing wrong with being poor and accepting alms when one is hardworking and does all one can to get by. The bad thing comes when you get used to living on that help. Moreover, it seemed to me that this and the other gifts from Manasseh and Leah were contributions from all the good men of Israel to the cause of the Messiah, even though they had not the faintest idea of what was brewing in my belly. If generous alms were given to the Temple, why, then, would donations that might enable the Messiah to carry out his mission not be accepted? And we must not forget that helping the works of God is a good fortune, so that almsgiving is not a favor done to Him from whom everything comes, but the occasion of being able to contribute, with something of what He Himself has given us, to the best of causes, His own. But this was more difficult for Joseph to understand, so it was I who accepted it and kept it. Soon, on the other hand, we would need it very much.

We arrived in Bethlehem at mid-morning. It was the last stage of our trip. We had to settle there and register, to return to Nazareth as soon as possible, for which a few months would have to pass, because the birth was already upon us and I did not want to travel with the newborn child. We knew, from other pilgrims we met on the way, that the city of David was overcrowded. It was small and could not accommodate all the people who claimed to be descendants of the great king of Israel. In fact, many had decided to settle in Jerusalem or in other villages, waiting for the Roman registration to take place. But we, beset as we were by the rush of childbirth, could not afford to be going back and forth, and Joseph by no means wanted to leave me alone. So, we had no choice but to find a place to stay in an inn or in a house that would take us in.

If you only could have seen, dear John, what we had to go through in Bethlehem. Joseph had no acquaintances there and the letters of recommendation that Manasseh gave us were of no use to us. The two hostels in the village were full and, frankly, I was glad not to find a place there because of the mess and the bad atmosphere. Joseph was nervous; leading the colt by the bridle, he took me from house to house begging for a place. He even showed me to the women so that they would take pity on me, claiming that I was about to give birth. All the places were full, mostly of relatives, although in some houses they had also accommodated strangers like us, but who had been lucky enough to arrive earlier. It was not that they treated us badly: many women felt sorry for me, they promised me help for when the birth took place, but they showed me the house, full of people and unable to accommodate anyone else.

Finally, a lady, seeing our anxiety, told us about some caves that are at the exit of the village, beginning the fall towards the valley. "There —she told us—, only the cattle is kept there, but it is probable that you can find a place to stay, at least for the night". In fact, time had passed and going from house to house, the day was already ending, and the shadows of the night were upon us. We decided to give it a try and, asking around, we found the caves, which, indeed, were not far from the village. There was no one in them. The sheep, the main livestock of the village, were further down in the valley, where the winter pastures are. The caves were labyrinths of more length than width and in the one closest to the entrance we decided to settle in, partly because the smell was less intense there.

Your heart sank, dear John, when you saw that. It was a cave like so many others, which also served as a sheepfold for the cattle, and it was filled with their excrement. The smell was unbearable, and we were afraid to look at the blackness of its nooks and crannies, in case some vermin came out of there. Joseph went through them with a lit torch and returned, assuring me that they were empty. Exhausted by the hustle and bustle and helped by him, I cleaned as best I could a corner of the first cave where we entered and there we spread our blankets and prepared to spend the night. The colt stayed with us, to keep us warm and to protect us with his body.

I had to reassure Joseph again, although, I must confess, John, that night I would have needed someone to reassure me too. But you know how we women are, we always have to act strong, even if we are trembling inside. He, my poor, good Joseph, was demoralized at the sight of that miserable stable.

"This is not a suitable place for the Messiah to be born", he said emphatically. "We are leaving this place tomorrow. At whatever cost, I will find a decent place for you and him. What kind of a man am I" added the poor man, "if I cannot find a decent place for my son to be born, who is also the one sent by God to save his people?".

"My dear", I replied, "don't be nervous. Remember what happened to your ancestor, King David, for whose sake we are here tonight. He too wanted to build a great temple to the Lord, and Yahweh did not accept it. Perhaps he wanted to teach him a lesson. It is possible that he also wants to teach us and other men something with this humiliation that we are now going through. Because the truth, Joseph, is that there is no palace in Jerusalem worthy enough to house the Messiah. Anything is too little for him. Is this not, then, a sign from the Most High, telling us that what the Messiah has come to seek is not luxury or honor, but humility of heart? If he were born in a palace, how would those who live in caves feel him to be theirs? How could they aspire to give him something if he already had everything from his cradle? And without giving, how can one experience love? Deep down, and this is what a woman who is about to become a mother tells you, you only love that which costs you a little, that which in some way you have built, that which depends on you. If God presents Himself to us in a very high way, we can adore and fear Him, but if, in addition, He presents Himself to us as humble and needy, we can also help Him, and thus it will be easier for us to love Him. Do you not understand, dear Joseph, that the Messiah is about to be born and that the Lord is giving lessons to you and to me, so that later we can give them to Him and to all the people? This will be one of the first lessons we will give him:

> "Son, we wanted to offer you a palace and we could only give you a cave. Many men will do the same, they will want their soul to be a holy and perfect house for you and instead they will only manage to make room for you in a place where the filth of sin abounds; do not reject them, do not run away from the poor in body or soul, rather look at their good intention and if they cannot give you more than a stable do not refuse to live in it, because you were born in a cave refuge of animals and not surrounded by marble and silk".

That is how we fell asleep that night. We were a little cold, despite the warmth of our donkey, but that too we offered to the Lord. The "for You" was, once again, more effective than the best reward for facing something that would have made anyone recoil who was not animated by the greatest motive: love.

In the morning Joseph went out to look for another place. He said he would not rest easy unless he tried to find something better. I was sure that all this was not a coincidence and that, for some reason that I did not understand but that I was beginning to sense, everything was part of the Almighty's plans. So, I set out to make our piece of cave a relatively clean and comfortable place.

So, when Joseph returned, disheartened and with all the denials in the world upon him, he found a much more welcoming place than the one he had left. He brought food and some clothes, which he had to buy at usurious prices, since the Bethlehemites were getting rich in a short time by exploiting foreigners like us.

We were eating our bread with oil and cheese when a farmer arrived. He had a cow with him and was surprised to find us there. Irritated, he asked us who had given us permission, because that cave was his and he used to keep his cattle there, among others that cow that he had just milked and that he had not been able to leave there the night before because he had not had time. But now the animal had to take its place and we had to leave the cave immediately. I thought: "Even this, Lord, must be accepted. That a cow should be preferred to your envoy. That the savior of Israel should be born in the field, in the cold and fear, so that an animal should be sheltered. Not only are we homeless, but animals are preferred to us. But, Lord, in this as in all things, may your will be done. In your hands we are, my son included, and I will not be the one to doubt your loving providence" So I took Joseph by the hand, who was arguing with the farmer and reasoning with him about my state, and I asked him to be quiet and to leave the cave. We left. I could not avoid a tear, but it was only one. Inwardly I forgave the man at once, so that there would be no trace of anger in me, for I felt that any bad feeling would do more harm to my son than the worst frost we could suffer facing the night in the open in the middle of winter.

Soon we were outside, where we found our little donkey, which we had not wanted to bring into the cave during the day. The cow was there too. She looked at us with those astonished and a bit silly eyes that these animals have and continued eating the scarce grass that was on the ground. I got on the colt and we were about to leave when the countryman appeared with one of our blankets in his hand. He was grumpy, more with himself than with us. He threw the blanket at us without saying a word and grabbed the cow by the cowbell to put it inside. But the animal did not move. The farmer turned in surprise and began to curse. "What's the matter with you?" —he said. "You are the tamest in the village, come on, move or I'll beat you to death".

Joseph and I looked at the animal with surprise and a little pity. The cow, impassive, spread her legs a little further apart and resisted the countryman's attempts. He grabbed a stake and began to beat it ferociously, unloading on it the anger he felt against himself for his bad deed. The animal did not even moo. With its head bent down, it endured the blows. From time to time, it looked at us and continued to resist the sovereign beating. The only noise that could be heard was that of our donkey, which suddenly began to bray and get nervous, so I had to get off for fear that it would drop me. And so on, until the man got tired. He looked at Joseph and me, who were dismayed at the outburst of anger that possessed him, but we did not dare to intervene so that he would not unleash his fury on us. Finally, sweating profusely, he stopped beating the animal, which was bleeding in several places, and turned to us. "There you have the cave", he said to us, "and also the cow, God knows who was on the verge of foreign a woman to give birth she won't go in. Maybe she has more heart than I do, who have been on the point of forcing a woman to give birth in the street. Stay in peace"; he said, his voice cracking with fatigue, "and you will give me what you can for the rent of the cave and the animal. I wish you well". And he left. I wanted to thank him, but Joseph prevented me. The atmosphere was not conducive to anything but silence. Later on, we had the opportunity to be friends with him and to understand the bitterness of his spirit.

Joseph took me gently by the arm and helped me into the cave, taking care that I did not slip.

Smiling, he said to me, "Remember about Balaam's donkey. In this case, the cow has not spoken, but she has been very explicit in defending the rights of the Messiah. We will have to take care of her".

That is how we settled in that blessed cave that brings me so many good memories. That is how we arrived in Bethlehem, by a decree of a distant emperor who neither knew of us nor cared about us, but who allowed the Scriptures to be fulfilled and that of my son, of the descendants of David, it could be said what the prophet Micah had announced: "And you, Bethlehem, land of Judah, are not, no, the least among the chief clans of Judah; for out of you shall come forth a leader who will shepherd my people Israel".

The Lord knew, John, the importance that our race gives to the ancient prophecies and did not want to leave any loose end. Yahweh looks down from heaven and sees everything, the past, the present and the future; we, on the other hand, are blind to anything beyond what is in front of us and already believe that we know everything; that is why, when we do not understand something, we get nervous and even doubt that God exists or that he loves us. An old woman tells you, this John be calm, always have confidence and you will see the resplendent face of God shining in the sky, dissipating the darkest clouds.

As for how the birth of Jesus came about, I will tell you another day. Now I am going to rest for a while and remember, that these stories so far away are for me sweeter than honey and more precious than the best of treasures.

CHAPTER 7

The Word became flesh

We did not stay long in the cave, as we were soon able to find a house, a very poor one, in which to stay. But in the meantime, the birth of my son took place.

How would I explain it to you so that you, a man, could understand me? I hardly think a woman would understand me, because what happened that night in the month of Tebet was like no other birth. And yet it was. It was just that, a birth. The child was born. Joseph was there, by my side, breaking the custom that keeps men away from women at such times, but it was just that we were very much alone. Not quite alone, though. Two women from the village had agreed to accompany me when the time approached, Joseph had time to go and warn them before it happened. So, three people were there to help me, although my good husband did not know how to do anything but keep the fire burning and twist his tunic in his hands.

The child was born as if a ray of light went through a crystal, cleanly. The women didn't notice, with all the blood and the attention given to the little boy. Least of all Joseph. I noticed something strange, but I wasn't in the mood for details either. The fact is that it hardly hurt, and the efforts and contractions produced more anguish and nerves than harm. But don't be surprised about this, dear John, remember that nothing is impossible for God. It was more difficult for me to become pregnant without any contact with a man, and it happened. I have thought about it many times and, to tell the truth, perhaps everything could have been otherwise, I am referring to the birth, but it was like that; perhaps the Most High wanted to show, once again, his presence, his power, his very special paternity; perhaps it was to protect me, so that my virginity would not be undermined, although I think that most probably he wanted to teach me a lesson, right from the first moments of my son's life: He had not come into the world to make anyone suffer nor to break anything that was whole, but to redeem everyone and rebuild what was broken. Just as sin did not enter by the will of God, but against it, so it was with my son: the suffering that was linked to his person —and it was and has been so much— is not his fault but the fault of those who oppose him and who, in doing so, cause harm to themselves and to others.

But all these are minor details compared to the most important thing of all: my son was there; He was born, and I was holding Him in my arms. How can I explain it to you, John! He was just another child, and yet He was unique, different; He looked like a star, but what can I say, more than a star, for he was the sun itself. When I took Him in my arms, so small, so fragile, a tiny, wrinkled little thing, with his little eyes closed and his little mouth looking for my breast and crying when He could not find it, it seemed impossible to me that He was anything else but a normal child. Joseph also looked at him with curiosity and with a little bit of fear; that fear that usually assails parents when they hold their child in their arms for the first time; fear of dropping him, of squeezing him too hard, of hurting him, of breaking that delicate doll. Maybe I thought it would be otherwise, that He would be born with some distinctive power, that He would be, from the very beginning, stronger, more awake, more superhuman. But none of that happened. He was a completely normal child, so normal that neither of the two women noticed anything, so, after a while, they congratulated me on the happy birth and went home.

Joseph and I were left alone. I was very tired, but unable to fall asleep. I had Him there, in my arms, curled up under the blankets, receiving the warmth of my chest and not too far from the two animals that blocked the entrance to the cave and prevented the cold wind of early Tebet from passing through. It was night outside, and yet by the light of the small fire that Joseph kept burning —not too big so as not to fill everything with smoke— the cave seemed illuminated by the greatest of brightness. Don't think that rays of light were coming out of the child. He was the light. His little angel face was very white, and the glow of the fire multiplied on his cheeks as if it were a mirror of those used by noble ladies.

I could not stop looking at Him. I looked at Him and, for the first time, there, in that cave that I would have liked to turn into a palace in honor of Him, I noticed a feeling that I had not had until then. I looked at Him and, suddenly, I began to adore Him. I was frightened. You know that in our religion any representation of the Most High is forbidden and that we are very severe even when it comes to mentioning the name of God. The Almighty cannot be shaped by the hands of artists so inclined to make idols which they then honor as much as they manipulate. Who is this child? I asked myself as my eyes were caught in his dream. He is the Messiah, I said to myself at once. But what Messiah? And, above all, if He is only an envoy of the Most High to rescue his people from slavery, like Moses or the judges or the kings, why was He not born in a normal way? Why was He not begotten like other men, from the love between husband and wife? If He has come into the world in this way and with this origin, who is his true father? For if it is clear that I am the mother, only God can claim his paternity.

Don't think it was too many guesses for a woman who had just given birth, John. On the contrary, it was the least I could think of on that blissful night. There, giving him from the abundance of my breast, holding his weak little body and caring for the fragility of the one who had been announced as the Messiah, the only thing to do was to stay in awe of God's plan and meditate on the why of things and how they would unfold.

"I love you". I said kissing his forehead. "I love you and I thank God for having you with me. It hasn't been easy, and I've been very scared. But now that you're here I'll give it all up for good. I would almost say, my little one, that I wouldn't mind if none of what the angel announced to me were to happen. I never dreamed of greatness beyond my capacity, nor did I aspire to be respected and admired. Now, having become the mother of the Messiah, everything seems so strange. What Messiah are you, born in a sheepfold, whose court is a cow and a donkey and whose parents are two humble yokels? Where is your power, where is your greatness? And yet I am not disappointed. You are worth more than anything they will ever get from you and I know this, I am your mother, and I hope the whole world learns it when you grow up and fulfill the mission you were born to do. Perhaps men will love you for what you give them, for what you represent, for your message, for your victories or, even, for your miracles. I, my dear child, will love you for you. It is not that the rest does not matter to me, because it would be like despising God's plans, but, understand me, I am your mother and, in this chest, you can always find pure love, love for you and not only for what you bring with you. You are the gift, you are the treasure, and if there were nothing else, it would be enough for me".

Joseph listened to me, sitting next to me and always keeping an eye on the fire. Suddenly, he asked me for the child, who was sleeping peacefully. Before, as I told you, he had already held Him, as required by law, because, as soon as He was washed, the women of the village had taken Him away, joyfully announcing to him that He was a boy. But he had given Him back to me at once, as if he were afraid that he might drop Him. Now, on the other hand, it was he who asked me for Him. I sat up a little so that I could hold Him without waking Him up, and he held Him in his strong arms, wrapped in the finest cloth we could get in town.

Thus, in the arms of that man whom I loved so much and who had agreed to pretend to be his father without being so, and even more, to stop being the father of other children forever, my boy was like that for a long time, warm and asleep. Joseph, always so quiet, hardly said anything. Only, after looking at Him for a long time, he kissed his cotton forehead and said, softly, so as not to wake Him up: "My son, I love you too. I don't know what blood runs in your veins, apart from that of your mother.

I don't know who you are, if you are a normal man or an extraordinary being under this simple appearance. I don't even know if I should kneel before you, as the Messiah that you are. What I do know is that now, at least now, you need me and with all that I am you can count on me. I thank the Most High for having noticed me in order to take part in his divine work. To help Him, the Almighty, is the greatest honor, the greatest blessing. I do not know what your followers will say someday, if you have any; perhaps some of them will resent your service; it will be because they have not understood anything. To be an instrument of God is not a burden, but a privilege. To spend my whole life for Him, through you for Him, is the greatest fortune I could ever have aspired to. That is why I call you today, my son, and tell you that I am here to give my life for you, to watch over your dream, to take care of your mother, to make it possible for you, when God wills, to undertake the work for which You have come". He kissed the child again and gave him back to me.

We hardly slept that night. Joseph laid down beside me, to give me warmth, and every now and then he would get up to add some wood to the fire. It was soon dawn. Fortunately, our landlord's cow was already giving very good milk, after having been without it for several days because of the beating. Joseph milked her and heated the milk for me, crumbling some bread in it and mixing in some honey. He gave it to me to drink, made sure everything was in order and left for the village. He had to fulfill the registration requirement, as the law mandated, and it was urgent for him to do so, as if, after the fact, he had been relieved of a great burden.

When he returned, he had already registered the child, he and I, in the Roman registry. He had managed to pay, for the three of us, the first tax, thanks in good measure to the generous help that Leah had given us. This is, John, how the good people began to collaborate in the work of my son's redemption.

And others soon followed. The first day I hardly moved from the bunk that Joseph had built for me, which, stuffed with straw as it was, was comfortable and warm. He was going back and forth to the village, preparing the food and very attentive to my every need. As crafty as he was, he had even prepared a cradle with an old crib that was in another of the caves, so that I could, the next day, leave my child there for a while. The two women who had helped me with the birth had shown up in the middle of the morning; they had brought me, in a clay pot, chicken broth with a boiled egg in it and some delicious honey cakes. For the rest, it seemed that the world was ignoring us and we were not in the mood for more visits.

It was late at night and Joseph was sleeping, as the day before, very close to me to give me as much warmth as possible, when we were awakened by footsteps at the mouth of the cave. The donkey got up and began to bray. The cow threatened to stand up but chose to remain lying down. Joseph jumped up and rushed outside, frightened and imagining the worst, ready to risk his life to defend us. A hoarse, wine-scorched voice reassured him at once. I, from inside, heard everything, worried at first, then surprised, clutching the little boy to my chest and ready to flee through the other end of the cave to seek refuge outside, in the darkness of the night.

They were shepherds who told a very strange story, which contrasted with how normal everything had been at the birth and in the first hours of my son's life. Although it was already winter and it was the coldest time of the year, they slept down in the valley with their flocks of sheep, because even at that time there is still grass in our land, as you know. To defend themselves from thieves, they took turns keeping watch, and while some took shelter in a cave, two stayed by the animals and by the generous fire that they always kept burning. In the previous days Joseph and I had seen, at night, those points of light that sowed the bottom of the valley with shy stars and we knew that those rough and good men were warming themselves around them.

There were eight or nine of them. The one who had begun to speak, the eldest of the group, told Joseph a strange story. An angel had appeared to them and, after reassuring them, had said: "I bring you good news of a great joy, which will be for all the people and not only for you. Today, in the city of David, a Savior has been born to you, who is Christ the Lord. This will be a sign to you: you will find a child wrapped in swaddling clothes and lying in a manger". The chief shepherd, Rason by name, also said that they had seemed to hear choirs of angels in heaven and that some thought they heard a kind of hymn, like the one sung in the holy temple in Jerusalem, which went something like this, "Glory to God in the highest, and on earth peace to men whom the Lord loves".

That had taken place in the early evening. They had run to the village and asked at the inns if there had been any births in those days. No one knew anything. They were already in despair when a scribe, one of those who had gone to Bethlehem accompanying the Roman official to take note of the inscriptions in the register and to collect the taxes, had told them that that same morning, very early, a man had come to register with his wife and his son, who, according to him, had just been born and whom they had named Jesus. But he did not know where he lived. Another, then, remembered that his wife had told him that the couple staying in the caves on the outskirts had had a child and that she had been helping the mother, who was as young as she was beautiful and poor.

They didn't need any more directions. In four strides they stood before our cave and there they were, begging Joseph to let them see the child, because the child who, according to the angel, would be the savior of Israel and whom the heavenly messenger had even designated with a title that is reserved for the Most High God, that of "Lord", had to be very special. They did not want to do us any harm, only to pay us homage and rejoice with us.

They were very surprised that the Messiah had been born in such a miserable place, but they did not dare to doubt the words of the angel, at least not until they had seen with their own eyes whether or not he was someone extraordinary.

Joseph was hesitant, suspicious of a trap. I sensed it and, from inside, half incorporated in my bunk as I was, I asked him to let them pass. "Perhaps", I thought, "my son should start his work soon".

They entered the cave in line and one at a time, preceded by my husband. They carried their caps in their hands and on their shoulder straps their leather jackets, into which they had hastily stuffed some poor present. They looked at me, they looked at Jesus and me, very surprised. For a few minutes that seemed eternal to me, no one spoke, and the silence was not even broken by the noise of the animals. Suddenly, one of them exclaimed: "This is a farce. There is only a normal child here, in the same cave where we put the sheep. I don't see the Messiah anywhere. We must have made a mistake and perhaps another child was born in some other house in Bethlehem. Let us go and leave these starving people alone, for they are as much the fathers of the savior of Israel as I am the prophet". Immediately Rason jumped up as if bitten by a snake and struck his companion with a blow that almost knocked him to the ground. "Shut up, you animal! —Who made you the identifier of the Messiah? Wasn't David born in a humble house, and didn't Samuel himself get confused and Yahweh had to correct him, warning him that God's gaze is not like man's, because man looks at appearances while God looks at the heart? If we, who pride ourselves on being descendants of the great King David have not learned that lesson, you will tell me who will remember it in Israel. This child may be as great as Samson or Gideon. Who are we to doubt it? Besides, not only is there the word of the angel, but here, in this cave, something I have never noticed before, not even when I am in the synagogue or when I go to the temple in Jerusalem. I don't know what it is, but looking at this creature and his mother, I feel something inside that is as if my guts and my heart were asking me to be a little kinder".

Having said that, Rason put one knee to the ground, as one does before the nobles and great lords. The others, even the one who seemed most reluctant, imitated him at once. They asked us to pray to the Most High for them and their families, and left by my bed the few things they had brought with them. Then, realizing that it was not the time to disturb a mother who had just given birth, and although the child had not even woken up all the time, they made a gesture to leave.

They were already taking their leave when Joseph stopped them to ask them a great favor. "I would like to ask you, my friends", he said, "to keep the matter of the angel a secret. If word gets out, perhaps the child's life may be in danger, for there will be no lack of those who feel threatened by the coming of a Messiah. So do not tell anyone and I even ask you to help us keep a low profile in Bethlehem. We will be here for a few days and as soon as we can, since we have already registered in the census of Augustus, we will return to our village. Of course, if you know of any work for me, as I am a good craftsman, I would be grateful if you would let me know".

"You see", he told me when they left, "we are not left out of God's hand, even if at times we seem to be so alone. The Lord carries out His plans in mysterious ways, and what has happened with the shepherds should help us to persevere in our faith in Him. Now rest while I place these gifts, for tomorrow we will surely find a good place to move to until you are strong enough to return home".

This was not the case. We still had to stay in the cave for two weeks, until the number of people who came to Bethlehem for the census began to decrease and we were finally able to find a place to stay in an old cottage on the outskirts of the village that was given to us by the family of one of the shepherds who had visited us that night. By the way, they behaved very well. We hardly saw them, but almost every day we found some gift at the door of the cave, something always humble but very appreciated from someone who needed everything like us. They left it at night, while we slept, and only on some occasions did they come during the day in very small groups, to beg us to let them see the child and to ask me, as the greatest of gifts, to let them hold him in their arms for a little while. They said they hoped to tell their children and grandchildren that they had helped the Messiah to get ahead and that this, being useful to God, was for them, who knew so little, a blessing from heaven.

With the shepherds, John, I learned how different we humans are, sometimes because of something that escapes us, such as our origin. For the poor, any gift they receive is a reason for joy; for those who have everything, they are grateful for nothing and nothing is enough for them. For the humble and simple, to help God is a blessing, for they understand that they are honoured by being able to be useful to the Almighty. On the other hand, those who could give so much, consider that if they help, they will lose something and that, furthermore, God is not doing them a favor by asking for their help, but on the contrary, the Most High should be grateful to them if they agree to meet their demands. With the shepherds, John, I had the opportunity to realize that our elders are right when they say that the sin of the Evil One is pride. Pride separates us from God and from his grace more than anything else, and pride appears, with full hands, when we do not realize that God deserves everything and that we, in giving it to him, are only doing our duty.

A week later, as required by law, we called the *mohel* to come and circumcise the child. We had to do it in the cave, but neither I was ashamed, nor were our new friends, because poverty is only shameful when it comes from idleness, and that was not our case. Ageo, the *mohel* of Bethlehem, asked Joseph the ritual question, "What name do you want to give the child?" And my husband, to everyone's surprise, answered just as the angel had shown him, "He will be called Jesus, because He will save the people from their sins". The circumciser, with a clean cut, left on my little one the mark of our race while he said: "Blessed be the Lord our God, who sanctified us with his precepts and commanded us to be circumcised". After this, Joseph, the ten witnesses commanded by the law, and myself replied, "Blessed is He whom thou hast taken and chosen". Meanwhile, the child wept disconsolately in my arms. It was almost the first time he did so, as a symbol that that law was to serve Him with pain and suffering. His little piece of skin and his blood lay on the table, staining a clean linen cloth, the red on the white, the detached flesh. I don't know what cloud then troubled my sight, what dire omens crossed my heart, but I pressed my little son to my breast and, turning around, I gave him to suckle, so that he would calm down.

Anyway, the days went by and, in the meantime, Joseph spent his time working to gather anything for the house.

Generally, he was paid for his small tasks in kind: bread, wine, an old hen on one occasion that gave us a very good broth, vegetables, some clothes. We had cow's milk and that's how we got by. Finally, as I said, we were able to leave the cave.

We were in the new house when the forty days from the birth were completed, the time prescribed by the law to redeem, in the temple, our son, who was the firstborn. And also, to proceed with my purification since, according to the same law, I was defiled by conception and childbirth. Not that I felt at fault, as you will understand, for having accepted that God's will be fulfilled in me and that the Messiah could have been born, but we decided that it was much better not to give much to talk about and we set out to fulfill scrupulously what had been ordered. Again, as on so many occasions, prudence prevailed. It was not a question of cowardice. It was simply the wisdom of the poor. It is not worthwhile to draw attention to anything but truly important things, as my son would later do when he did healing on Saturdays to relieve someone. Peace is almost always better, even if you have to pay the price of not doing exactly what is best, because the best is often the enemy of the good. Conflict should be avoided whenever it can be avoided, whenever the good at stake is not greater, because peace is something so great that there are few things worth losing it for.

We bought the two turtledoves in the marketplace and offered them to the Levite, along with the five shekels of ransom for the child. It was then that that woman, Anne, who had a reputation as a prophetess and who had spent almost her whole life in the service of the temple, approached me without my noticing. Apparently, that was one of her occupations, to scrutinize the mothers who came to the house of God with their children and, after pronouncing a few kind words, to pass on to others, as if she were always in search of someone she could not find. Some thought she was crazy, while others thought she was simply a good woman who had not had any children and who liked to cuddle with others' children. As soon as she saw Jesus, she was full of praise for Him, not at all comparable to what she said about the other children. But I hardly had time to thank her for the beautiful words and blessings she was uttering, because Anne asked us not to move from that spot for a moment.

She soon returned. She was accompanied by an old man, Simeon, another of the regulars around the temple. Anne said to him: "Look, look, look at his eyes. Look at the light in his hair. Make use of your God given sense Simeon and notice the purity of the mother. He's here, it's Him, we've found Him at last". Simeon approached me, slowly. I, at first, pressed the child to my breast and made a gesture to leave, because all this frightened me. I was always so afraid that something bad might happen to that fragile creature! I seemed to feel that I was being stalked by the breath of the Evil One, that he could not bear that the redeemer of mankind had been born. Then Simeon said something that left me motionless. He called me with the same title as my cousin had done: "Full of grace", he said to me in a hoarse, plaintive voice that could make children shiver with fear on winter nights. "Let me, I beseech you, let me see Him". I looked at Joseph and, when he hesitated, I chose to show him a little, but without letting Him out of my arms. The little boy was awake and was already beginning to smile, something he did frequently and to almost everyone who approached Him. That smile was what Simeon saw when he brought his face close to my son's face.

He stood like that for a few minutes, hunched over the boy, tall as he was. He looked at him with those charcoal eyes of his that rose from his wrinkled face and gave him an almost terrible expression. He remained like that until he separated from me and raised his arms to the sky, standing another while in silence with his gaze set high above, contemplated, also in silence, not only by Anne, Joseph and me, but by a group of curious onlookers that was growing larger and larger. Suddenly, he exclaimed in a loud voice: "Now, Lord, according to your promise, you may let your servant go in peace, for my eyes have seen your savior, a light to enlighten the nations and the glory of your people, Israel".

His words were very beautiful, which were received by those present with signs of joy and surprise, and which helped us to reaffirm our certainty that behind the apparent normality of our son, a mystery of salvation was hidden, which holy men were able to grasp. So, with Joseph's permission, I let him hold Him. He took Him in his trembling arms, always under our gaze, alert that he might drop Him. He kissed his forehead and then handed Him back to us. To our surprise, then, having Jesus with me, he knelt down before Him, which, as you know John, we Jews never do before any human being, for it is strictly forbidden to us. Joseph helped him up quickly, lest he should be seen by a priest and be accused of blasphemy.

We had already said goodbye to Anne and him and had turned our backs on them, walking hastily towards the exit of the temple to get away from the mob of curious onlookers who wanted to contemplate the child, when we heard a cry from behind us. We spun around, fearing that he had collapsed and needed our help. Then we saw him, standing upright, with his legs spread wide and both arms outstretched towards the sky; his gnarled staff was on the ground beside him. He really looked like a prophetic figure of the kind our elders tell us about.

His scream had been one of pain, of tearing, of terror almost. His gaze was fixed on the sky and remained so for a few minutes. Quickly a circle formed around him again, this time more numerous. Many of the regular temple attendees knew and respected him, so everyone was aware that he had just received an inspiration from heaven. After a while he lowered his arms and his shoulders slumped, as if under a heavy weight. Then he looked into my eyes. Joseph and I had moved closer to him, always ready to support him if his strength faltered and he fell to the ground. We were very close, so I could almost feel his breath on my face. He spoke to me in a low voice, with a tone akin to agony. "This one is set", he said, "for the fall and elevation of many in Israel, and to be a sign of contradiction, that the thoughts of many hearts may be laid bare; and you yourself a sword shall pierce your soul". Joseph put his arm around my shoulder and pulled me to him, but I could not stop looking at Simeon, whose eyes had begun to shed thick, almost reddish tears. We were stunned, rigid, in the midst of that circle of curious onlookers who began to comment on the strangeness of the prophecy that the old man had cast over that child and that mother, not knowing whether it was a blessing or a curse because of the ambiguity of its content. Simeon suddenly turned and walked quickly away from us, sobbing. Anne followed him, asking him what he had seen, what he meant, why he had told me that terrible thing about the sword. Motionless, we watched as they made their way through the crowd and disappeared into one of the temple courtyards. The people turned, curious, towards us and it was hard for us to get rid of them and leave the temple, with a huge fright in our bodies and souls.

As we walked toward Bethlehem, we had time to meditate on what had happened to us. Joseph tried in vain to minimize its importance. We both knew that it was important, that it was a new warning from heaven. And the worst of it was that we did not know what the elder Simeon had meant when he had uttered his strange prophecy. Then I felt as if an angel was passing his sweet hand over my oppressed heart. It was dusk and the sky was, as befitted the season, covered with clouds that lowered the brightness of the afternoon. However, I noticed that the clarity of the Lord was enveloping us, and I recovered my peace. "Look", I said to my husband, "we should look on the bright side of things. It was a wonderful lesson given to us by those two elders, who spoke, no doubt, on God's behalf".

»The most important thing is that this child we have to take care of is, indeed, the Messiah. And that his task will be to redeem his people. But we should not be surprised that this task will bring him difficulties. In any case, He will always have the Almighty behind Him, who will watch over Him as he has done up to now. As for me, I am afraid of the sword, but I believe that this is the role of all mothers, to live always suffering for our children, fearing their misfortunes and suffering more than they themselves do when they befall them. More over, when I accepted the angel's invitation, I did not do it to cover myself with glory and be honored by the other women of Israel as the mother of the Messiah, but to be useful to God. I only ask the Lord that whatever happens to me may be a release and a relief to him. Let me suffer but let him not suffer. May the sword that pierces my heart, as the good old man prophesied, not enter, in return, into the heart of our son. And may God give me strength to bear it all".

That was how that strange day passed. We arrived at our humble home and, in the days that followed, we were preparing to return to Nazareth as soon as possible when something happened to us that brought the mystery back into our lives.

CHAPTER 8

Rachel's cry

It was mid-morning. I was already well recovered from the fatigue of childbirth, which, as I told you, had not really been that much. The child was very awake and was already opening his little eyes to fix them, still clumsily, on his father and on me, as well as on those things we put in front of him. He was as calm as a sunset on Lake Galilee and as beautiful as a full moon. We were already making plans, John, as I told you yesterday, to return to Nazareth and we even planned to make a short stopover at Ain Karem, which is north of Jerusalem, to spend a few days with Zacharias, Elizabeth and little John.

At this, as I tell you, about mid-morning, I heard a great commotion in the village. Our hut was on the side of the hill, on the opposite side of the road from Bethlehem to Jerusalem, but, as far as I could tell, something big was happening in the village. I was alone, for Joseph used to go out to look for work, either in the fields with the land or the cattle or doing some repairing in the houses. Now in Bethlehem there was money in abundance after the passage of so many strangers, and many were taking advantage of it to improve their homes. At this moment, my husband suddenly pulled open the mat that served as a door to our house and went inside. He was very agitated. "Mysterious characters have just arrived in town, in a caravan with camels and horses. They've come asking for the Messiah. The whole village has come out to greet them and no one knows who the Messiah is. I saw two of our friends, the shepherds, who looked at me worried and I signaled them to be quiet. One of them went in search of Rason, while I ran here. I don't know if we should run away or if we should let them find us".

He was still talking when a well-dressed man appeared at the door of the hut. Behind him, a short distance away, was that shepherd who had insinuated that our son was an impostor because he had not been born with outward signs of greatness. Despite the warnings of the others, he did not hesitate to tell the noble lords that he did know where the alleged Messiah was and immediately, after negotiating a reward, brought them to our house. He did not know whether what he led to us was good or evil. He had acted out of spite and greed. But, without knowing it, as it happened years later with our poor Judas, he had served God as an instrument. Again, the crooked paths. Once again God who acts by bringing good even out of sin.

Because the fact is that he was right. The first one to show himself was a servant. Then his lords did the same. There were three of them, dressed in very different ways. One of them was of the color of the Nubian slaves we had sometimes seen in the Roman retinues, but, unlike them, he was not ragged, but elegantly dressed, like his companions. Joseph, as he always did when there was any danger, stepped between me and the boy and asked them, without raising his voice but firmly, who they were and what they wanted.

They replied, "We are wise men who have come from the East. We dedicate ourselves, in the lands from which one day this chosen and numerous people came out, to study the stars. We know the Most High God and we worship Him alone, even though we are not your race. That is why one day, months ago, we received from Him a message inviting us to leave our land, as your father Abraham did, in search of someone who would reveal to us the fullness of wisdom. This someone could be none other than the king of the Jews, the descendant of David and the great Solomon. So, we went to the capital, Jerusalem, and went to Herod's palace because we assumed that it would be there, from among his descendants, that Yahweh would have chosen the Messiah. But Herod knows nothing and has even asked us to tell him where the Messiah is, so that he too may come to pay him homage and give him his throne. The wise men of Israel have told us that it is in this village of Bethlehem, the cradle of David, where it is prophesied that the redeemer of the people will be born, and that is why we have come. Now this man outside has told us of the angel's appearance to the shepherds, and although he has told us that he thinks you are impostors, he has agreed to show us the way. We want to know if the Messiah is here and, if so, that you will let us see Him". Joseph was blocking their way, although he remained silent, undecided. Then I looked out and with the child in my arms, protecting Him but without hiding him, I said to them: "Here He is. I don't know if it will happen to you as it did to the shepherd who brought you to this house and you will be disappointed by its smallness and our poverty. It is not our task to convince you of anything, because we did not call you and we do not need you. I tell you only that this is the Messiah. Whether you believe in Him or not is your business". At this, the child opened his eyes and looked at them. I assure you, John, He did nothing else, not a single extraordinary gesture or one unbecoming of a little one like Him. But that look was enough for the three of them, in unison and without looking at each other, to fall to their knees. Not only that, but almost immediately they burst into tears.

One of them, Melchior by name, said then, calling me for the first time with this title that so many of you now give me: "Lady, mother of the savior of Israel and of all nations, you cannot understand what we feel. We have spent our lives seeking wisdom. We have given up our youth and so many possibilities of pleasures in that endeavor, and we have given everything for the good of our lives in order to obtain it one day. We are famous not only in our city, but also in Greece, in Rome and even in faraway India. Our friends are the most renowned sages in the world, and they regard us as the first of all. Well, what we have just seen is the ruin of our knowledge. Wisdom, most worthy lady, is not an idea, a thought, a concept that is caught and formulated, with which we work day and night, turning it over and over and polishing it as rivers smooth stones by incessantly striking them. Wisdom, madam, is a child. Wisdom is life. Wisdom is that God has remembered mankind and has decided to intervene again to help them. Wisdom is the love in that creature, so fragile that a tyrant can kill, but so powerful that, without violence, it can change the world. Love, noble lady, is the sum of all the knowledge and the summary of all understanding. And this, though neither you nor your husband know it, is what you now protect in your arms". The magi gave us gifts of great value and full of symbolism. Gold, frankincense and myrrh. I was a little disturbed by their words and had a long time to meditate on them, as well as on the fact that so many cried when they met my son. I was shocked, but not afraid. The whole town of Bethlehem was crowded at the door of our house, for they had followed the strangers, and only the servants of the three foreigners were able to keep the people out. Joseph invited them to sit on the stools he had made himself. They wanted to know everything, and we told them everything. They were more and more amazed. Curiously, they too, like our shepherd friends before them, like old Simeon in the temple, asked me to hold the child in their arms for a moment. It was as if touching him appealed to them all irremediably. "To take care of him", they told me, "is the greatest of gifts. Just by being able to serve him for a moment, we already feel rewarded". They warned us of their fear of Herod and how a noble old Jewish man living in the palace had secretly advised them to try to outwit the King's vigilance, for the last thing he was willing to do was to place his throne at the disposal of the Messiah. So, they told us that, on our departure, they were going to tell everyone in Bethlehem that they had been mistaken and that we were not the ones they were looking for, to remove suspicions, but that we would do well to leave as soon as possible.

They said this, took as a courtesy some of the poor food and fresh water that I offered them and, as quickly as they had come, they left.

For a long time, we could hear the noise of their procession and of the people who followed them. Some loitered about the house, but Joseph,

Rason and the other shepherds, stationed at the door, prevented them from disturbing me. Night fell early, for we were in the middle of winter, although the day had already begun to lengthen, and with the shadows all was quiet again.

"What shall we do, Mary", asked my husband, sitting beside me on the hearth, as Jesus slept in the old manger that still served as a cradle. "These strange messengers of God have advised us to leave as soon as possible. As much as they try to mislead Herod, his spies must have followed them here, and it is very likely that by now he has been informed of this visit. Tomorrow or in the next few days we may be attacked by his henchmen. That is why I think we should leave at once. Besides, we had already planned to leave, so it is only a matter of hastening our return to Nazareth, without passing by Elizabeth's house as we had planned".

I recall that I reassured him and agreed to his plans. I was very puzzled, so surprised and, deep down, so happy, that even if a Roman patrol had appeared at our door at that moment, I would not have been worried. I advised him that we should go to bed as soon as possible and that, at dawn, we should start preparing everything to leave that very day.

But that was not the end of the day's events. We were already asleep when a vivid light startled us, including the child, who woke up but did not burst into tears but kept staring at the one who, little by little, was glimpsed behind the light. You might think, dear John, that we had become so accustomed to the apparitions of angels, the oracles of venerable elders and the visits of portentous magicians that this had become routine. It was not like that.

Neither for Joseph nor for me, of course, although nothing seemed to surprise the little boy, who was just a month old. The fact is that the angel knelt before the cradle of Jesus and touched the ground with his forehead. Then, as on the first occasion, he kissed my hand with one of his wings, and finally, with a bow and a voice full of respect, he addressed Joseph: "Arise", he said to him, "take the child and his mother with you and flee to Egypt and wait there until I tell you. For Herod is going to seek the child to kill Him". He said no more, and we did not ask any questions. It was all very clear. The only difference was that if before we were planning to go north, now God was telling us that it was safer to go south.

The angel disappeared and Joseph and I did not hesitate for a moment. In a short time, we had gathered our few things and had rigged the little donkey. With the child well tucked in and very close to my chest, we started to flee. We left the village in the middle of the night, but just in case anyone saw us, we took the opposite road to the one we wanted and headed for Jerusalem. Then, after having traveled a prudent distance, by shortcuts and paths, we set out for Egypt.

The thing I regretted most was not saying goodbye to our friends. Rason and the others had been very good to us and now we had to flee like this, without saying anything. But Joseph had quieted me when I told him that, claiming that it was better for them not to know anything about us in case Herod's envoys questioned them. Besides, not all of them could be trusted, as had become clear when the magi were brought to our house. They, on the other hand, would understand perfectly well what had happened, for they been with Joseph, after the magi had left, commenting on the risk the child ran if Herod should happen to locate him. "Fortunately". Joseph said to me, "I have not lied to them when I told them this afternoon that we intended to leave for Nazareth as soon as possible, for that was what I believed at the time. The thing is, if anyone asks them, that's what they'll say because they won't know otherwise".

For the rest of the night we hardly spoke. We tried to pay attention to the road, to avoid stumbling, which was not difficult thanks to the beautiful moon shining in the sky. At dawn we were already far from Bethlehem and we were even farther away when we made our first stop to take food. It was then that Joseph started venting.

"I have not understood anything from the first moment, although I have made efforts to accept everything and put myself at the service of the plans of the Most High. But to run away like criminals in the middle of the night, that really overwhelms me. We have been taught, Mary, that

God rewards the good and punishes the bad and that, therefore, when He punishes someone it is because he is bad. What have we done so bad that we have to flee? Why does the Almighty not send an army of angels to confront even the Roman legions if they dare to attempt against his Messiah? Is this always going to happen to us? What dangers await us in this strange land to which we are going, in which our ancestors suffered so much? Will we have to remain in it forever, and will Jesus have to return at the head of an army to liberate Israel?"

Since I had also been meditating during the long hours of travel, and the questions he asked me were similar, I was able to answer some of them. "Dear Joseph", I told him, "remember that it is not up to us to understand, but only to have faith. What has happened is not the fruit of human intelligence, but of God's plans. So, our duty is to obey and second the divine will as faithfully as possible. It is true that we are like a reed blown by the wind, like a dry leaf that is carried to and fro without being able to avoid it. It is true that, for almost a year now, your life and mine have changed so much that it is nothing like what we could have planned. But neither you nor I have the slightest doubt that God is behind everything, so we must trust no matter what happens. As for what you say about reward and punishment, I know that this is how it is taught in the synagogues, but it is also true that some prophets speak otherwise, and there is even the story of Job, who suffered while innocent. Suffering is a mystery, and it has always seemed to me too easy to attribute it to a punishment from God for the sins of the one who is suffering. Our son, in any case, is absolutely innocent and you see, He was not born in the best of palaces as He deserved, nor does He have a court of servants at his service, nor can he grow up without a thousand dangers threatening him. But, in short, what I tell you, Joseph, are things of an inexperienced girl as I am. So, I ask you to be calm and be sure that neither in Egypt nor anywhere else will God cease to protect us, even if we have to wander until the end of our days. The important thing is to save our son, and so far, we are doing that".

Joseph came up to me and kissed my cheek. He did it rarely and always with great respect. But on that occasion, I had the feeling that it was the kiss of a son to his mother, as if, despite the fact that he was the man of the house and older than me, my words had given him support and he had found in me the encouragement that he had begun to lack.

The trip to Egypt was difficult. We made many stopovers and met many different people. We always moved in caravans of Jews, since the commercial traffic between Alexandria and Jerusalem was constant, given that in the great Egyptian city there was a very considerable Jewish colony. We lived there for a few years, until, once again, the angel warned us that the danger had passed. The death of Herod and the strife that broke out among his descendants meant that our case was forgotten, and we were able to return safely. However, since Archelaus, Herod's son, reigned in Judea, we made a great detour and, without even passing through Jerusalem, we settled in Galilee, in our beloved Nazareth.

But it was on the way back, traveling with a caravan from Gaza to Jerusalem, that we learned all that had happened after our departure from Bethlehem. Joseph sometimes stayed at the gatherings that were organized in the evenings around the campfire. The story they told that day immediately caught his attention and then he was able to tell it to me. They were discussing the latest political events, the difficult inheritance of Herod and the last years of that bloodthirsty king. One of those who spoke, to emphasize his cruelty, said that four years before his death and Herod being very worried about his succession, three magicians from Babylon had appeared in Jerusalem, in search of the Messiah. According to these astrologers, He had been born and they thought they could find Him in the palace of the king, as it was logical. Since Herod had not had any new children for some time, despite the number of his concubines, he knew that it was not in his house that the Messiah had been born. He tried to kill the magi, but first he sent them in search of the one who, according to their prophecy, was to be the deliverer of Israel, because if his existence reached the ears of the people, he would become a serious rival to inherit his kingdom, displacing his sons. The fact is that the magi managed to outwit the vigilance of his spies and that he could only learn that the birth had taken place in the village of Bethlehem.

As there had been so many people in that village on the occasion of the Roman registration, it was difficult to know who had been born there and who had not. Nor did he know how long ago the child had been born, for the magi had not been precise in determining his age, although they told him that it was certainly a small child. In short, Herod showed his cruelty by ordering his soldiers to kill all the children under two years of age in Bethlehem and its surroundings, to make sure that the one who claimed to be the Messiah was not left alive. That was —the narrator concluded— one of his last misdeeds, for years later he died in terrible pain. Another of those present, who also knew the story, like many in Judea, recalled that some wise men in Jerusalem, upon hearing the terrible news of the slaughter of the children, had quoted an oracle of the prophet Jeremiah: "No one knows, said the narrators, if Herod succeeded in his attempt to kill the Messiah. Probably he did, they concluded, because nothing has ever been heard of him again".

Joseph said nothing and just listened. After a while he got up and returned to the tent, where I was waiting for him with the boy, who was already five years old. Nobody suspected, he told me, that we were the main characters in the story. Everyone saw us as a family returning to Israel after having been in Egypt to make a fortune, a fortune which, by the way, was none other than the splendid gifts that the magi had given us when they left and which, wisely administered by my husband, allowed us not only to survive in Egypt, but to settle in Nazareth comfortably.

Neither Joseph nor I could keep from tears as he related to me the story I had just heard by the fire. We thought of the children of the village who had perished at the hands of the tyrant, and also of the fate of some of our friends, brutally interrogated by Herod's henchmen for clues to our fate. And all for what, we wondered. But then our little son woke up. He sat up without getting up and asked us why we were crying. Then

He got up, came over to us and began to shower us with kisses. I hugged Him, in a fit of fear and tenderness. We wiped away our tears and set out to move on. The reason for what had happened was there, in that five-year-old boy, who made everyone happy without realizing his own gift and to whom everyone felt strangely attracted to. But the reason lay, above all, in the wickedness of men, in their rejection of God's plan. It was the sin that my son had come to defeat which was giving its last terrible blows, harming the just and the unjust, just as the sun rises on the bad and the good. Was it God's fault? Was God responsible for the evil of the world and the sin of men for having made them free? Was God ultimately guilty of the slaughter of the innocents, having set in motion the process of redemption with the birth of my son? No. God had done everything right, from the creation of the world to the conception of my child. God had done everything right, including creating us in his image and likeness. It was we who used that freedom to turn it against Him and against ourselves. And now it was again God who wanted to intervene in history to give us a new chance. But, unfortunately, it was not going to be easy to achieve this because the Evil One was not going to abandon the conquered terrain without putting up a fierce battle.

CHAPTER 9

Educating God

Our arrival in Nazareth caused a sensation. They had not heard from us for more than five years and some even thought we had died. The story of my premature pregnancy had been forgotten, or at least no one remembered it. In the end, it was not so important since it had taken place within marriage, for I was already engaged to Joseph, even though we had not yet begun to live together.

I found my parents very old and very worried about us. Anne told me that at no time had they ever feared for me or for the child, nor for Joseph, for that would have been doubting God. They were sure that we were well, but the fact that they had no news from us confirmed their suspicion that we had been in trouble, otherwise we would have sent them a message. They, for their part, had contacted Elizabeth in Ain Karem, who also knew nothing about us. The employees of Manasseh, our friend from Cana, had asked here and there, when they traveled with their caravans, and everything seemed to indicate that the earth had swallowed us up. However, my parents insisted, for them the certainty that God never abandons his children was stronger than the total lack of news, so, in the midst of worry, they never lost hope of seeing us again someday.

The news of the slaughter of the children in Bethlehem reached Nazareth, as well as the other villages of Galilee, but the version that circulated in our land had nothing to do with what had really happened. For those peasants of the north, so involved in their own affairs and so far, removed from political life, the king had great prestige and it was difficult for them to believe the criticisms that the more educated addressed to them. That is why they thought it was a settling of scores, cruel and inhuman, but with the purpose of to clarifying the line of succession to the throne. Even, Joachim told me, some even justified this action, claiming that this way there would be fewer pretenders and that we would not run the risk of a civil war.

The fact is that in Nazareth no one suspected that we might have been involved in the terrible slaughter and that Herod had sought us out in his day to eliminate Jesus. We told them all the part of the truth that seemed prudent, to justify in some way our absence, and so we told them that Joseph had been called to Egypt by a powerful lord who offered him a good job and that, having finished the task, he had dismissed him saying that he could return again to his homeland. As we did not come ill-equipped, since Joseph had been able to increase moderately the goods left to us by the magi, it was easy for them to believe us. We were able to settle in Nazareth, in Joseph's old house, which had remained closed all the time, and he was able to acquire some new tools for his business, also putting into practice certain techniques he had learned in the craftsmen's workshops in Egypt. This allowed us to live with a certain degree of comfort, always within the humility of our lineage, which also coincided with our desires.

Everything began to return to normal. We were so eager for this kind of life that, for many years, we did not even ask ourselves about the possibility that things could or even should be otherwise. Joseph and I lived, always looking out for each other. Looking out for each other and, above all, for the child. But we were not closed in on ourselves, on our family. The first thing in our house was the honor due to God. Also important were our own, my parents and Joseph's and my relatives, with whom we had a very close relationship, all the more so since the small abundance we enjoyed enabled us to help them on several occasions. Friends also counted. We continued to maintain our relationship with Manasseh and Leah from Cana, who by the way had already had two other children. In spite of the distance, we did not miss the opportunity to send and receive news of Zacharias and Elizabeth, as well as of little John, who from the very beginning gave many signs of his resolute character as well as of his rapturous fidelity to God. And not least of all there were all the others, the villagers, the poor, the sick, those who passed through Nazareth as migrants. We tried to help them as much as we could, with our hearts and prayers first and, when they needed it, with money as well. That was the environment in which Jesus grew up, in which he was educated and in which he learned to live like a man.

Our life was very normal and that was, for us, a great gift. But if it was so outwardly, it was not so much inwardly, and I am not referring to the relationship between Joseph and me, which ran along the paths of chaste love that we had proposed at the beginning. I am referring to the development of our son.

At first glance, Jesus was a child like any other. Well, not exactly like the others, because He was very handsome. Others would say, John, that I exaggerate and that it is a mother's passion, but you, who loved Him almost as much as I did, know that my son was truly a beauty, even though you knew Him as a man, and I had the immense fortune of seeing Him grow day by day by my side.

Jesus was a child like all the others, and yet He was very different. He played, like everyone else, but He laughed more than anyone else. He was the one who could most easily become the leader of the gang, but He refused to do so when it meant having to fight with some other child who aspired to the same. Thus, He gathered a group of friends who had other tastes and who did not enjoy playing at killing Romans, throwing stones at the nests or playing pranks in the fields. One of those faithful friends was his cousin James, whom many believed to be his brother, because of their resemblance and because they were always together.

But that was not the most significant thing. His inner dominion and a kind of lordship, which He did not claim and for which He did not fight, was noticeable to everyone. What Joseph and I saw were, in addition, other things, which did warn us that behind the apparent normality, the public appearance of the Messiah was being prepared. I remember, for example, when Joachim, my father, died. We had not been settled in Nazareth for long, just a few months. I think Jesus was already six years old. He was at that age where everything has to be asked. My mother accepted my father's death with serenity but with great sorrow. They had always been very close and had had to spend so much together for that loss not to be a very hard blow for her. Jesus, six years old and with a smile on his face, met death face to face for the first time. He stared for a long time at his shrouded grandfather, as if spellbound by the burial mound. He stayed like that for so long that Anne and I realized that something strange was happening to him and we feared that his sensitive spirit, full of life, might have been struck a hard blow by the direct contemplation of death. Then I reached over and gently pulled him out of the room where grandfather's corpse was lying. "Don't cry", I said to Him. "Grandfather rests in *Sheol*, the place of the dead, and there he awaits, together with the patriarch Abraham, the redemption that Yahweh will one day grant them".

As soon as I told Him this, He turned to me. His face was lit up, as when He discovered something He was very excited about and came running to show it to me so that I could enjoy it too. "The time of the resurrection is near", He affirmed, "Besides, grandfather is a righteous man, and it won't be long before he will be admitted to heaven, which has nothing to do with the *Sheol* they talk about in the synagogue".

"And you, what do you know about it? Who told you about the resurrection", asked my mother, who had listened with interest to the child's answer, "when that is something that not everyone in our town believes in, and that not even those of us who believe in it know what it will be like? What I would give to be sure that my Joachim rests in peace and that he will soon be able to rejoice in the presence of the Most High!".

That was the first time He said the crucial word, the first time He alluded to Yahweh, to God, as his "Father". At first, we did not realize it, for, as you know, John, that word had other meanings. Only later did the misunderstanding disappear. The fact is that He answered my mother, with his evernerlesting calmness, as if it were the most natural thing in the world: "Grandmother, my father told me so. And he also told me that Grandfather Joachim is well and that we should not suffer for him. He told me that he is alive".

That was too much for Anne, who burst into tears and had to leave. Then I picked up the boy and pulled Him to me. I sat down in front of Him, so that my face was almost at the same level as his. I looked Him straight in the eyes as I held his shoulders with my hands and asked, "Has Joseph told you that grandfather is alive? Has Joseph told you about the resurrection of the dead?" "No, not Joseph", He answered, "It was my Father. And He let go of my arms to go out into the street, to run with his cousins who were calling him to come with them.

"It was my father". That sentence shattered the veil of naïve normality in which we thought we were living. Of course, I asked Joseph if he had told the child about his conception and birth. As I expected, Joseph had not told him anything, nor had Anne and, although he was no longer alive, we could be sure that neither had Grandpa Joachim told him anything. What did my little Jesus know, then? What was He discovering on his own? But was He alone, or was God Himself educating Him to teach Him what we did not know? Were night angels coming to his bedside to tell Him who knows what secrets? Joseph and I asked ourselves a thousand questions and, above all, we decided to continue living normally but more attentive to the child's growth. We agreed that I would take it upon myself to talk to Him more and not only to answer his questions, but also to ask them myself so that I could find out what God was teaching Him and so that we too could learn from Him.

Above all, I was concerned, we were concerned, about this identification of God as his Father. We had never heard anything like it in our religion. Certainly, in our house it was never called that. We talked a lot about God's love, but we always said that this love was the love that the Creator had for his creatures; it was a love from the superior to the inferior, from the Almighty to his humble servants; it was a great, infinite love, because it came from the Almighty and was directed towards us, who did not deserve it. But from there to considering God as "Father" there was an abyss.

A father is certainly a superior to whom obedience must be rendered, but he is also an equal, someone who has your own blood, and even someone whom one day you will have to take care of, when the curve of life bends for him while for you it is at its peak. True, the child could say, in his own right, that God was his "father", for only a woman and no man had been involved in his conception, but to hear him say it, so matter-of-factly and so young, filled us with wonder. We believed his relationship with God would be more like that of a prophet, an envoy for a great mission, the Messiah in short, but we had not realized the intimate relationship that existed between Him and God, as if only the task He had to perform in the service of the Most High was important.

That made Joseph and me reflect deeply. I won't say it was easy for Joseph, because it wasn't. It wasn't easy to hear his beloved child call someone else "father", even if that someone else was God Himself. The tension eased somewhat when, almost immediately, Jesus addressed him as "daddy", as if nothing had happened. But the seed had been sown and both my husband and I were aware from then on, that normality was no such thing, but that, beneath appearances, God was at work in our son's spirit, and we had to accept that because that was what he had been born to do.

But that was not the only occasion we were given to meditate and be surprised. I will tell you, John, some more cases.

The child was now seven years old and his life was like that of any other child in Nazareth, except that He gave us, his parents, no cause for complaint. One day, when Joseph was out of the village and I was at home, there was a great uproar. The boy was preparing some wood in Joseph's workshop, as Joseph had ordered Him to do; He had recently begun to help him and to learn the trade of a craftsman, as all children of his age did in the fields, either with the cattle or, as in our case, in our own house. The commotion was tremendous, and we could not help but look out into the street to see what was going on. He was next to me. Almost at that moment the procession passed our door. A group of men were pushing and shoving a woman down the street towards the outskirts of town. The woman, Sephora, was known to us. She was a neighbor who lived in the upper part of town and with whom we didn't have much contact, but we knew her. Her children didn't hang out much with Jesus and his friends, and on some occasions, they had even hit him, as often happens among children. Behind the first group, a few steps away, there was another, larger group, in which there were many women. I had no need to ask anything, because another neighbor was questioning one of them. "What happened, where are they taking her? Actually, the answer was obvious: "She has been caught in adultery", a man answered, "and she is going to receive the punishment that the law establishes for those who cheat on their husbands. The rabbi —he was no longer the good old man we had had in the village for years— has passed sentence and we are going to stone her. This will serve as a lesson to others, who take advantage of the fact that their men are away, working or suffering under the Roman yoke, to behave like harlots". And indeed, Sephora cheated on her husband with a neighbor and took advantage when he went to the country side to bring the other one into her house. In the end, rumors reached the cheated one and he set a trap for the couple, catching them at the worst moment.

I shuddered. It had not been so long since I had almost found myself in a similar situation, although for completely different reasons. The boy was next to me, close to my skirts, and he was watching, curious, the parade of the procession. He must have noticed something, because he said to me, looking at me fixedly and very seriously this time, like a little man coming to my defense: "Mom, don't worry, nothing will happen to you". And then, without giving me time to answer or to recover from the surprise of what he had just told me, he asked: "Are they going to kill her? What are they going to do to the man who was with her? What is going to happen to her children?"

I grabbed Him and we both went into the house. I closed the door and, as the commotion moved away down the street, I made Him sit next to me. "What do you know about your birth?" I asked Him. I saw, again, surprise painted on his face, and a certain awkwardness, as if I was asking Him something obvious, something self-evident, and it made Him feel small to have to talk about it. "Mom", He said to me, shying away from the answer, "why do women who have done something wrong get punished and men don't? Is it that only women do wrong and men can do whatever they want to do?"

I insisted, "Son, we'll talk about that later, but first, tell me, what do you know about your birth? Has any boy in the village said anything to you? Do the other children pick on you?"

When He saw that He could not trick me into talking about anything else, He agreed to answer my questions. He told me that He knew that God was his Father and to my questions about his conception He did not know what to answer and even asked me if something extraordinary had happened. He only insisted on telling me that God was his Father, and that Joseph was also his Father, but in a different way. Then, a little annoyed, He asked me again about the reason for the punishment given to the woman caught in adultery.

I understood that the mystery had not yet been revealed to Him in its fullness, but that little by little the butterfly was emerging from the chrysalis and it would not take long for Him to understand who He was and what He had come for. I understood and was frightened. He was a child, a seven-year-old child; He was too fragile to get into a fight in the world of men. So, I asked God to give Him more time before He had to begin that mission that the angel announced, and the old man Simeon prophesied to me in the temple. But I didn't have time to be absorbed in trought, Jesus was already shaking me, restless, repeating to me the question whose answer He urgently needed to know. So, I had to tell Him something.

I tried first to give him an answer that did not even satisfy me: "They do it", I told Him, "to serve as a lesson to other women so that none of them will cheat on her husbands". "Why, then, don't the husbands do the same thing to them so that it will serve as a lesson and no one else will cheat on his wife? Is it that men can sin and women can't?" He answered me. You know, John, that in our town it is said that the important thing is to find the right question, not the answer. My son was a true Israelite who knew how to tenaciously follow the strand of the question until He found what he was looking for. So, I had no choice but to keep answering his questions. I was going to do it in the traditional sense, in the sense that everyone uses to justify the difference in treatment between men and women, when I understood that this was not from God and that, therefore, neither I should say it, nor He should listen to it. Then I affirmed: "They are old customs that God will make change one day. In reality, son, the sin is the same in the man and in the woman, for if she does wrong by cheating on her husband with other men, he does the same with regard to his wife. All should suffer the same punishment and it should not be, in any case, so terrible, even though one cannot pretend that nothing happened".

That answer of mine seemed to satisfy Him. With a quick gesture, as if his interest was suddenly elsewhere, He threw his arms around my neck, kissed me and said: "In any case, thank goodness nothing happened to you". And He went to the street to look for his cousins.

The kiss still caressed my cheek, and He was no longer with me. But there were his last words, similar to those he had addressed to me at the beginning of our conversation. Evidently, God had told Him something and He didn't want to talk about it, or maybe He still didn't know exactly what He knew, remaining only mere intuitions that would later become conscious. Perhaps I should be the one to help Him understand, to speak to Him clearly about his origins. I was afraid and embarrassed at the same time. And Joseph on that occasion was of little use to me, because he, less than I, dared to say anything, not even to give an opinion on what should be done. So, we decided to wait a little longer and remain attentive to what was going on in our son's soul.

But what was happening was a mystery to us. The child was so normal that it seemed to us that nothing was happening. Nothing, until, suddenly, something happened. A few months after Sephora's anecdote, I was collecting water at the fountain in the lower part of the village, next to the road, and He was with me. He was already eight years old and very strong, so He helped me with this and other chores around the house, although He had already started going to the synagogue with his father, and so the other children told him that He should not do women's work. He, as I tell you, John, was that morning with me. We had already filled two large pitchers, the ones I was to bring up, and we were filling the two small ones for Him. At that moment we heard, on the road, the shearing of the leper. They make themselves heard from afar, as the law requires, so that people can stay away from them and not be contaminated by the terrible disease. They never enter the villages, and you know that everyone thinks they are cursed, victims of some grave hidden sin. My boy put down his pitcher and peered out into the road. I ran after Him, without thinking anything of it, whereupon the pot fell to the ground and shattered to pieces. I managed to catch Him when He was already at the door and gave Him a tug to pull Him inside. The leper's bell indicated that he was about to pass. Jesus was struggling to get loose; He wanted to see up close what one of those men his cousins had told Him so much about looked like. I allowed Him to do so, but from the inside. As he passed, the poor man looked over to where we were, and our eyes met. At that moment, the child gave a jerk and let go of my arms; without my being able to do anything and in spite of my scream, He ran towards the leper. When He got there, He stopped. The man had also done so and had even stepped back, aware that He was a child who did not know the danger He was in if He came near. The two looked at each other and Jesus said to him, "What is your name? Why are you like this? Is it true that you have done something very bad? Don't worry, I will ask my Father to heal you. Are you thirsty? Wait, I will bring you some water". I was already at his side and I had already grabbed Him to prevent Him from touching him. You understand, John, that I did what any mother would have done. But, at the same time, I understood that there was something mysterious behind that gesture of my son. He let go of my arms again and went inside the fountain enclosure. He returned with a small gourd bowl full of water. This time He asked my permission: "Mom, will you let me give him a drink? Don't be afraid, nothing will happen to me". I wanted to hold Him so that his fingers would not touch the rotten flesh of the sick man, but then He told me: "Let me do it, I have to do it myself. I must do what my Father commands me to do. "Wait", I then said to Him, "I also want to fulfill what your Father asks of you". So, I kissed the bowl He was holding and let Him give the man a drink. In any case, I was not entirely calm, for I could not shake off the fear that my child might be infected just by touching the leper; that was the way we all thought, and I was a woman of my people and not an exception.

Jesus gave him the bowl, with a smile on his face that was the very expression of kindness. The leper was surprised that someone was so kind to him, for the most he received was food and drink that some good people left for him on the roads, but without coming near him. I myself had done so on many occasions and sometimes Jesus had accompanied me, although He had never seen one up close. The sick man took the bowl and a grin-like grimace lit up his face. That's when I shuddered, because my child stroked his hand, while letting him take the bowl. The leper drank and then, talking to me, asked my permission to keep the gourd bowl. "Thank you", he said to me, "it has been a long time since anyone has treated me like this. Thanks to you, little one, may Yahweh bless you, although I believe he has already done so because you bear in your eyes goodness and peace". He turned and walked away. I saw him walk away more upright, with a firmer step, as if he had regained his dignity.

Some days later news reached Nazareth that a leper had been miraculously cured by drinking water from our spring and that he went about saying that two angels had appeared to him, one in the form of a child and the other in the form of a woman, who had given him to drink from a gourd bowl which he still had. The townspeople were very upset, because the news had spread throughout the region and there were many lepers who came to the spring to see if the same thing was happening to them, so they had asked the authorities to place armed men on the roads so that Nazareth would not become a place of pilgrimage for the sick.

"Do you know about the leper?" Jesus then asked me, very happy. The children of the village, like the other inhabitants of Nazareth, spoke of nothing else. "It is ours", He added, "He is cured. I asked my Father to do it, and He has listened to me. I am very happy, Mother". I was close to tears, so I had to sit down. Again, the mystery was knocking at my door and this time, as when I carried Him in my womb and my prayers were used to heal Leah's son, it manifested itself through an extraordinary healing, a true sign of God's power, although in this case there was something more. My son had taught me that there are no barriers to love and that the real miracle lies in breaking those barriers.

The other event, the one you already know, John, took place years later. Every year, for Passover, we went to Jerusalem. Not everyone did, but for us it was very important. That time Jesus would have been a little over twelve years old. He was a little man. Tall, strong, very handsome and so good and quiet that He attracted attention. Everything went very well, as usual. Perhaps, more than on previous occasions, Jesus, who was no longer a child, had been self-absorbed, very attentive to the Passover rites and a little regretful at the spectacle of the slaughter of the lambs. "Poor things", he said one day to the astonishment of his father and mine, "they are but symbols. The real lamb is already here and only He will truly be able to make sins be forgiven". But He gave us no further explanation, nor did we ask for it.

When the feasts were over, we returned to Galilee. After the first day's journey, when we were preparing to rest, we went to look for Him among his cousins, who had come down to Jerusalem with us that year. We thought He had been with them all day, for they had become inseparable, especially with James. But He was not there. So Joseph on one side and

I on the other began to look all over the caravan. Night fell and Jesus did not appear. You cannot imagine, John, the anguish and fear that my husband and I felt, and also the rest of our family. Anything could have happened to Him, from being lost to lying in any corner of Jerusalem, wounded or even dead. We realized that there was nothing we could do but wait until the next morning to retrace our steps and return in search of Him. I spent the night praying and crying. Joseph, at my side, tried in vain to console me. "He's already a little man", he said to me. "You'll see that nothing has happened to Him. He must have lost his way and is in Jerusalem, perhaps at the house of those acquaintances of mine who live by the market, or at the house of your cousin Rachel's relatives. Tomorrow we will find Him. Be calm and rest". His strong hand gave me warmth and encouragement. I thought, once again, that pain was present in my life. I could not stop suffering for Him, but I understood that on that occasion, as on so many others, the Lord was waiting for a yes from me, an act of trust in Him, and that my son's fate was not only my business, but above all God's, who was the Almighty and would not let anything bad happen to Him. At least not yet. What a dreadful time we had, John! Joseph and I searched through all over Jerusalem for a day and a half. We went to the houses of our acquaintances and relatives, however distant they were. We already feared we had lost Him forever when we set out for the Temple. It was late in the afternoon, the sun had not yet set, and the rabbis and Pharisees were assembled in the Royal Portico for prayer. As we entered, we saw a group of people arguing. We did not give it much importance, because it was normal, given how much we like to argue and question each other, and if it is on religious grounds even more so. We approached to ask if, by any chance, they had seen a lost boy. And we saw Him there, in the center.

He sat in the middle of the teachers, listening and asking questions, leaving everyone surprised. I could not stand it any longer and, contrary to custom, I entered the circle and stood before Him. In front of everyone, nervous as I was, I said: "Son, why have you done this to us? Look at your father and me, in anguish, we were looking for you". Later I realized that I had made a fool of Him, for I had burst in there, where He had everyone gaping at his wisdom, to scold Him and treat Him like a child. However, He did not answer me angrily. Calmly, as if He understood my nerves, completely in control of the situation and without giving importance to the laughter of some of his opponents, who wanted to take revenge for the dialectical defeat he had inflicted on them, He smiled at me and said: "Why were you looking for me? Didn't you know that I should be in my Father's house?".

With the same calmness with which He had spoken, He stood up, said goodbye to those wise men and, opening the circle, went to Joseph, who had not dared to intervene. I, still surprised, quickly followed Him, while the group broke up behind us. The three of us, in silence, left the Royal Portico and started our way back home. The mystery, John, always the mystery, all around Him and enveloping us all. But a mystery that began to become more and more tenuous, that flooded from day to day with light and struggled to show itself to everyone, beginning with us. That was what Jesus soon did with Joseph and with me. But that, dear boy, I will tell you tomorrow.

CHAPTER 10

Thirty years of glory

If I were asked what I hope to find after death, dear John, I could only say one thing: to be in heaven again. And the fact is that I have already lived in heaven. And not for a fleeting season. I have lived in heaven for at least thirty years in a row. I have lived in heaven because I have been with God, that is, with my son, living with Him, enjoying being with Him, learning from Him while teaching Him what little I knew. But the fact that Jesus, the son that was conceived in my womb, was God, of the same caste as God or, as the Greeks say, of the same divine nature, was not very clear to me from the very first moment. Neither Joseph nor I did. It was Jesus himself who helped us to understand the profound meaning of what we, by intuition, already knew.

It must be said, John, that neither did He know everything clearly from the first moment of His existence. Otherwise, He would not have been a normal child. In Him, too, the light broke through little by little. I have already told you how He had begun to refer to God as his "father", to our great surprise and even with a certain fear, for that designation sounded to Joseph and to me, who were good Israelites, like blasphemy. God is the Most High, the Almighty, the One who watches over His chosen people from generation to generation, but from there to calling Him "father" in the way He did, there is a long way to go. And even more so if one pretends, as my son did, that this fatherhood was not only symbolic, but real and exclusive to him, even if he later extended it to us.

After that event in the temple, when He got lost and we found him explaining a new way of understanding the law to the doctors, we finally had to make things clear. Joseph and I understood that the time had come and that He was ready, not only to understand where He had come from, but also to give us explanations about His behavior and even His mission.

We did so immediately. Already on the trip to Nazareth, which we made alone because the caravan of Galileans was three days ahead of us, we turned to Him and asked Him to explain to us more clearly why He had stayed in the temple without telling us. First of all, He apologized for the hard time He had given us, but He assured us that it had all been the result of a confusion. He reminded me that, on the day of our departure, He had told me to wait for Him because he had to urgently resolve something in the Royal Portico, where He had seen that some doctors of the law usually met to discuss among themselves; the day before He had been listening to them, deep in thought, and I had had to take Him away from there almost by force. I, indeed, realized that He had told me about it, but I did not think that the wait should be so long. With the preparations for the trip, I had forgotten, and we had left believing that He was with his cousins. He, missing us, thought we would soon come back for Him and so he spent two and a half days at the house of one of the teachers with whom He was quarreling. His tranquility and his absolute trust in God never ceased to amaze me, especially because of his age.

Having clarified things, we wanted to know what He had told the rabbis and doctors, what they were discussing with so much interest. Jesus told his father and me that everything had centered on finding out what was essential in the law. For some of the Torah experts, the most important thing was faith in God and the absolute rejection of all idolatry; for others, on the other hand, the most important thing was the rigorous fulfillment of the precepts laid down by Yahweh to Moses at Sinai and even the minor laws derived from them; there were those who went further and referred to the survival of the people themselves and their visible structures, among them the temple, as that which, whatever happened, should not disappear. Jesus, as He Himself told us, had posed the question to them on the basis of the first revelations of the prophet Isaiah, those in which he says: "What to me, is the multitude of your sacrifices?", says Yahweh. "I have had enough of burnt offerings of rams and fattened animals; I have no pleasure in the blood of bullocks and goats, when you come to present yourselves before me. Who has asked you for such a trampling in my courtyard? Bring no more vain oblation: the smoke of incense is detestable to me. Novilunium, Sabbath, convocation: I do not tolerate falsehood and solemnity. Your noviluniums and solemnities abhor my soul: they have become a burden that I find it hard to bear. And when you extend your palms, I cover my eyes so as not to see you. Even when you pray, the prayer, I do not hear you.

"Your hands are full of blood: wash yourselves, cleanse yourselves, put away your misdeeds from before my eyes, desist from doing evil, learn to do good, seek what is right, give the oppressed his rights, do justice to the fatherless, plead for the widow. Come, then, and let us contend", says Yahweh. "Whether your sins be as scarlet, they shall be as white as snow. And if they are red like crimson, they shall be as wool".

That intervention ignited the dispute in the circle of scholars of the law. While some said that the words of the prophet could not be applied to the letter, to the current situation, with the nation occupied by the Romans, others affirmed that there was a risk of forgetting that good works come first. When evening fell, a young Pharisee from a very rich and God-fearing family, seeing that everyone was leaving and that Jesus was left alone, while still a boy, offered him his house. Jesus went with him and slept in his house for the two nights He stayed in Jerusalem while we were looking for him.

That man, whom we could not even greet when we took Jesus away from the group of doctors he was teaching, was someone you met many years later; he was Joseph of Arimathea.

Once Jesus had explained all this to us, we wanted to know more. We had both realized that God had already revealed to our son the most essential aspects of his mission, and we were eager to learn what the Most High's plans were for Him and for us. So, we asked Him, "What about you, son, what do you think of Isaiah's prophecy, what do you think is most important to please God?" I remember that we were walking under the shade of some olive trees, yet even so I could perfectly notice the surprise on Jesus' face when He stopped and looked at me. "Why are you telling me this, Mother?" He answered me, "Don't you know?" Joseph, who intervened very little, as if he were afraid of asserting his status as a father in matters in which he was not a father, came to my defense and told Him: "Son, she does know, but I'm not sure. I would like you to teach me and tell me what God has revealed to you. In what does the glory of God consist? What can a man do that is most pleasing to the Most High?"

Calmer, as if the fear that I was not aware of all that He knew had passed, Jesus said, with absolute ease, as if everything was obvious: "Listen, Israel: "You shall love the Lord your God with all your heart, with all your soul and with all your strength". And also, "You shall love your neighbor as yourself".

Joseph, more expert in the study of the Scriptures than I, recognized at once both fragments and said to Jesus:

"Those two texts are from Deuteronomy one and Leviticus the other. But why those and not others?". The boy, encouraged by the opportunity to be able to explain what was inside Him, answered Him excitedly, "Father, don't you see? The essential part of God's revelation to our people is not the law, nor is it the temple, nor is it even the meticulous fulfillment of all the legal prescriptions. The most important thing is love. If there is no love, if there is injustice, resentment, hatred, envy and all the rest, no matter how many sacrifices we offer, no matter how much we pray, God is not pleased with us not can He be.

"Mother", He said, turning to me, "am I not right, am I not right that God is love and that only love unites us to Him and enables us to be like Him?" I noticed that my heart was pounding. His words found an absolute echo in my soul, as if they contained something I had always known but had never dared to formulate. So, touched, I hugged Him. I kissed his head, which now almost reached my shoulders, and I agreed with Him. Then He turned to Joseph: "And you, father, do you agree that without love everything else is like an empty shell or a whitewashed sepulcher that looks beautiful on the outside but is full of death on the inside?" Joseph found it harder to say yes. Not for nothing, in spite of his enormous goodness, had he been educated in the strictest traditions and had adhered to them. He understood what Jesus was telling him and knew He was right, but he doubted. So, like a good Israelite, he answered his question with another: "And then, what is the use of sacrifices and prayers? Wouldn't this theory of yours lead, as a consequence, to the disappearance of the law, the disappearance even of the temple and therefore of the people themselves as chosen ones? If love is what pleases God most, as anyone can love, why does God need a nation to call his own? And how to prevent everyone from deciding for themselves what is love, and what is not love?"

Jesus broke away from my embrace and, still walking, approached Joseph. "Look", He said to him with that tone of his so characteristic, with that authority with which He spoke later when He met you and which He already then had on certain occasions, "perhaps the hour has come, announced from ancient times, when they will come from East and West to worship the true God, and that worship will not be with animal fat or with sacrifices and offerings, but with a clean heart. The true worshipers will worship God in spirit and in truth. And this does not have to destroy what we already have, the temple, the law and everything else, but only to purify it, to cleanse it of everything that is not pleasing to God. At least, this is how my Father has taught me".

Jesus always spoke with the same matter-of-factness, as if what He said was as evident to others as it was to Himself, but on that occasion even He understood, with His last words, that He had entered dangerous terrain and that He must necessarily give more explanations. One could not begin by calling Joseph father and end by invoking the paternity of another, even if Joseph himself and I sensed that he was speaking of the same God. Besides, that paternity that He continually had in Joseph's mouth made him very nervous, and it also made me a little uneasy; not in vain, I was also Jewish and, as you know, calling the Most High in that way was something that almost sounded like blasphemy to our ears. As I noticed Joseph's uneasiness and I also noticed that this time Jesus had taken notice, I hastened to intervene.

"Son", I said to Him, "I think it is time you tell us what you know about yourself, about your birth, about your mission and also why you call God with the title of Father".

"Mom", He answered, a little nervously, "I don't know when I knew it all. I don't even know how I knew it, but the fact is that I have always known it, although I was not always aware of what I knew. I know that Joseph" he lowered his eyes a little embarrassed, of having to talk about these things in front of him, as far as He was concerned, and me, because I was a woman, "is not my real father. I know that I was conceived after the angel asked you and you consented. I know also, and I do not know how I know it, that this God whom you all call the Most High and the Almighty, is because He is in truth, is my Father. He is so in His own right. I cannot feel it otherwise, and those are the words that come to my lips when I think of Him. He begot me. From Him I come and to Him I will go. I sense that there is something more about myself, about who I am, and about the task I am to fulfill, but I do not yet know what it is. But I also know I should not worry. It is as if, little by little, He, my Father, is teaching me everything, and what He teaches me I know that I already knew, that I have always known. For example, what I have told you about love, or what I said one day to Grandmother Anne when Grandfather Joachim died. Everything is already in me, although I still don't know what that everything is. But I", and now He turned to Joseph and took his hand, something He never used to do since he stopped being a child, "I love you very much and I call you father because you are too. And I tell you that you will be blessed for generations, and that in you the prophecy made by Nathan the prophet to David, from whom you came, will be fulfilled, and has already been fulfilled: "Your house and your kingdom shall stand before me forever; your throne shall be established forever". This said, He embraced him. Father and son embraced as they had never embraced before. I knew that all the doubts had disappeared in Joseph, even the resentment before a paternity that was not his and that, innocently, my son reiterated before him without realizing that it bothered him. I also knew that I no longer had much time left to enjoy the company of that man, whom I loved so much and to whom I owed so much. But this thought quickly disappeared from my mind, as I was asked by the two of them to join in their joy.

Nevertheless, and now almost within sight of our village, Joseph turned to Jesus and warned him in a solemn voice:

"Son, you must pay attention to what your Father in heaven teaches you and no one else, not even your mother or me, if we ever tell you something, in our clumsiness, that does not coincide with what the Most High reveals to you. But I advise you to be very careful, to measure well what you say and before whom you say it. Your words sowed confusion in the temple and perhaps they could seem very dangerous to some, especially if they find an echo among the young, for I am sure that they will listen to you with delight, since the subject of love is always pleasant to hear for those who have little experience, but very frightening for those who know how hard life is and how many compromises have to be made to survive. So, don't be too hasty. Wait until you are sure that your time has come".

"Father". Jesus answered, "I know you are right. I feel within me two opposing forces, at the same time powerful". One tells me: "prudence" and the other invites me to run, to gallop, to throw myself into the street to shout what my heart is shouting at me. The latter was the one that won when I was in the Royal Portico and that is why I could not avoid asking those questions to the doctors. But I also know that God has not yet revealed everything to me, although I already know that I carry it all within me. And I know that I will notice, I don't know when, that the time has come. Until then, I will have to continue to struggle to contain this untamed colt that would like to gallop and to whom this village of ours is too small.

From then on, time passed very quickly, at least for me, although it was not so for Jesus. But he learned to contain himself and learned —as He himself told me on more than one occasion— that it was not enough to know things, but that wisdom was authentic when it was translated into deeds. He understood that this was the cause of the expectation that God imposed on him. God commanded Him to experience, without haste, all that he knew about love so that he would really know it and not just as a beautiful theory that had nothing to do with his life. That lesson, dear John, could not just be learned with the head; it had to sink in, like water when it falls gently, and that took time. Time became the means by which Jesus assimilated in his own flesh what was in his head. Time became, therefore, my first ally, since it was thanks to it that I was able to enjoy his company for thirty years.

As I tell you, John, time passed quickly. Two years after that trip to Jerusalem, my mother died. Anne was already wrinkled and very old. She was not the strong woman she had been in her youth, but she had all the inner vitality that she had been able to transmit to me, and all the love for God that her grandson spoke of. Grandmother and grandson had long conversations, from which she always came out crying with joy. They talked a lot about Joachim and Jesus told her things about life in heaven, things that I was not allowed to hear. I only know that she was eager to leave and that, when her time came, she died with infinite peace. I held one of her hands and Jesus held the other. First she blessed me, making an enormous effort, and then, to the surprise of all the family around her, she turned to her grandson and said: "Bless me, Lord, and commend me so that I may soon be with the Almighty and my husband in heaven". Jesus made a strange sign on His forehead; strange it seemed to us then, although now we know that it was the sign of the cross on which He would die. Then He kissed her hands and her forehead, while tears served as balm and ointment. Thus, she departed to heaven, from where she never ceases to intercede for us. To her I have commended myself, John, on many occasions, and I have not failed to obtain what I asked for. The neighbors and relatives commented on the strange request of the dying woman, especially that of calling her grandson " Lord ", but they did not give it much importance, because they attributed it to a delirium in her last moments.

As for my husband, we were still able to enjoy some happy years together. Joseph died when Jesus was twenty years old. There was already talk in Nazareth of a wedding for our son, although we, his father and I, knew that this was not in God's plans, nor in those of the boy. Joseph's death helped to remove that problem for a while, because we were able to tell everyone that Jesus did not want to leave his mother alone and that He had decided to postpone starting his own family.

This is how Joseph passed away: a neighbor of ours had a herd of goats in the mountains, a day's walk from Nazareth. It was a wild and lonely place, where the animals grazed among the rocks during the day and gathered in the sheepfold at night. The wolf was on the prowl, so the sheepfold had to be well protected, both for the safety of the animals and for that of the farmhand, who stayed with them day and night. Heavy rains in the fall had collapsed part of the old building and it was urgent to repair the damage. In the mountains, the cold was more intense than in our village and, in addition, vermin were able to enter through the cracks. So, our neighbor, Maltake was his name, had been asking Joseph insistently to go to the place with his tools to repair the damage and, at the same time, to build new stalls for the goats. Finally, a date was agreed upon, and when the time came, it was clear that the day would not be long before water or even snow would get there, due to the cold weather. I was afraid for Joseph to go out in that weather, especially since he would have to stay in the hills for several days; he was not very well, had had severe back pain and was complaining of cramps in his legs. Although it was foreseen that Jesus would accompany him to help him in his work, as He always used to do, I did not feel safe. Joseph teased me, with the affection with which he always treated me, and told me that I was turning into a fearful woman; he also told me that if we disappointed our neighbor Maltake, we ran the risk that no one would ever order any work from us again, because clients must always be kept happy. "We poor people", I remember him adding, "we cannot choose. We have to accept the work that is given to us, when it is given to us. And we have to thank God that at least we have that". So he took advantage of the fact that it was not raining at dawn and, wrapped in a thick fur jacket, he left. Jesus went with him. The donkey also went to carry the tools, because the work they had to do there was heavy and they needed many tools.

He said goodbye to me with his best smile, to dissipate my fears and, as he always did when we said goodbye, he kissed my forehead and gave me his blessing. I instructed our son to take care of his father and not to let him catch a cold.

They had not been out for two hours when it began to rain. What was rain in Nazareth was snow on the mountain. I understood that they had not had time to reach the shepherds' shelter and, very worried, I began to pray, asking the Lord, whom I now and then dared to call "Father", to protect my husband and my son. As the hours passed, even in Nazareth the rain turned to snow, and although it took a long time to set because of the humidity, little by little the roofs of the houses were painted white. I could not be more anxious, even though my faith in God gave me the strength, at that moment, to remain calm. I was alone at home and the darkness of the evening was beginning to fill everything, so I lit a candle and began to pray again. That's how I spent the whole night, serene and worried at the same time, wanting to run out to look for them and realizing that I could do nothing but wait. In the meantime, I kept praying and praying for my husband and my son, while begging God to give me the strength to accept His will at all times.

The next morning Nazareth was a completely white village. The cold was intense, but it was no longer snowing. The children were running through the streets and throwing snowballs at each other, enjoying the strange spectacle. I went to my cousins' house and told them what had happened, how Joseph and Jesus had gone to the mountain and how afraid I was that they might be in trouble. They were also worried and told their husbands. It was decided to leave in search of them, taking advantage of the fact that, for the moment, it did not seem that the storm was going to rekindle. It did not take long to organize things. Five men set out, accompanied by two horses.

Not two hours had passed since their departure when they were already back. They were all back, but not all of them returned well. Jesus was bruised, with hands, feet and face that looked pitiful. But the worst was Joseph. Although he was riding on the donkey and wearing the clothes of his son, who had spent the night almost without a coat in a desperate attempt to take care of his father, his condition could not have been more pitiful. He could barely hold himself up on the animal and his breathing was choppy and agonizing.

They took him home and there we rubbed oil all over his frozen body. We did the same with Jesus, who kept crying and telling me that He had really done everything possible to help him, but when they realized the seriousness of the situation it was too late to return and they just looked for a bad refuge in which to shelter from the storm. There they had been, all night long, unable to light a fire because all the wood was wet and feeling the bite of death on their bodies.

Joseph did not last many days. A very high fever consumed him and two days later he had already lost consciousness, although he later regained it. The pains oppressed his chest and, when he coughed, he thought he was losing his life. However, dear John, in spite of everything, you cannot imagine the serenity he displayed. Between crises and crises, making remarkable efforts, he tried to console me and assured me that everything was going well and that at that moment, as in the previous ones of our life, the important thing, the only important thing, was to continue believing in God's love. He was already talking about God's love, for it was not for nothing that both he and I had learned what that meant from our son. "God is love", he said, holding my hand, "God is love, and we must believe that not only in times when everything is going well, but also and especially in difficult times. It is for the difficult moments that friendship must be reserved, and it is now that we must put our faith in God's love to the test. Mary, I now repeat to you what the angel said to you one day: 'Do not be afraid, what the Lord has said to you will be fulfilled'. Nothing will happen to your son, to my son, until the time comes, and when the time comes, whatever happens, it will also be the will of the Most High, of his Father, of our Father". Then he wanted to be alone with Jesus. They talked for a long time, as had happened with Anne, my mother, when the hour of death came for her. Jesus also made on his forehead the then strange sign of the cross and kissed, as He had done with his grandmother, the hands and forehead of his father; his tears, as with Anne, flowed abundantly through his eyes and were a balm that descended on the dying man.

After this, Joseph never lost his peace. His face was transfigured, and not even the severe pain he was in could tear the image of serenity from his face. He was still conscious for almost a day but could hardly say anything more to me. Only, at the end, he asked Jesus and me to hold his hand and, in a whisper, I heard him say:

> "Mary, only God knows how much I have loved you. God alone knows how lucky I have been to be able to live with you these years. God bless you for the love you have given me. Now we are separated, but this will not last long. Soon we will be together again, as we are now, with God between us, forever".

To Jesus he said, "My son, I am the only man in the world who can call you that, and therefore all generations will call me blessed. I have loved you as a normal father would have loved you, and I have received more from you than if you had been a son of my blood. Thank you for honoring my lineage with your presence. Thank you for announcing to me the world of happiness that now awaits me. I cannot bless you, for it is you who must bless me. Do it soon, for the departure is at hand". Jesus blessed him and made, like with his grandmother, the sign of the cross on his forehead, his eyes, his mouth and his hands. Shortly afterwards we both lay down on his body, which had just died. He had departed and with him went my soul mate, the one with whom I had shared so many difficult moments and so many joys. His death was a tremendous loss for me, and also for Jesus.

I loved Joseph very much, John, I loved him very much. I don't know if this will surprise you: I don't know if you will understand that this affection for him was compatible with my total consecration to God. I don't know if you will understand, but I assure you that it was like that. I loved him at the same time that I loved the Father, at the same time that I loved my Son. Perhaps everything depends on how big one's heart is. Perhaps it depends on the priorities established in that heart. My consecration to God, which included my body as well as my soul, did not prevent me from loving others. I never experienced God as a "jealous husband" who wanted to reign exclusively in my soul. God wanted to be the first, but not the only one. On the contrary, He asked me to love everyone, starting with those closest to me, except that the first one I had to love was Him.

I loved Joseph very much and so it was not easy to accept his death. I wondered why God had not heard my prayers. I also wondered why Jesus had not made some extraordinary gesture to prevent his father's death. I asked myself all that and at the same time I answered myself that God had his plans and that I could not pretend to understand them. But it was not easy for me to accept God's will, which hurt me so much, although I did, and without any room for rebellion. It is true that the certainty that he was still alive greatly eased my pain, which, without it, would have turned into despair. For twenty years we had been three at home, united like the great stones that form the foundations of the temple of Jerusalem, which not even an earthquake seems to be able to separate. For twenty years, our home was the gateway to paradise. Love was the bread we ate every day, tenderness was the water that quenched our thirst, joy was the clothing that protected us from the cold and covered the holes of our poverty. We were the happiest family not only in Nazareth, not even in Israel, but in the world. For Jesus, he was always and only a father. Well, not always, because from the time he was 12 years old, from that time in the temple, both he and I had also become disciples, without ceasing to play the role of parents and to teach our son what it means to live subject to authority.

I have not stopped talking to him a single day since then. In the most difficult moments, even at the time of Jesus' death, I always felt his presence at my side. His last words, so similar to those of the angel Gabriel, still ring in my ears: "Do not be afraid, Mary". Yes, this is how I have always continued to live with him, certain that he is alive, that he is with this God whom my Jesus has taught me to call "Father", and that, from there, he watches over and intercedes permanently for us, especially for those who, like Jesus and me, have been called to a full consecration to the Lord.

Fortunately, his last words, spoken almost in a whisper, were not heard by any of the many who filled the house. Joseph was loved by everyone in Nazareth, and the whole town crowded to the door of our home to accompany him. Some said they had seen angels take Joseph's spirit to heaven, while others claimed that it was Father Abraham who had come to fetch him. The fact is that the rumor spread that his death had been extraordinary, as in fact it had happened, and since then until today you can see that there are many who entrust themselves to him in that final moment, so that the transit may be mild and they may enjoy the presence of God eternally.

In the midst of the commotion, Jesus was by my side at all times. He was suffering a lot, and everyone could see that. But perhaps only I sensed that in his pain there was a point that made it even harder. As soon as we had a moment of peace, I was alone with Him, sitting on one of the benches Joseph had built and which adorned our house. I held his hand and waited for Him to speak to me. He rested his head on mine and burst into tears.

After a while, when He calmed down, I said, "I have nothing to ask you. I know that you could have saved him if you had wanted to. But I also know that if you didn't, it was for a just reason, which I don't understand but which I fully accept". He sighed. He needed to unburden himself and give me an explanation, but He couldn't be the first to face the subject, because He didn't know if I knew that He was capable of performing miracles, although I had already seen some from Him".

"Mother", He said, "I thank you for your faith, I thank you for your trust. I knew that his time had come. As one day mine will come, and then yours. And I knew that if I prevented him from leaving, men would not understand why I let their loved ones die while I had not let my father die. One day I will have to heal the sick and raise the dead. But it will always be with strangers or with a very dear friend. Everyone will understand that, even if it is hard for them to accept why some will and some will not. However, if I had done it with Joseph and not with them, not only would they not have understood, but they would not have forgiven me.

"It was very hard for me to be able to save him and not do it. I took off my clothes to do for him what any son who loves his father as much as I love him would have done. I could do no more, without paying consequences that would have been very costly for the mission my Father has entrusted to me. Do you understand?".

I listened to Him without daring to look Him in the eye. His words had only remained engraved on me, like an iron that pierced my soul, like the sword of pain that the old man Simeon had prophesied to me, that He was going to die before me. I felt an enormous desire to ask Him, to rebel, to tell Him that it could not be. And yet, I understood that it was neither the time nor my role. I had to support my son, not increase his pain by rebelling against what was God's will for Him and for me. So I pressed Him tightly against my chest, covered his face with kisses, thanked Him and after a while I told Him: "Everything is all right, son. Joseph is with God. That's the only thing that really matters". And I left Him by himself.

I understood that he had to talk to his Father and that he had to unburden himself to Him as he had done with me.

After this, John, everything went back to normal. With the excuse of my widowhood, we were able, as I told you, to postpone Jesus' wedding without attracting too much attention. He had decided to be, body and soul, God's, as I had been, as Joseph had been, and we did our best to remain unnoticed while keeping firmly to our purpose. Jesus was for me, from that moment on, not only the main reason for my concern, but the only one. My parents and my husband had died and I had no more children, so I was able to consecrate myself to Him entirely, with that certainty I had from the beginning that in doing so I was not loving the Lord through a mediator, but I was loving the Lord himself.

Those were ten years of particular teachings and tremendous confidences. Little by little, He knew everything. Long before the wedding at Cana, everything was ready for God's plan to become public and notorious. At the age of twenty-three or twenty-four, He was already fully aware, and I with Him, of who He was and what his mission was. We were both aware, too, of the capacity He had to transform the normal order of things, to work miracles. That was something that worried me a lot, because I was always afraid that his good heart would lead Him to do things that would attract attention, so I asked Him, before doing anything, to think carefully whether he should do it, because it would probably be the sign that would set in motion his public performance as Messiah. He agreed with me, although it was hard for Him to hold back and not help the suffering people, the poor who begged for their food or the sick who were tormented by pain; it had cost Him not to save Joseph and He had done it for another reason; now it was a question of not making Himself known before his time. That is why He always told me the same thing: "My time has not yet come". And He did not know how to tell me more, because He did not know exactly what I had to notice to be sure that that moment had arrived. It was not easy for Him to wait, because time was passing, and He was getting older. He was approaching thirty years of age and He was still at home, taking care of His mother and working as a carpenter, He, the Messiah, as if He did not have more important things to do. Once again, God was testing Him. With such a prolonged wait, which He did not know when it would end, God taught Him to listen to His voice and to discern His commands. In a way, by suffering, He was teaching Him to obey. And, above all, as I told you before, He taught Him to love. He taught Him that the important thing is not to work miracles, nor to preach great sermons, nor to convert the multitudes; but that the important thing, what really pleases God, is to do everything out of love and from love. The one who loves is the one who reigns, and one can love by performing a miracle as much as by making dinner. This lesson is so important that Jesus had to experience it by curbing his desire to run and spread his message to all the ends of the earth. But if He had not done so, that same message would have been incomplete and today you, his disciples, would believe that you can only be like Him by doing great things; since that is not an everyday thing, you would have the impression that he is inimitable, even more unattainable than He is because of his divine nature.

Thus, the years of waiting in Nazareth, years apparently lost, were the greatest lesson that God gave Him and gave me about the true importance of things. Jesus knew, from very early on, everything He had to know, but it was not enough to know it all, He needed to live it all. He needed to live it not just for a day, not just for a month, not just for a year, but for a long, long time. So long as if the end would never come, as if it didn't matter that the end would come. He learned what patience means and, by its hand, humility. He learned that it is not enough to say "Lord,

Lord", but that you must do the will of the Father, even when you do not understand where that will is leading you. He learned that words are convincing only when the listener hears at the same time a tone of voice that only the one who has lived them intensely emits and that, for that, time is essential. If He later spoke with conviction about love, it was because for many years He lived loving and not only in the big things, but also in the little things, in the everyday things, those that no one but God sees and values.

CHAPTER 11

Love became public

If one day, dear John, thirty years earlier, love had become flesh, now love wanted to become public. The moment had come, although we did not know it until the very moment it had to happen. I am referring to that wedding in Cana of Galilee to which we had been invited.

You know how weddings are in our land. The festivities last at least a week. The friends of the two families come and the house is full of people to attend to, especially when it is a rich and well-known family, as was that of our dear Manasseh and Leah, for it was the wedding of one of their children. But before that other things had happened, which you already know because they refer to your friends and yourself.

I am referring to the group of disciples that had begun to form around my son and also to the meeting with his cousin John, the son of Elizabeth, whom you all call "the Baptist".

John had not waited as long as Jesus to begin his public activity. His parents had passed away many years prior, for they were both much older than Joseph and me. For a short time, he tried to lead a normal life, managing his house and attending to his social duties. Soon, that way of life became too constricting for him, and the Lord took him first to one of those communities of Jews who live among the rocks of the desert, near the Dead Sea. But that did not convince him either and, after a few years, he threw himself into a solitary life as an itinerant preacher, repeating everywhere a call to conversion and penance because the Messiah was near.

We had had no contact with him since the death of his parents. We knew, always with much delay, of his departure to the desert, and of his stay with the Essenes who lived there, but we had totally lost track of him until his name began to circulate by word of mouth throughout Israel, as that of a prophet similar to the ancient ones, who launched invectives against the powerful, priests and nobles included, and who even reproached the tetrarch Herod for having married Herodias, his brother's wife, while the latter was still alive.

John's preaching about the imminent arrival of the Messiah alerted my son. He knew who he was, but He didn't know if John did too, or if he was just talking about a stranger without knowing exactly who he was talking about. I had already told Him what happened when I went to visit my cousin Elizabeth and how she told me that the child had jumped in her womb when she noticed my arrival. But then, the few times we had seen each other, John had shown no sign of knowing who Jesus was.

So Jesus decided to go to him. Perhaps this was the sign he had been waiting for so long. Perhaps the time had come for him to announce his message to all of Israel. He had to meet John and see what happened.

He did not go alone. In Nazareth, as I have told you on other occasions, he had a group of friends, among whom were some of his cousins, especially James. He persuaded them to go to meet John and receive the baptism of penance which he imparted in the Jordan. His friends joked about it. I remember it well because when they were talking about the trip they were at home and his cousin James said to Him, laughing, that what was he going to repent of if he had never done anything wrong, unless He had hidden sins that no one knew about. Jesus then became very serious and cut short all the jokes to assure them that God had his plans and that John's baptism was not only of penance but also of revelation and that he should receive it. Finally, more calmly, He asked them whether or not they wanted to accompany Him, because He was ready to leave at once.

Five left, although not all of them persevered at my son's side, and many more returned. You already know what happened. I am referring to the baptism in the Jordan, there by Bethany, how when John saw Him coming toward him, he was transfigured and began to cry out, calling everyone's attention: "Behold the Lamb of God, who takes away the sin of the world. This is the one about whom I said, 'Behind me comes a man who has gone before me because he was before me. And I myself did not know him, but I have come to baptize in water, that he may be revealed to Israel'".

James told me all this when, a few days later, we met in Cana for the wedding. The boy was excited. He had always loved his cousin very much and followed him almost blindly. But he had never imagined that He could be the Messiah. That is why he found it hard to believe John's words, for, he said, it was difficult to understand why, if Jesus was the Messiah, he had not done something extraordinary for so long as he had been in Nazareth.

Later, it was my own son who told me of the joy He had felt on seeing his cousin John, and the peace He experienced on knowing that the moment had indeed arrived. He also told me that He had not even had time to greet John, for he had rushed, seeing him from afar, to meet him, not even knowing that he was a relative of his. He refused, as you know, to baptize Him, saying that it was he who should receive from his hands this sign of penance. Jesus insisted because He wanted to take on all that is reserved for us and because he knew that something had to happen for the manifestation of God's support to be public. And that was when the event with the Holy Spirit took place. Everyone was crowding around John and Jesus, immersed in the Jordan, astonished by the words that the Baptist had just pronounced, when, as soon as Jesus was immersed in the waters of the river, the dove was seen flying over him while it was heard: "This is my beloved Son, in whom I am well pleased".

From then on, as if the sign had been received by all, things went very quickly. The next day He met two of you; one of them Andrew, the one who would later introduce Him to his brother, Simon, whom we now call Peter. Also Philip, who was, like Andrew, Peter, you and your brother, from our Galilee. Philip introduced Him to Nathanael, whom, after his conversion, you called Bartholomew. And He also met your brother James and you, when you were helping your father in the boat.

This is how you presented yourselves at Cana, as a happy bunch of excited and good Israelites, ready to leave everything to put yourselves at the service of the Most High and collaborate with the one whom John the Baptist had pointed out as the Messiah. When I saw you arrive, my heart skipped a beat. I knew at once, before James or my own son told me the details, that everything had begun. I was overjoyed. I was happy for Him, who was looking forward to it, and for God, since at last, his saving will was going to be fulfilled. But, I confess John, I also felt a little bit sad. With your presence at his side, I felt that, in some way, I was losing him. I knew that it would never be like before, that the sweet years of mutual companionship in Nazareth were over. Don't misunderstand me, I knew that this had to happen, and I didn't object. But you will understand that it was proper for a mother to feel pain when she saw that her son was moving away from her; otherwise, she would not have loved him, and, for me, Jesus was always my son, the fruit of my womb, and not only the one sent by the Most High to carry out a marvelous mission. For me, He was more important than what He represented. For you, who hardly knew Him, he was only an idea, a symbol, but not a human being with a heart of flesh, much less a God.

How long it took you to understand Him and to love Him! How difficult those moments were for me, and for Him. I saw you ciraling around Him, from that first moment when I met you in the house of Manasseh, sometimes as footmen around his master and sometimes as legionaries around his centurion. But He did not want that. I, accustomed to read his eyes and his smallest gestures, knew what was wrong with him. I knew that He neither liked flattery nor was He satisfied with the eagerness that some of you showed for victorious war campaigns. But, accustomed as He was to patience, He let things take their course and trusted that God would show you, also you, which was the true path.

It did not take long to happen. We were almost at the end of the wedding festivities of the son of Manasseh and Leah, a boy born after the two I have already told you about. For that family, with so much prestige and so many relations, it was very important that nothing was lacking, that no unforeseen event should occur that would cause them to be on the tongues of the envious. And that event happened. Elihu, one of the main servants, whom I had known all my life because he had been in the house since I was there for the first time, told me with concern. They had run out of wine. It was partly due to the large number of guests: among them was the large group with whom Jesus had presented Himself; and partly because the preparations had failed. If things were not remedied, the party would collapse, and it would be a great disappointment for my two friends. I owed them a lot, and, above all, I loved them very much. They had always been by my side, from the first time I stayed at their house. When Joseph died, their support was a great comfort to me, as was their generosity. I loved them as if they were my siblings and their problems were my problems. So, I turned to my son. Not that I knew what He was going to do, but I knew that He was capable of solving any problem. Notice, John, that I did not ask Him to cure his father when he was dying; that, painful as it was, it was within God's natural plans, since death is not the end of the road, but a forced transit for everyone, a transit to a better life. This was different. You may think I was selfish to claim his attention for something seemingly so small; Jesus could have been doing miracles every day in Nazareth, healing our neighbors or multiplying food so that no one would go hungry when the winter dragged on. He did almost none. That was another time, the time of silence, and now both He and I knew that the time of public life had begun, the time to speak and to tell what we had previously kept hidden.

So, I explained the situation to Him. His first reaction was surprise. He even answered me with a certain anger: "Who put you up to this, woman?", He added, "My time has not yet come". I, who knew Him well, knew that no more was needed. If John the Baptist had given Him the signal to start, now, in another way, I was giving it to Him. John had indicated to Him that it was time to preach; I was telling Him that it was time to love, even with extraordinary gestures. The message was John's thing, it was a man's thing; the favors and even the miracles were my thing, they were something that perhaps we women can understand better than you men, who are always more concerned with ideas than with what is cooking in the kitchen.

My Jesus understood perfectly. And I knew He understood. So, I told Elihu to do whatever He asked them to do. The chief of the servants stood before Him and all he had to say was, "Your mother sent us. What do you want us to do?" Jesus shook his head, shrugged his shoulders and, laughing, said to his friends, to you who surrounded Him: "Who can resist a mother? It would be better to listen to her as soon as possible, otherwise she will insist until she gets what she wants". And He said to the servants, "Fill the jars with water". Elihu, who had witnessed, years before, the healing of the then little Levi, didn't refuse. The other servants did, because they did not understand what the Nazarene was proposing to do, as if by putting water into the stone jars it was possible that the sediments that remained inside would give it the taste of wine.

Laughing and joking, they obeyed. "Take it out now and take it to the master", He asked them at once. You know the rest, John, because you yourself were among those who tasted of that wine again and again until you were convinced that it really was such. You and all of you.

That, dear boy, is how it all began. With the passing of time, especially after his death and resurrection, now that I no longer have Him with me as I did then, I have wondered if I was right to encourage Him to perform that first miracle. I did not realize the meaning of those words He said to me when I pointed out that they had run out of wine: "Woman, my hour has not yet come". I did not know what time He was referring to. I thought it was the time for the public demonstration, the time for everyone to know who He was. But in reality, He knew then that that hour was not the hour of applause, but the hour of death on the cross.

Both were the same hour. I did not know it and He did. He had known it for a long time, and that was perhaps the only secret He had not wanted to tell me in the long conversations we had had since Joseph died and in which He had revealed so many things to me about life in heaven. He knew that his end would begin to approach as soon as it was made public and, perhaps, He was lazy, He wanted and did not want at the same time, and not because of doubts but because we were both so well there, in our Galilee, that it was hard to leave all that paradise to get fully into the task.

So, you see, it was I, precisely I, his mother, who hastened his hour. Have I regretted it? There was a moment when I had doubts, when I saw him hanging on the cross. But not now. Now I know that I did what I had to do and that, without knowing it, I was God's instrument so that everything would begin in due time. That miracle made him known to you, strengthened your incipient bonds, served to confirm you in the faith that John the Baptist had sown in you towards him. And it also served to make me known to you. I mean that, since then, I did not cease to receive requests to obtain from Him this or that favor. The truth is that I paid a hard penance with that gesture of mine, because you cannot imagine how hard it is to discern when there is a real need and when there is a whim. Besides, I couldn't be continually pressuring my son either, among other things because He hasn't by my side for much longer after that. It's easier for me now. Now I am really insistent with Him and, to tell the truth, there are few things that He does not grant me when I ask him for them, although I always notice that He smiles, shakes his head and says to me, as He did then: "This mother, always the same, but let's see who denies her anything". After that first public miracle we all went together to Capernaum. The news had spread quickly in that part of Galilee, because many of the guests were from that area and they told it to all who wanted to hear it. That is why He went away into the desert and left you by yourselves. He needed calm. After so many years of waiting, now everything was suddenly rushing. He did not want to lose control of events and He did not want you to follow Him because of the miracle you had just seen. So he said goodbye to you, summoned you forty days later in Capernaum itself, and left. I returned to Nazareth with my nephew James and the other boys who had gone out with him a few days before to see the Baptist.

Then my battle began. Everything was already known in the town. They knew about the Holy Spirit in the Jordan. It was known that Jesus attracted disciples as if he were a prestigious rabbi. They also knew about the miracle at Cana. They waited for Him, with more curiosity and skepticism than anything else. His own friends, those who had gone with Him and had seen it all, were not convinced. Even James, who loved Him so much, had difficulty accepting that this cousin of his was something more than a good and admirable man. John, it is so difficult to see God walking beside us! We are always ready to believe that great things happen far away, but when we are told that they have happened at our side, we doubt and do not believe it. Deep down this is because we do not know God. We believe that the Lord can only act amidst thunder and lightning, as happened to the prophet Elijah, who had to convince himself that the Almighty spoke in the gentle breeze and not in the hurricane.

It was not easy in Nazareth. When they saw that He was not coming with me, the criticisms worsened. There were even those who said some rude things to me and those who dared to call Him an imposter in front of me. James defended me from the first moment, the same as the rest of my family, but I knew that in general the mood was hostile. Not a day went by without me receiving comments and gossip; one had said that what happened at the Jordan had been prepared by John, who was his cousin, and that he had lied to say that Jesus was the Messiah; another claimed that Manasseh had prepared the wine to deceive the boys who accompanied him. And the fact is, John, when you don't want to believe, miracles are useless. You can witness the greatest and they will continue to look for hidden reasons to explain the incomprehensible. It is rightly said in our land that there is no worse blind than he who does not want to see. This is what happened to the people of Nazareth. Deep down, they were angry that they had had Jesus among them for so long and had not recognized Him. That He had gone unnoticed was like an insult to them, because it meant that they were very clumsy and that they had not known how to value the treasure they had had at their side. It also bothered them that He had not worked miracles in the town. It is true that some of them remembered about the leper at the spring, but most of them even reproached me for not having cured their husband, their wife, their son and even their cow or their goat. They believed that being from there, Jesus had to establish a kind of office to solve problems, similar to the telonium set up by the tax collectors. They all believed they had the right to be helped and they did not ask or beg for help but demanded it and even threatened to attack Him if, once He was back in town, He did not satisfy even the smallest of their demands.

I went through all of this alone, while He was in the desert, allowing Himself to be tempted by the devil. My temptations were quite different. They had more of a the bitter taste of disappointment. Those days, I came to know a side of humanity that I could have never imagined. I saw their angry and threatening faces close to mine. Faces that until then had been kind to me, faces of people with whom I got along well, but that had been transformed once interest intervened. Before, if the son of one of them died, they did not even dare to reproach Yahweh for it; now, however, they blamed my son and were eager to treat Him as if He were a ruthless murderer. And I understood how dangerous my son's mission was, how dangerous his power was. If He worked miracles, if He let Himself be carried away by the goodness of his heart, it would be very difficult for Him to preach any kind of message. What people wanted was to be healed, to be fed and even to be resurrected. They did not want to change, or to be better people, or to love God or their neighbor more. They just wanted to be on earth as well as possible, to suffer as little as possible and at the lowest possible cost. That was all. That was, in the end, what God was for them: a kind of insurance for beyond death and a shoulder to cry on for this life. Not all of them were like that, of course, but most of them were. There were those who were more cultivated, like the Pharisees, who were more religious and spiritual. At first, I thought that with them my son would get along better, that they would not approach Him to see what they could get out of Him, but to listen to the content of his message and to second the redemptive plan that the Most High had entrusted to Him. I was wrong too. James was the first to realize that they could not be trusted either, perhaps because he looked a little like them. They turned my son into a flag, into an idea, into something unreal, impersonal, theoretical. They did not care much about Him as a human being; they cared, above all, about what He represented. That is why, when He ceased to be the symbol they thought He should be, they abandoned Him. His personal fate, his sufferings, his joys, did not count; what counted was only what they could get out of Him, as it happened to the others, even if they were not concerned with material miracles but with political ideals and theories.

What I am telling you will help you understand what happened in Nazareth when, at last, Jesus appeared there. He arrived, surrounded by many of you, on a Friday morning. It was cold, I remember well. We had just entered the fourth month, the month of Tebeth. From the very first moment people swarmed around our house. My cousins and I were busy taking care of you all, and He kept listening to those old friends who came to see Him. Especially his cousins, James, Jude and Simon, who had always been his companions and one of whom had been with him at his baptism in the Jordan; he wanted to know if they were willing to accompany him in the itinerant life he was about to lead from then on. He could hardly speak to me until late in the evening, when everyone had gone to bed.

By the fire, with his hands in mine, as when he was a child, we opened our hearts to each other. I told Him of my fears, I spoke to Him of the selfishness of the people, of the expectations that had been raised after the miracle at Cana and after the story of the manifestation of his messianism in the Jordan; I even asked Him to forgive me for having been responsible for that first miracle of his, superfluous ultimately. He reassured me; He told me that the days in the desert had helped Him to know well what his task was and the steps he had to take until "his hour" arrived. "Mother", He said, looking me straight in the eyes, "I cannot and do not want to hide anything from you. I am about to begin the last stage of my life. It will end badly and, therefore, it will end well".

"Whatever happens, never doubt me or the love of God. I will later tell you the details, but from now on I want you to know that everything is foreseen by my Father and that it has to be fulfilled as foreseen, so that all may believe. Do not stop praying for me and, I repeat, whatever they tell you, never doubt that I am doing the right thing, however surprising it may seem to you. Tomorrow I will go to the synagogue, as I do every Sabbath, and there my journey will begin. Then I will leave, and it will be a long time before we see each other. If you have problems in town, let me know at once, and I will find a place for you in Capernaum".

I did not cry, and it was not for lack of desire. Nor was I frightened; much less did I try to dissuade Him. I knew that was what He had come for and, with that special intuition that we mothers have, the previous days I had come to understand that, indeed, everything would end badly. But I also knew that, in the end, everything would turn out just as God had foreseen. That is why, putting on a brave face, I said to Him: "My son, now I am the one who asks you never to doubt me either. What I have seen these days in Nazareth was enough for me to understand the suffering that awaits you. I know that you will win, but I also know that you will have a hard time. That is why I want you to always be sure of me. Whatever happens and whatever they tell me, do not have the slightest suspicion: I will be at your side, believing in you and convinced that what you are doing is right. I would like to go with you, but I know that I would only be a hindrance to you. So, I will either stay here or go and live with my cousin Mary of Alpheus, or else I will go to Cana, to our friends' house. Besides, wasn't it you who once told me, looking at some birds, that God loves us more than the sparrows and that we shouldn't worry about anything because even the hairs on our heads are numbered? I have lived in that faith since my childhood and thanks to that faith you were born. Therefore, rest assured that your Father, my God, will watch over me as much as over you".

"I hope he does more over you than me, otherwise I'll have to settle the score with him", He said jokingly, as He stood up. We hugged and then I kissed his forehead. Then I tried to kiss his hands too, those hands that had made the miracle of the wine at Cana with the same naturalness and with the same love as they had made furniture in our workshop. He prevented me from doing so. On the contrary, He took mine and said to me, solemnly and emotionally: "These blessed hands, Mother, you must always keep them open so that whoever sees them will understand that you are waiting for their burdens to be presented to heaven. I promise you that what is placed in them will never be unheeded, neither by me, nor by the Spirit, nor by my Father".

That's how we said goodbye. When I was left alone, naturally, I cried my eyes out. I knew I would not see Him for a long time, and that distressed me. I knew He was going to suffer, and I even feared that his inability to dissimulate would endanger his life. But my tears were not tears of despair. They were of pain and of venting, just that. Because I was sure that, whatever happened, God would be with Him.

The next day everything happened as He had predicted. He went to the synagogue, you were there too, with the others. Everyone had gone there that morning. They expected to hear from his lips some exceptional message and perhaps even to see some miracle. In fact, several sick people were crowding at our door while others were waiting for Him there. I was with the group of women, behind the lattice, and I felt strange, surrounded by the expectation of so many, but protected by my cousins, who did not leave me alone for a moment. My son looked for the text he wanted to read and proclaimed it in a solemn voice: "The Spirit of the Lord is upon me, because He has anointed me to preach good news to the poor, He has sent me to proclaim liberty to the captives and recovery of sight to the blind, to set at liberty those who are oppressed and to proclaim a year of the Lord's favor.

A murmur of approval greeted the prophet's words. I breathed a sigh of relief. But the tranquility was short-lived. When silence fell, He began to speak: "This Scripture that you have just heard has been fulfilled today. I am in your midst; I have lived with you here for most of my life and you have not known me because the hour had not yet come. But now I tell you that I have been sent by the Most High to carry out a redeeming mission, to fulfill the ancient prophecies, to announce the grace and mercy of God, to summon you all to conversion, to reconciliation, to the fullness of revelation".

His words divided the assembly. While some nodded and even wept with emotion, because they believed in what He was telling, supported by the manifestation made by the Baptist and the miracle of Cana, others began to shout: "Who are you to consider yourself the Messiah? We know who you are, you are the son of Joseph, a carpenter. Do you think we are going to believe that the Messiah was born in a poor man's house?". There were even those who went so far as to insult: "They say that you performed a miracle at Cana, and they say that a voice from heaven was heard when John baptized you in the Jordan. All this is a lie. You are an impostor and a liar. Here, in your town, we say to you: physician, heal yourself. If you have the ability to perform miracles, why haven't you performed them here, where you have lived for so many years? Why don't you perform them now so that we can see them and believe in you?"

Then He stretched out his arms and held them out until silence fell. He was standing, surrounded by everyone, most with anger on their faces and only a few willing to give him their support. No one knew what might happen, whether He would make some extraordinary gesture or reveal some secret, but He simply said: "Truly I tell you, no prophet is welcome in his own land. There were many widows in Israel in the days of Elijah, when the heaven was shut up for three years and six months, and there was a great famine throughout all the land; and to none of them was Elijah sent, but to a widow woman of Zarephath of Sidon. And there were many lepers in Israel in the time of Elisha the prophet, and none of them were cleansed but Naaman the Syrian". Then he fell silent.

Then they all threw themselves onto Him, while shouting: "Imposter, you tell us that you do not perform miracles because we are not good, because we do not deserve them. You are going to find out who we are". In spite of your efforts, they seized Him and dragged Him up the village to the ravine, intending to throw him down there and kill Him. I trailed behind, anguished, begging to let Him go, trying to make my way through the crowd. Since everyone knew me, not only did I not go unnoticed, but I even had to suffer insults and taunts; one woman even scratched my face and would have pulled out my hair had it not been for the fact that you, dear boy, were there. Only later did I learn that Jesus had told you that, whatever happened and whatever was done to Him, you were not to leave my side as soon as you saw me leave the women's enclosure in the synagogue.

And so, we arrived at the edge of the ravine. We were a little late, but we could see what was happening. When they had Him in front of the cliff, He shouted to them: "Let me go" And they, as brave and angry as they were, suddenly flinched. His voice was powerful. He had been totally passive, as if gone, as they had carried Him almost flying. Now, however, as if He had awakened, He towered over the crowd. "Let me go", He repeated, "this is not the place, nor is it now the time for me to give glory to the Most High. You have lost the opportunity to participate in God's plan. Let me go and be at peace. I do not want you to be harmed by hatred. I have lived with you for a long time and that saves you". Then, the hands that were holding Him and that had torn his clothes released Him. Those who had stones, they dropped them. Those who carried sticks, they left them on the ground. He started walking and passed through their midst, surrounded by a complete, painful and strange silence. He came towards me, kissed me again on the forehead but this time without saying anything to me and continued down the hill. Only then, when He was already walking away with that majestic and solemn walk of his, the people woke up from that kind of stupor that had left them stunned. You ran after Him, and they, without moving, resumed their insults. "Go away and don't come back, impostor", they said to Him. "If you come back you know what awaits you", others commented with laughter. Then, although He was already some distance away, He turned and looked at them. We could all see that He was crying, and those tears made those bullies keep silent. My cousins came to me, because you had already left. They took me by the shoulders and together we started down the hill, toward our homes. Two of his cousins did not need anything and went with Him; they were Simon and Judas. The other, James, had followed Him from the first moment.

It was the last time I saw Him in many months. Contrary to what might have been expected, peace was made in Nazareth and no one bothered me. Even that woman who had hit me apologized after a few days. Only a few extremists continued to insist that He was an impostor. Most of them felt a deep regret and spoke among themselves, commenting on his words in the synagogue and admitting that He was right, that they had lacked faith and that they had been fools for not having been able to recognize the Messiah himself, who had lived among them for so many years in the most complete secrecy.

This, of course, was helped by the extraordinary fame that soon accompanied Him and that did not take long to reach our town, with the news of the portentous miracles he performed everywhere. But I believe John, that what really changed the hearts of my countrymen were his tears. This is what more than one confessed to me. When they saw Him crying, with that solemnity with which He was covered in that difficult moment, almost impassive and totally serene in spite of the threat that loomed over Him, they understood that He was the Messiah. That was a foretaste of what would happen years later.

Your tears, John, are the ones that convert, the ones that attract and the ones that heal. His tears, much more, infinitely more than his miracles.

CHAPTER 12

From the rearguard

I was telling you yesterday, John, what happened when Jesus was in his town, in Nazareth, shortly after he began the public manifestation of his mission. I told you precisely because what I saw and experienced, neither He saw, nor you saw. And so it happened during the almost three years that followed. He, with you, went back to and fro, going up and down to Jerusalem, going to Tyre and Sidon, crossing Galilee and even passing through Samaria. I, on the other hand, was at home in Nazareth, until my life was in danger and I had to take refuge in Cana. From there, from the rearguard, I had news from your adventures almost daily, which reached me many times distorted, incomplete, riddled with threats of mistakes. It was not easy to be away from the one who was my life's everything. It was not easy to remain serene when those voices that claimed to be my friends put anguish in my throat as they told me in detail the dangers that my son was facing. It was not easy, either, when I heard that my Jesus was going to lead a rebellion against the Romans, or when they told me that He had become a danger to the survival of the people, and even less so when they claimed that He was a blasphemer and that He violated the sacred laws of our religion.

But I had promised Him that, no matter what happened, I would never stop being calm, without losing my peace and without losing my trust in God. I had also promised Him that I would not doubt Him, although it was easy for me to keep that promise, because the rumors that reached me questioning his honesty or his faith, hurt me because of how unfair

I knew it was, but they did not even touch me in terms of making me doubt Him. It was not in vain that I had brought him into the world and had lived with Him for thirty years; if others could doubt, I could not, for I knew Him and I knew that whatever they said, it was all due to misunderstandings or to the sin of those who were reviling Him.

Problems arose immediately, even during the first period, the one in which you walked from triumph to triumph, wrapped in the fame of the miracles that my son performed and carried away by the fervor of the crowd. For example, when, on the first Passover, you went up to Jerusalem.

Not five days had passed since the expulsion of the merchants from the temple when the whole of Galilee knew about it. Even faster than the fastest mail, the news spread throughout the whole region. Not only in Capernaum, where you had settled, but even in secluded Nazareth it was all any one could talk about. What I was told was not, of course, what happened. It took me a long time to find out exactly what had happened. First they told me that a riot had broken out against the Romans in Jerusalem and that my son was one of the ringleaders; they claimed that it had all started in the temple and that the merchants had been expelled from there because they were collaborators with the invaders of our homeland.

They spoke of blood and deaths, of destruction and reprisals. You can understand, John, that anguish filled my mouth with bitterness and my eyes with tears. I was sure that my son was not involved in any violent operation, but I did not know what could have happened and, above all, what his fate had been. A mother always imagines the worst and although my heart told me He was alive, I could not help but shudder at the possibility that something bad might have happened to Him.

Then came the other version. According to this one, Jesus would have confronted the priests and criticized them for the business they had been turning the worship of the Most High into. I was told that He had affirmed, quoting the prophet Zechariah and while expelling the merchants: "Remove this from here, do not make my Father's house a market house". But I was also told that He and you had vented God's wrath on the people, that you had beaten them with whips and that the blood of the merchants had run mixed with that of the sacrificial victims. That zeal of my son for the things of his Father fit better with his way of being, but not so the violence against the people. No, that could not be Him. So I was adamant in rejecting any kind of story that was contrary to the image I had of the one I had carried in my womb. But that did not lessen the fear and anguish. How had the expelled merchants reacted? How had the priests, who received a share of the profits, taken it? And the Romans? Had they remained impassive in the face of a problem that disrupted the order in the beating heart of our restless state?

Yes, John, that was the beginning of a long series of stories that, as I told you, reached to me with delay and necessarily distorted. Then, after some time, either because some of you came to Nazareth, or because in the end the truth would come out, I would find out what had happened, but sometimes it was weeks later, and in the meantime, I had to endure the anguish, the fear and also the doubt.

That was my contribution to your cause. From my pigeon-house in Nazareth, I could only pray. I shared my son´s suffering, and I asked God to unload on me the blows that were reserved for Him. That was how the prophecy of the old man Simeon began to be fulfilled. That was how the sword of pain began to pierce my soul.

The anguish became terrible when, shortly after the events of the Passover, John the Baptist was arrested. He was baptizing at Ainon, near Salim, when the men of Herod the Tetrarch threw themselves upon him and took him away to Machaerus. The news of John's arrest spread quickly throughout the land. Don't forget that I was his aunt and that, although we had not had much contact with him because of the early death of his parents, I had been at his mother's side when she gave birth. Besides, John was loved by all of us. And, as if that were not enough, he had been the one chosen by the Most High to give my son the sign of departure;

from him, finally, some of you had started out, being among the first to accompany my son in his preaching.

But I did not only suffer for John. I also suffered for Jesus. And my cousins suffered for their sons: James, Judas and Simon, who were with Him announcing the good news of God's love to his people. As concerned mothers, we met frequently to exchange the smallest news and to pray asking God for mercy for the Baptist and for our boys. They did not have the faith in Jesus that I had, so I noticed that, in spite of the affection that united us, they sometimes felt bitter and regretful that their sons had gotten into that adventure. On one hand, my cousin Mary, the mother of James, was always firm; on the other hand, the wife of Cleopas, perhaps because she was older, had more difficulty in believing that what Jesus was doing was from God.

The fact is that we suffered because we had no news and we suffered when we received them. And so it was until we learned that, after John's arrest, Jesus had decided to leave Judea and return to Galilee.

You may not believe it, John, but I knew about the Samaritan woman long before we met at Manasseh's house in Cana and He could tell me about it. And, as on so many other occasions, I knew it was wrong and had to suffer for the version I was given.

They did not dare to hurt me directly, so they told Mary, my cousin. First, they said that Jesus had been caught at Jacob's well with a prostitute of Sychar and that his own disciples had found Him talking to her, which is forbidden between us and the Samaritans, and much more so if it is a man and a woman who are alone together, especially if she is a woman of that class. Then they told us that, while it was true that it had only been a conversation, with that fact Jesus had wanted to show that we were all equal and that was an intolerable scandal, because it was unthinkable that we who are good Israelites and worshippers of the true God should be made equal to the Samaritans; just as it was intolerable that an honest woman should be put on the same level as any other woman. In the face of these rumors, which set the virtue of my son on people's tongues and made those who considered themselves zealous defenders of the law gnash their teeth in rage, my cousins and I could not but be more and more anxious.

As soon as we had overcome one cause of anxiety, another would come upon us, always mixed with new ingredients, with rumors of his safety or news of scandals.

That is why we sent you that somewhat desperate message, which I know upset Jesus because it forced Him to change his plans. But it was not that I was a mother with doubts; I was simply a mother. My faith in my son had not been shaken in the least, but I needed to see Him and hold Him in my arms and, if He wanted, to hear from his mouth what had really happened during all that time.

As you know, Jesus agreed to meet us in Cana, in the home of Manasseh who, by the way, died shortly after that visit, leaving Leah desolate. There, in that welcoming home, much more open to the winds of the world than the old-fashioned walls of hilly Nazareth, we were able to spend a few days of rest. And there another miracle took place, although it actually took place at a distance, in Capernaum. I am referring to the healing of the son of the royal official, who came up to Cana from the shores of the lake to beg for the healing of his boy. I was next to my son when that man pleaded insistently with Him. I saw Jesus very tired. So much so that he exclaimed, "Unless you see signs and wonders, you do not believe". I did not dare, as I did in the past, to mediate, among other things because I did not have time. The good man, in spite of his high position, humbled himself before Jesus and again asked Him to go down with him to Capernaum before the child died. Then I saw Him become serious, close his eyes and shudder softly. Then He said to him, "Go, your son lives". That boy lived, John, because of the miracle my son did, but also because of his father's faith, because his father accepted Jesus' word and stopped insisting. If he had continued to beg, of course the healing would have taken place just the same, because when Jesus told him he had already been healed, but who knows what dreadful disease of the spirit would have taken root in the heart of a father who discovers that he has doubted the one who has just saved his child.

Although that meeting between my son and me lasted only a short time, I was able to talk to Him calmly. I took the opportunity to ask Him about his soul, about his peace. I saw Him, as I said, tired. I found Him, even though He was still at the beginning of his adventure, a little disappointed. It could not be said that He had gotten into that mess in ignorance of human nature. We had both talked about it, and his father, Joseph, had told Him so a long time before. Men ask for small miracles from the one who wants to give them the greatest of miracles, that of knowing that God exists and that He is love for each one of them. But it is one thing to know men in theory, but it´s another to immerse yourself in that sea of selfishness that surrounds you as soon as you begin to give and to give of yourself. He told me that He had the impression of being like a large loaf of bread that is placed in the square and from which the hungry come to eat, each one taking a piece, the biggest they can tear off, without worrying about the fate of the bread or the reasons why it is there, within their reach. I understood that, in shreds, they were beginning to tear his life away from Him and that each miracle was not only a proof of His love and a sign of God's power at work in his hands, but also a disappointment to him. A disappointment that came from the fact that most of those who benefited from his favors immediately turned their backs on Him, without even thanking Him or taking an interest in his message.

But, all in all, I at least had the opportunity to see Him and to hold Him in my arms. When you left for Capernaum, I stayed at Cana for a while. I felt at home in that house and, as I tell you, shortly after Manasseh fell ill and I wanted to be at Leah's side. She knew my son's ability to work miracles and had even been able to understand that my prayers were heard by the Most High. Levi's life was proof of this. However, like me, she had noticed that Jesus was exhausted.

Still, I asked her, "Do you want us to send him a message to Capernaum? Perhaps He will save him from a distance, as He did with the son of the royal official". She hesitated, because of the love she felt for her husband, but it didn't take long for her to answer me with a soft smile. "Mary, you pray. But do not ask God to give Manasseh life, and to delay his death. Ask Him to do His will and that, if possible, and if he must to die, that he die in peace and without suffering". I then embraced her and invited her to pray with me. Then we went together to the dying man's bedside.

He was still lucid. I did not dare to make on his forehead the signs still mysterious to me that I had seen Jesus make on his father and grandmother. But I took his trembling hand and told him about heaven. I told him that this was the most important part of the message my son was preaching: that God indeed exists and that it was not exactly as we had been told, that God was Father as well as Almighty. I also told him that heaven was open to all those who had done good and that, when the Lord so desires, he could be accompanying Abraham in the presence of the righteous, but that even that stage was transitory because God's mercy would not take long to manifest itself to redeem us from our sins. He looked at me with his now almost dark eyes and thanked me for having illuminated his last anguish with my words and for having blessed his home with my presence. Then he turned to his wife and blessed her. Finally, he sent for his children and grandchildren and begged them, with the last remaining strand of his voice, to take care of me and, whatever happened, to always keep their doors open for me and my son. Thus, he fell asleep in the Lord and rested in peace. I confess to you, John, that I myself meditated, surprised, when I was able to be alone, on what I had said to Manasseh. It was something that came from within me, that my son had undoubtedly put inside me, but that I myself did not fully understand. Later, after the death and resurrection of my son and the coming of the Holy Spirit at Pentecost, I was able to understand the profound meaning of what I already knew then. But what I did sense was that it was new and that it was a very big change from what we had been taught until then. And I knew it was good, because that righteous man had died in peace.

My son did not go up to Cana for the funeral of Manasseh. He sent three of you as his messengers. He was very busy in Capernaum and was preparing to return to Jerusalem. It was not easy for me to understand. I was his mother and my things seemed very important to me, so I thought they should also be important to Him. It hurt me that He was not at the side of that good family to whom we owed so much. It hurt me that He had not performed a miracle to cure Manasseh, when miracles had been performed to restore the health of strangers, and even more that He did not have time to travel to Cana and be present at the burial of that good man. However, I remembered that scene in the temple, so many years before, when he was a boy and left his father and me to stand there arguing with the doctors. "I have to take care of my Father's business" He told us when we found Him. Yes, He had to do his own thing, which was really what was best for me, for Leah and for her late husband. He had to carry out his Father's mission, even if it was hard for me to understand why those things did not coincide with mine. But all that was also good for my spirit, because it placed me again and again in the mystery and in that mystery, I encountered God. A God whom I now also called Father, although I always had the feeling that for me, He was also something else. That is to say, I called Him Father thinking of myself, but I had a relationship with Him similar to that of a husband and wife who have a child in common.

In conclusion, John, the three short years of my son's evangelizing work, as you now call it, were for me years of suffering, a suffering that I would have liked to alleviate by being at his side, as you were, and even as some of the women who followed Him and helped Him with his belongings. But He did not want me there, glued to his tunic. He wanted me home, safe and oblivious to the problems He was continually getting into. He knew of my pain because of the separation, but He knew that I would have suffered more if I had witnessed the insults that were sometimes directed at Him, the threats that weighed on Him, the plots that his enemies were devising.

When I learned that He was planning to return to Jerusalem for the Sabu'ot holiday, a little over a month after He had been forced to leave the city following the arrest of his cousin, my anguish was enormous. True, the news about John was not bad. It was said that Herod was fond of him and that he even consulted him on matters of state. But there he was, in a prison, and my son could follow his same path. Yet you left and there you were, performing miracles like the one of the sick man He cured at the pool of Bethesda, the one so close to the house where I was born. Of course, you did not only that; Jesus tried to convince the dignitaries, He insisted in his dialogue with the more open-minded Pharisees to make them understand that the message He was spreading was not opposed to what was announced by Moses and the prophets, but was its continuation and its completeness. Finally, you spent many months in the holy city, until that unfortunate feast in which the girl Salome, instigated by her mother, forced Herod to kill the Baptist.

When the news reached us it was already the month of Sebat, although this happened a few days earlier, at the end of Tebet. Once again, fear and pain took hold of me. Fear and anguish for the fate of Jesus and yours, pain for what had happened to John. But I always kept in mind the promise I had made to my son: whatever happens, do not lose hope and do not doubt that God is behind everything. How hard it was for me to accept that God could be behind that murder! But it must be so. I learned to distinguish between what God wants and what God allows. When a person slaps you, that is that person´s will and responsibility; when his hand reaches your face, it is God's will. I learned, I actually had not really stopped learning since that day when the angel appeared to me, to love in the mystery, to love in the darkness. And tremendous darkness was the darkness I endured, without news, until I learned that, after John's death, you had again left Jerusalem in haste, where you were not safe.

So, we had you back in Galilee, even though I was still in Nazareth and you had settled in Capernaum. My cousins and I were anxious to see our respective children. Jesus had sent Judas to reassure us, but his arrival in Nazareth had only made things worse. The people had not forgotten Jesus' stay in the village. Although many had been moved by his tears as He walked away down the hillside, with the passage of time most of them had again become deeply resentful of Him. Above all, they considered his refusal to perform any miracle there as an unforgiable contempt, especially since the news of the miracles He was performing in other places were continuously arriving. So it was probably in Nazareth where He was the least popular in all of Galillee. This pressure had repercussions on all his family and, especially, on his cousins. With the exception of those who had followed Him, the rest were annoyed of having to endure the attacks of those who accused them of being relatives of an apostate, of one who violated the Sabbath, who had pretensions of greatness and who wanted to change the teachings of our elders. I realized that a storm was brewing, and I did not know what to do, for it had been a long time since my words had been heard even among my own people. Only my cousin Mary was still very close to me and, with the others, I could hardly do anything else but bear their reproaches and ironies in silence. Then, when you had been in Capernaum for some weeks, and after Judas' stay in the town, it was decided to form a family retinue to go to where Jesus was and ask for explanations. He, they said, could not do he whatever wanted because his behavior was endangering the rest of the family. He had to be reasonable, moderate his pretensions, submit to the rabbis and the chiefs of the town, not to provoke and, if possible, to benefit his own people in some way, as they all did when they gained power and influence in some way.

As you can understand, John, it was a terrible disappointment for me. What could I do? They wouldn't even let me speak. They only told me that I could go with them or, if I didn't want to, I could stay in town. I couldn't refuse to go with them, I wanted to see Him so much! Besides, perhaps I could mediate to avoid a clash that would cause my son to lose what little support He had among his own people.

It was winter, but the days were mild. Adar was advancing and the fields were beginning to fill with flowers. We arrived in Capernaum and immediately we were told that "the Master", as everyone knew Him in the town, was teaching in the house of a notable. We went there. The house was full. One of my nephews asked one of those who craned their necks from outside to tell them what was taking place in the courtyard of the house. "What is he talking about?" he asked. "Something about a sign of Jonah", he answered, to add, "He says that the Ninevites will rise up against us on the day of Judgment because they were converted by the preaching of Jonah, and He is more than Jonah, and yet we are not converted. And He also says that the queen of the South will do the same, the one who came to listen to Solomon, because He is more than Solomon".

"More than Jonah and more than Solomon", my relatives exclaimed indignantly. "This is too much. He has gone mad and if we don't stop Him, He is going to bring disgrace upon us all and even upon all Israel".

At the commotion, some of them turned and ordered them to be quiet. "He is talking about Satan, so shut up and let us listen to Him. If you don't believe Him, that's up to you, but for us everything He says is true because we have seen so many of his miracles that neither Solomon nor David himself can match Him". My cousins protested and the commotion, instead of abating, grew. Then they identified themselves:

> "We are his family who have come to see him from Nazareth and here with us is his mother". My heart skipped a beat. How could they dare to involve me in such a mess? How dare they mention my name, as if I agreed with them and had doubts about my son's identity and importance? But there was nothing to be done. As soon as it was heard that I was there, and that no one knew me, the news spread like lightning: "It's his mother", they said to one another with reverence, making way for me. And so it went on until someone managed to get close to Jesus, who was still speaking, and said to him, "Your mother and your brothers are outside and want to talk to you". They could all hear him and turned to where we were. How much I suffered then, John! I still did not see Him, as far away as I was still from Him. And I carried within

me the enormous pain of being the companion of people who did not love Him and did not understand Him. I was afraid that He might doubt me and suspect that I was also with those who criticized Him. I wanted to go ahead of everyone and give Him explanations, but at that moment, I myself like the others, heard Him say, in a calm but very excited voice: "Who is my mother and who are my brothers?", and then He added, while pointing to you, his dearest disciples: "These are my mother and my brothers. For whoever does the will of my heavenly Father, he is my brother, she is my sister, my mother". The murmur grew then, all spoke, one to another, wondering about the meaning of those words. If they were a disdain for his family, including me; if the Master had just given another lesson opening to anyone the possibility of being one of his closest friends; if what really matters is not the bond of blood, but the bonds established by love.

The truth is that there was no time for many comments. Jesus had gotten up and they had cleared a path for Him so he could get to me. His cousins, so irritated before and rather confused now, were behind me. My son, in full view of everyone, with that calmness that now never left Him, threw his arms around my neck and kissed my forehead. I was still stunned; I wanted to talk, to explain, to tell Him what was happening, but He wouldn't let me. In my ear He said, "I know everything. Be calm. I don't doubt you, just as you don't doubt me. But all this has to happen, so stop suffering, because in God's plans everything is foreseen, even that the prophets will be despised in their land". Then He went to his cousins and greeted them with affection, as if He was not aware of their intentions, as if He did not know how to read their envy and selfishness in their eyes, or better yet, as if, even, knowing about it, he loved them just the same. Later, I learned that Judas, his cousin, had told him how things were in Nazareth and among us. Nevertheless, both to them and to me, He treated us with great courtesy. He asked his friends to put them up in their houses, and He took me to Peter's house, where he lived. It was then that

He came back to you and asked you, for the second time, to stay with me all the time and to move from your father's house to Peter's to accompany me. How much you had changed in a few months! But, anyway, this is not the time to talk about us, but to continue telling you what happened between his cousins and Him in the meeting that followed.

Jesus didn't let me go on with them. What I came to know, I learned from Mary, for He did not want his other cousins, those who were at his side, James, Simon and Judas, to be present either.

The meeting was difficult. It is true that the boys were less aggressive than in Nazareth. Now they were no longer in their own home. Besides, the atmosphere in Capernaum was very different from the one in our town. Here Jesus was admired and loved, He had many followers and people from all over Galilee and even from Judea and the Decapolis were continually coming to the little town to listen to Him and, above all, to be cured by him. They told marvels about Him, and they did not cease to flatter and bless me for having had such a son.

But, nevertheless, the family reunion was difficult. Past the first moment, his cousins told Him, more gently but clearly, everything they thought. They omitted some things, but reminded Him of his family duties and, above all, of the delicate situation in which his "adventures", as they called them, made them look in Nazareth. There was one who dared to go further and who advised Him more. "Confronting the priests, the Pharisees, the Sadducees and, above all, the Romans", he told Him, "will not get you anywhere. If you want to be recognized as the Messiah, listen to me and focus on performing miracles and getting along with those in charge. Afterwards, when you achieve power, you will settle accounts with your enemies. You have to be smarter, more astute", he added, "and less confrontational. It's no use telling the truth, it's enough to be honest and to be a bit discreet. Otherwise, I assure you, you will never be anything in life. If you think that the friendship of all these people is worth something, you are wrong. They will all abandon you as soon as the powerful attack you directly".

As I tell you, John, I was not present at that meeting. My son wanted to spare me that displeasure. I learned from Mary that He listened to his cousins with his head in his hands. And that he did not dismiss them angrily. My cousin told me that His eyes were even wet when they finished giving Him their advice. I know, although He never wanted to tell me about what had happened there so as not to make me sad, how much He must have suffered. After all, they were his family and we loved each other. For years we had lived together and had spent very good times together; we even had debts with some of them, and not only of affection but also of money. And now they asked Him to fight for power with trickery, to lie if necessary, and, above all, to not make life difficult for them.

Jesus had already begun to drink from the cup of bitterness and disappointment, but I am sure that this was a considerable gulp. If his own people did not recognize Him and did not believe the signs He performed, how could the people understand Him? How could the wise and knowledgeable accept His message, those who looked at Him with suspicion because He was not of the priestly caste or because He did not comply strictly with the legal prescriptions?

The fact was that He sent his cousins away without making any promises to them and keeping his disappointment in check. It was not the last time He saw them, for He still had to endure another family "delegation" a few months later, even harsher than the first. However, with that one he had enough to know what to expect from his family.

The only good thing about that unpleasantness was that He would not let me leave. He did not want me to return with them to Nazareth. He didn't tell me why, but I guess He must have understood how much I was struggling it in the mountains, without Him and surrounded by people who continually filled my head with gossip, doubts and even criticism of my own son. Without giving explanations to anyone, He asked me to stay, so I had to beg Mary, my cousin, to close the house and to send me my things as soon as possible to continue the rest of my life outside Nazareth, where, since then and to my regret, I have not returned.

I was a little hurt by that loss, for I was very fond of my people, but that sorrow was nothing compared to the joy of being able to be with my son. This joy was short-lived, for he soon sent me to Leah's house in Cana, where I stayed almost until the end, a little before His time had come. But at least I was able to be with you that Passover.

We have spoken many times of the significance of the multiplication of the loaves and fishes on that spring day. We have talked about it after the coming of the blessed Holy Spirit. Now we understand much better what Jesus wanted to do that day. It was a symbol of what was to come. But with the few lights we had then, we did not realize that it was more than just a great miracle. For it was indeed that: the most spectacular miracle of all. It seemed that He had decided to heed the advice of his cousins and that he was willing to keep the people happy at the cost of satisfying their needs, even their food needs. It was not so, but that is how the people took it.

That is why they wanted to make Him king. King of a world full of wars and selfishness, when what He wanted was to be king in the hearts, king of peace and justice.

He had not told me what was going to happen, which makes me think that He had nothing prepared. Those days, even though He was always on the go and surrounded by all kinds of people, we saw each other from time to time. I liked to be in a corner, close to Him but without standing out, without making myself present so as not to disturb. He liked having me around but without drawing attention. We both cherished that time together, which reminded us of the sweet intimacy we had lived in our home in Nazareth, both when his father was alive and after his death. Thus, I listened to Him preach and saw how He behaved. I was also able to observe you and the others more closely, as well as the women around him, which, believe me, did not stop worrying me, because you never know what can happen between a man and a woman, especially if she tries to win him over with tears and by playing the victim.

I was able to witness with my own eyes several of his miracles, which were no particular revelation to me, for I knew well what He could do with the

Father's power. But I, too, learned much in those days. Above all, I became more and more aware that He was not only my son, but that he was also the Son of God and, as he himself said, your brother. I do not understand much of these concepts that you now handle in this Greek world; I am referring to "person" and "nature". I get lost in these new categories, so foreign to our way of thinking. I only know, now with more clarity than at that time, that if He was my son, He was truly man, and that if God, the Most High, had begotten Him, He was his Son and therefore God was like Him, because pears do not grow from apple trees, nor turtles from fish. I know that this still sounds very scandalous in many ears, especially in the ears of many of our compatriots, who have approached our group but who have not been willing to take the step of accepting Him as God. I know, but since then I have been seeing it more and more clearly, especially since the conversation I had with him shortly after. Although I confess that it frightened me, and it still frightens me, to think what that meant, because, among other things, if that were so, I would mean that I would have carried God Himself in my womb and I would be, in that case, the mother of God.

Thinking about all that made me dizzy, so I did it rarely. But, anyway, I didn't have much time to think about the things in my head. Things that, far exceeded my capacity to understand and that, if I have come to understand something else, it has been thanks to the action of the Holy Spirit through Pentecost. I limited myself, as I said, to being there, in a corner, watching Him and enjoying listening to his words. From time to time, He would look for me with his eyes and that was enough for both of us. Also, from time to time, we could be alone, and we could give free rein to our affection as son and mother. However, He did not tell me anything about what was going to happen that morning when He multiplied the loaves. That is why I believe that, as on so many other occasions, He had nothing planned. The problem simply arose, and He wanted to do a favor to a hungry crowd, and at the same time He saw that it was an opportunity to give us a great teaching. Deep down, this reminded to all the good Israelites who were there of the appearance of the manna in the

Sinai desert. And perhaps that was why they decided to make him king. For that reason and because a king such as him, no Israelite army would be defeated and no man would have to work again, for the stones would become bread and the water would become generous wine.

And that is why He fled. When He saw that they still did not understand, and that what He had wanted to do with that miracle had been misrepresented, disappointment invaded Him again. What would he have to do to make them understand that He was not a doctor of bodies but of souls, that He did not want to feed their stomachs but to quench their thirst for God? Whatever He did, in the end their kindness would turn against Him. That seemed to be his fate, his irremediable end. The more He loved people, the less people understood his message. The more He helped them, the more they sought material and less spiritual help. Few, if any, came to Him to say: Help me to be better, help me to control my temper, ask God to make me generous. On the contrary, the requests were always the same: Cure my son, cure my wife, cure my husband, my servant or even my donkey. The spiritual, goodness, God in short, did not seem to interest anyone. Only the things of the earth, only what was material moved people. And also, at least a little bit, you as well. Because I realized that right away, as soon as I could be near you and observe you from the quiet. There was no doubt in my mind that you loved Him. You, of course, madly. And Peter, your brother James, and my nephew James too. You loved and admired Him, but you did not understand him. You too, who believed that He was sent by the Most High, thought that his mission was above all earthly and that one day He would take power in all Israel and would establish a kingdom that, even if it was based on the divine commandments, it was still a kingdom with its power, its economy, its ministers and even its police and its army. Hence the fights among you to see who was going to be the most important. That is why —and forgive me for saying so— your mother's intervention took place, claiming for your brother and for you the first positions in the future kingdom that you believed was about to be established.

The fact is that the multiplication of the loaves and fishes passed as the great miracle of Jesus, without anyone realizing that there was something more. There was the proof that God was with him, as he was with Moses in the desert, and there was also the foretaste of a food that would eternally satisfy our hunger, which He would later give us with his body and blood on the eve of his Passion, with the "Eucharist", as you now call it in this strange Greek world.

After that I could only be with Him and with you for a few days. He sent you, remember, to accompany me to Cana. But before that we spent a long time together. In that conversation, even more than on other occasions, He opened his heart to me. I was able to hold his head in my hands and tried to comfort Him, while encouraging Him to go on. He was, after all, a man and you men always need us women to encourage and support you. And that's what I was there for, just as I am still here for you and for everyone, as a rock, as a pillar for those who are tired and burdened to rest and lean on.

I told him, I remember it well: "What did you expect? Did you think that everything was going to be easy? Did you think that with the miracles and your speeches people would understand and would be converted and their hearts would be transformed? My dear son, you must accept things as they are, and you must accept us men as we are made. Of clay and sinners, although the latter is our business and not that of Yahweh. And, deep down, that is what has attracted you: our weakness. You did not come to save those who did not need salvation, but the sinners. As you yourself say, you came to look for the lost sheep. What happens is that that sheep is more lost and more rebellious than you thought. So, take heart and move on. God is with you and everything will be fine, you'll see".

I didn't know then what was going to happen, although I had an intuition, because we mothers always put ourselves in the worst situation. But I wasn't going to tell him either, because what I wanted to do was to encourage Him. He, who did know, who knew that the end would be the cross, looked at me sweetly and held me in his arms. My God, his kisses, how much I miss his kisses and his embraces! If I am longing to leave this world, it is to recover them again. Only the Eucharist can be compared to them, even though they are so different.

Then I seized to take the opportunity to ask Him something that had been weighing on me more and more. So I asked him, "Son, tell me clearly, who are you?". "I am your son, mother", he answered, laughing, to add, "You really are something!". I insisted, "I know for a fact that you are my son, but what are you of God? What did the angel Gabriel mean when he announced to me that the one who was to be begotten in me would be called 'Son of the Most High'".

Jesus broke away from me. He got up and went to the other end of the room. With His back to me, as I remained seated and expectant, He spoke to me: "Mother, I do not want to scandalize you, nor do I want to reveal to you now things that you cannot yet understand. In due time, the Holy Spirit who one day covered you with His shadow will cover you with His wisdom and teach you everything. I will ask him to do so. For now, you only need to know that the Father and I are one and that it has been so for all eternity. This is enough for you", and as He said this He turned and looked at me, "This is enough for you and now leave me, I must pray. You have already consoled me and now He must do so. I need to be consoled by both, because I am your son and each of you must do your part". He kissed me again and I went out. I felt like a kind of dizziness, as if my head was spinning, as if my intuitions were fighting their way through my little Galilean woman's mind. "For all eternity", those words echoed over and over in my ears. "For all eternity". Then, then he was not just a messiah, an envoy, a prophet. He was far more than the greatest of the prophets, more than the great Isaiah, more than King David himself, or Moses, or than our father Abraham. Who was He, then? Could it be possible that He was really God? And again the questions about me: If He is God, who am I? How should I treat him? By what right have I educated Him, corrected him, even scolded Him as a child? Whom have I held at my womb and upon my breasts?

It was too much, as I tell you, for a simple woman from a mountain village. So much so that I realized that my son was right when He told me that my hour had not yet come, that of understanding everything, and I decided to put a stop to my thoughts and to keep the mystery in my heart.

That is how I left Capernaum, with you, to whom I did not reveal then that conversation because I understood that you were not prepared for it, even less prepared than I was. Thus, I entered Cana again. With my soul a little more at peace because of my decision not to complicate my life unnecessarily and to wait for that mysterious Holy Spirit my son was refering to, in due time, to reveal to me what I had to know.

What I could not avoid was fear for the fate of my Jesus. If it was so difficult for me to understand, what about you? And what about the priests, the notables and the most religious men of our people? How could they, educated in respect and fear of the Almighty God, accept that this same God had become man? How could the people and a religion that did not even allow sculptures of God to be made because it was considered blasphemy, accept it? And now it was not only a matter of sculptures, but of a real presence in the world of men, of a man who pretended to be, at the same time, God. I understood that failure was inevitable and that really terrified me. Although, once again, I was helped by the certainty of knowing that God is behind everything and that nothing, absolutely nothing, escapes his merciful and benevolent designs.

After this, already in the autumn, in the month of Tisri, you went again to Jerusalem to celebrate Sukkot there. But first He had to put up with another delegation of his cousins, who did not hesitate to tell him, even though they knew the risk he was running: "Leave and go to Judea, so that your disciples there may also see the deeds you are doing, for no one acts in secret when he wants to be known. If you do these things, show yourself to the world". It hurts me, even though so much time has passed, to think about it again. It hurts me to know that it was his own relatives who put Him on the way of the cross and that they did it consciously, only because they wanted to keep Him away from them, because they did not want to continue to have problems in Nazareth because of the kinship with that man who had become an increasingly controversial figure.

But that interview was not like the first one. I found out later, just like last time, although I was already in Cana at the time. My son, hurt and determined to listen to them and to lay his cards on the table, said to his cousins: "My time has not yet come, but your time is always at hand. Do not worry so much about the hatred of the world. The world cannot hate you, but it hates me, for I testify that its works are evil. You go up to Jerusalem to take part in the feast; I am not going because my time is not yet fulfilled".

He said that but didn't do it. He simply did not want to go with them. He wanted to set up his own program. So, when they, who were not to be trusted, left, He, with you, made his way to Jerusalem. I can imagine his pain at having to move in secret, at not being able to manifest himself in public. And not because he feared death, but because He knew that it was not yet the time to pass from this world to the Father, that He still had many things to do, even though that decisive hour was drawing nearer and nearer.

Of what I knew of that long stay in the holy city, John, I can tell you little that you do not know. At Cana, news reached me more quickly and with more accuracy than at Nazareth. There I was among friends and did not have to endure the insidiousness of my former neighbors in Nazareth. But that did not stop me from worrying, being surprised and also rejoicing.

They told me, amazed, about the adulterous woman whom He saved from being stoned to death after having said to her accusers, "He among you who is without sin, let him cast the first stone at her", How pleased and proud I felt then of my son! For I could not but remember that I myself was about to have found myself in a similar situation, precisely because of his birth, even though I had not committed adultery of any kind. Yes, the lessons I had taught him about what we women suffer in this society of ours had taken effect and I had every reason to be happy for my son.

The same thing happened to me when they told me about the miracle He had done with that man, blind from birth, whom even his parents did not want to defend when the Pharisees questioned him. That was my Jesus, that was my son and the Son of the Most High: the one who does not hesitate to complicate his life to help someone, the one of whom the Scriptures told us: "Even if your father and mother forsake you, I will not forsake you". He loved us more, He risked more for us than our own fathers and mothers in the flesh. And so, He was right to speak of Himself as "the good shepherd" and to say that those who had come before Him were "thieves and robbers", while He was on earth to give "his life for the sheep".

But, as you will understand John, I could not stop suffering. When they told me what he said about his mission as a shepherd, they did not omit those words of his that were so premonitory of what was to happen. "For this reason, the Father loves me, because I lay down my life, that I may take it again; that is the command I have received from my Father". If you and the Pharisees were arguing about what was meant by the use of the term "father" in reference to God and applied to Himself as Son, if some were annoyed by its familiarity and others were scandalized by its pretensions, I only noticed that more and more frequently He referred to death, to that "giving of life" which could only signify the nearness of the final moment.

So, my life was one of constant distress, as I thought of the danger He was in, being in Jerusalem, surrounded by enemies who were lurking around Him from all sides? Moreover, on that occasion, your stay in the capital was prolonged for a long time, well into the winter, for you spent the feast of Hanukkah there, and only in the month of Shebat, when again they tried to stone Him in the temple, He agreed to leave Jerusalem and cross the Jordan to rest a little and prepare for the final assault. Of this, however, we will speak tomorrow, because just thinking about it hurts my heart again as it did then, and I feel again how those swords of pain of which Simeon spoke to me pierce my soul.

CHAPTER 13

Standing by the Cross

I have not spoken to you, until now, of our dear friends of Bethany because you knew them before I did and because, until this moment in our history, I had not had any knowledge of them. Perhaps, some people, at one time or another, spoke to me about the family of Lazarus, Martha and Mary, but I did not give too much importance to them, as I thought that they were just one of many who loved my son. I remember, however, that you had spoken to me, I'm not sure if it was you or someone else, about the time my son gave a lesson to a very anxious Martha, giving as an example to imitate her sister, Mary, who did nothing more than to listen attentively to his words. I remember it because, on hearing it from your lips, I thought of the profound wisdom of my son, who knows the female soul as well as He knows the soul of men, and who knows that we must both prevent the good in us from becoming so accentuated that we become unbalanced. Well, that was the only memory I had of a pious family from Bethany, in whose house you used to stop when you were in the area.

From there, from Bethany, they called you not long after having had to leave Jerusalem to avoid being arrested. The proximity of the holy city made it difficult to return; things had not calmed down sufficiently and it still risky to return again. On the other hand, the Passover was approaching, which was also a reason to return to Jerusalem, but, above all, the main reason was the desperate call of Martha, who claimed Jesus at the bedside of her dying brother.

You know that my son did not respond promptly to that call. Some of you advised Him not to go to Bethany, because of the obvious danger. You told Him that, if He wished, He could cure Lazarus from a distance, as He had done with the son of the royal official. He seemed to listen to those who told him so and waited two days. Then, suddenly, He decided to go up to Jerusalem, in spite of your opposition, which became greater when you learned from him that Lazarus was already dead. I also knew that Thomas, that wonderful boy always full of curiosity, said before all of you , expressing the common feeling: "Let us also go so we can die with Him". That was your spirit. You were aware that the danger was great and that this time it could not be easily avoided. And that was your merit: that of having decided to be with my son until the end, risking to suffer his death, when it was already known what could await Him.

As for Jesus, what did He know of what could happen to Him in Jerusalem? I was in Cana at the time, and only later was I able to see Him and speak with Him. Of that, of his state of mind when He decided to set out on the road that would lead Him to the cross, did not speak. However, I am sure that He was fully aware of what was going to happen to Him. Just as He was also aware that his hour had come and that the occasion given to Him was the right one.

You see, John, what happened to Lazarus was very similar to what happened at Cana. On that occasion, when He performed his first miracle, when He turned water into wine, He said to me that mysterious phrase that has given me so much food for thought: "Woman, leave me, my hour has not yet come". He was referring to the hour of miracles, but, above all, He was referring to the hour of the cross.

Because both times were linked. His time had come and that time began to count from the moment He made himself known, from the moment he went public. By doing a favor, by helping someone, He had taken the first step and had begun a kind of countdown that was stealing moments of his existence. Now, as if it were an agreed signal, the need to do another favor, this time not to some of his mother's friends but to some of his own, put Him before the last moments of his life. With an act of love for some friends, this countdown began. With another act of love, it ended. He was born only out of an act of love —that which existed between God and me— and to carry out acts of love. Of love for all of us, certainly, but in a special way for those who most needed that love: for sinners, for the poor, for the sick, for the suffering. Out of love He became man, out of love he worked miracles, out of love He drew attention to Himself and out of love He went up to Jerusalem to heal a friend even though He knew it was leading Him straight to torture. Anything else would have been unlike Him, it would have been like denying Himself. He was not, therefore, a daredevil who despised dangers, who ignored them or who enjoyed risk and adventure. He did not want to die as He died, because his death would be due to the sin of one or of many, and He could not wish anyone to sin. He wanted to live and live surrounded by converted, holy, happy men and women. But if He had to die crucified, let it be for the reason that had brought Him to earth: out of love. If his time had come, let the sign for Him and for all be precisely this: someone needed Him and he could not fail to respond to his call, even if it meant the beginning of the end. In reality, there was not much difference between that ascent to Jerusalem, invoked by a dying Lazarus, and his birth in Bethlehem, invoked not by one but by many, millions of dying people, who, without knowing it, were crying out to heaven from their misery, invoking a physician for their souls, a savior.

That is why He went up to Jerusalem that spring. And the proof that He knew not only what He was exposing Himself to but also what was going to happen was the fact that he sent you to get me at Cana. He wanted to say goodbye to me before the final moment. In reality, truly human as He was, he wanted to find the only support he could not do without, that of, his mother's.

When you arrived in Cana and told me that my son wanted me at his side in Bethany, I feared the worst. I thought that He was sick or at least that something serious was happening, for it was not normal for Him to call me to his side. No matter how much you tried to reassure me, telling me that it was only that He wanted us to spend the Passover feast together, I was sure that something was happening or was going to happen.

With this in mind, which I kept to myself so as not to pass on my fears to you, I accompanied you to Bethany. When we arrived there, the miracle of Lazarus' resurrection had already taken place, and the house and the whole village were buzzing with joy and with people. Many were those who came to see Jesus, to listen to Him, to ask Him for cures and favors. Many were also those who had come to see Lazarus, to see that he was alive and to hear the extraordinary story of how he had been raised from the dead. In this atmosphere of celebration and exaltation we were welcomed when we entered the town. I was surprised and reassured, and I even came to think that, if such was the fame of my son, perhaps my worries were excessive and were due more to the obsessions of an old woman than to reality.

However, when I met Jesus, even though I was surrounded by enthusiastic people and the affection of Lazarus, Martha and Mary, I knew from the first moment that my son was having a hard time and that the situation was serious.

That first day we were not able to talk at all. It was already late when we arrived at Bethany and He limited himself to greeting me, to receive me with kisses and hugs of welcome and to tell me that we would have time to talk calmly.

That did not happen. The next day, almost at dawn, an envoy from Nicodemus arrived with an urgent message for Jesus:

> "Leave Bethany quickly", his illustrious friend was telling him.
> "The Pharisees are plotting to kill you. What you have done with
> Lazarus has upset them very much, and they have decided that, at
> all costs, they must put an end to you and even to him".

All of you, then, became nervous. Everyone except Him. He did not want to leave, but to reassure you and to avoid endangering the family that was sheltering him, He decided to leave the village for a while, although He warned us that He would only be gone for a short time, for it was his desire, whatever happened, to return to Jerusalem for the Passover.

This time he did not go to the Jordan, but chose Ephraim, where He might not have been expected, to let the storm subside a little.

As for me, I remember that He said to me: "You see, mother, I have made you come at a bad time. It is useless for me to try to deceive you with words that you will not believe. Things are just as you see them. But you and I know that this is what I have come for. Perhaps I was wrong to call you to my side. I am sorry. I am sorry for making you suffer, but I assure you that I could not take this step without seeing you again, without holding you in my arms again and without receiving your kisses and your blessings. Now do not fear. You will be fine here. Besides, this is not a definitive separation. My time has not yet come, although it is near. We will see each other again".

And He left. You surrounded Him, both solicitous and uneasy. It seemed as if, suddenly, the overflowing joy that had followed the resurrection of Lazarus, the euphoria that had possessed you all, had dissipated in the twinkling of an eye. It seemed as if, once again, fear had taken possession of your spirit and you had forgotten even the power that he had and to which, once again, he had just borne witness to you. But, in spite of your fear and doubts, you went with Him.

I stood outside, at the door of the house, watching you leave.

Lazarus was with you, for he too was being threatened. Martha and Mary were with me, one on each side. Mary put her arm around my shoulders and Martha held my hand in hers. They were crying, I was not. I didn't want Him to turn his head to take one last look at me and see an old, defeated, desperate woman. He had called me to his side for support, not to receive more pain. He wanted me to be, as when He was a child, his pillar, his rock, his refuge, his comfort. And so, I was to stand, firm, as if I were suffering nothing. Otherwise, if I let myself be dragged down by what I felt inside, instead of helping Him I would only increase his own grief and add more pain to the bitterness He already had.

Indeed, as He was walking away, He turned back. It was an instant. Barely a glimpse of his face. Barely a quick movement of his hand in the air. Just a glance at each other. It was enough. How my son and I understood each other! That was enough, a glance to know that each one of us was in their place, before God and before our duty. He knew that He could count on me and I knew that I had to support Him so that He could do what he had to do. We both knew, moreover, that we were alone. And not because we doubted your affection, yours, that of the other apostles or that of those two magnificent girls who wept at my side. But because we knew that you did not understand what was happening and that you did not imagine what was going to happen. I was beginning to sense, moreover, that the loneliness was deeper, that the Father was also beginning to withdraw to make Him drink right to the bottom of the cup of bitterness that we mankind usually drink from. I was beginning to sense it, but He already knew that. And it was precisely for this reason, because perhaps without a father you can go on but not without a mother, and that´s why He had sent for me so that at least, the mother, would not be missing when everything else was denied to Him.

As Jesus had foreseen, the news that, together with his disciples and Lazarus, He had left Bethany heading north, soon spread. His enemies thought that He was setting out again on the road to Galilee and, pleased with this flight, which they had interpreted as a gesture of cowardice, they abandoned their machinations for the time being in order to devote themselves to the preparations of the approaching Passover feast. However, they redoubled their system of espionage, which included people who entered into the group of my son's followers, so that they would be informed of his steps if He tried to return to Jerusalem during the great solemnities that were approaching. So great was their fear that Jesus might organize a revolt in the temple, a kind of riot against them or the Romans. Not only, as you see, John, did his friends not know Him, but also those who feared and despised Him had not understood that He was incapable of violence, of resentment, of hatred.

My son returned, by surprise, a week before Passover. He entered the village, with Lazarus and you, all of you trying to go as unnoticed as possible.

He knew that they were spying on Him and that, no matter what He did, the priests and Pharisees would soon find out, but He wanted to gain time, to gain a few days of peace and quiet and prepare for the last and final assault of the fortress of death.

It was impossible to keep the secret. A few hours later, the house was full of people again, just as when I arrived in Bethany. And with those people, the rumors about the dangers that hovered over all of us.

Then Jesus changed tactics. As if nothing mattered anymore, as though He had decided to come out into the open and show his face, no longer hiding. He asked Lazarus to organize a big party that very night and to invite all his friends to it, even some who were frankly hostile to him. In the end, the party could not be held at Lazarus' house and was held at the house of another friend, Simon, whom he had cured of leprosy. It was at that feast, the last one He attended, that Mary, moved because she too had begun to sense what was happening, poured a pound of nard perfume on his feet and wiped them with her hair. The words of my son, answering the objections of Judas the Iscariot who complained about that waste because he thought it would have been better to give it to the poor, sounded in my ears and in those of many of you as an epitaph: "Leave it, for she was saving it for the day of my burial. For you will always have the poor with you, but you will not always have me". Mary raised her eyes when she heard him say those words and withdrew in tears. We all knew that He was speaking of his death and that He considered the girl's act of love as the tribute that loved ones pay to the deceased.

The party was over. Most of us had not grasped the message, although those of us closest to Him did not fail to comment on the meaning of his words. But soon other events attracted our attention. Indeed, the next day Jesus sent two of you to Jerusalem to prepare everything necessary to celebrate the Passover. You were all alarmed: "So He dares to go up to Jerusalem and provoke those who are looking for him to kill Him", you said. Some of you tried to dissuade Him and advised Him to wait and celebrate the feast at Lazarus' house, and not in the holy city. He insisted. He even told you to go to the house of Joseph of Arimathea, one of the richest men in the city and a friend of his, who lived in the most luxurious neighborhood, not far from the High Priest himself, to celebrate the great feast there. It was indeed provoking, but, as I said, it´s as if He had decided that since the end was near, it would have to be according to his own rules, and not when and how his enemies wanted. It was a challenge, it was not a show of strength, but that He was surrendering voluntarily and did not just hide to be caught like a rabbit by a ferret in its burrow.

As soon as the two disciples left to carry out their assignment, with quite a bit of fear in their bodies, He said goodbye to all of you and was left alone with me. He asked me if I was tired, and when I told Him I was not, He asked me to accompany Him for a walk in the fields around the village, fields of olive trees, wheat, barley and poppies.

It was a beautiful spring day. The month of Nisan was shining. It was still early; the sun was not too hot, and the temperature was gentle like a mother's kiss. Nature was putting on her best dress to envelop us both. Birds were singing and butterflies and bees were busy gathering their food from the flowers.

We walked calmly and silently. Mother and child. Master and disciple. We were like that for a long time. In silence. Without saying anything and knowing everything. He did not dare to start, and I was afraid of spoiling everything by opening my mouth. We were like so until He asked me to sit down. We were on a road, surrounded by orchards, with their low dry-stone borders as they are usually made in our land. There we sat down and there He began to talk.

"What a magnificent day, isn't it, Mother? It is a kindness from my Father, who does not want me to say goodbye to life with the memory of a storm or a hurricane" Having said this He waited to see my reaction.

I remained silent. Of course, I knew that my protests were useless and even more my pretending, as if I didn't know anything or as if telling him to forget those bad omens of death could have been of any use. So, I looked at Him and kept silent. I waited for Him to go on.

He understood. Then He took my hand and added:

"So you know everything. It was only natural that you wouldn't miss anything. I'm glad that's so, although I suppose you're suffering. It's no use trying to fool you, and that's why I want you to take what I'm about to tell you seriously. I am not telling you this as a false consolation, as if I intended to reassure you with kind words so that you would enclure with false hope the coming ordeal. I want you to know that I am going to die. Or rather, that they are going to kill me", then, John, and in spite of my efforts to be serene, I could not avoid a shudder that he noticed. "Yes, mother, I want you to know everything. Next Thursday night the hit men will seize me in order to have me killed. This is a terrible ending, but that is how it is written and that is how it must be. But I also want you to know that I will be resurrected. You have heard what happened to Lazarus and others whom I have rescued from death. The Father has given me that power and now He, myself and the Spirit will use it on myself. That is to say, dear Mother, that I will rise again, although it will be a different resurrection from that of Lazarus. You must, therefore, be calm. Look, it is very likely that they will all leave and betray me", I was still silent, but again a trembling of my hands, which he grasped tightly, made him notice that the pain was hitting me. "Yes, everyone will abandon me. Well, almost everyone; your dear John" he meant you "Will have only a moment of weakness. You women won't leave me either. Anyway, I don't want to tell you any more details about this. I only want you to know that, even if everyone abandons me and even if it seems that heaven consents to what men decide, everything is foreseen. After three days, that is, on the first day of the week, I will rise from the dead and I will see you again. Do not run to and fro as the others will do. I will come to you. You stay here, where you are safe, and then I will show you what to do. For the time being, be aware of everything and do not stop praying so that things may be fulfilled according to the will of the Father. We are gambling, dear Mother, the success of my mission. It is the final hour, the awaited moment, and we cannot let this opportunity pass to save this dear humanity, these men whom I love so much. So do not suffer more than necessary, although I imagine that to ask that of you is to ask the impossible. I am satisfied that you do not lose faith, and that, whatever happens, you never doubt that the Father is with me and that everything is being done according to His will. I need that faith from you. I need it more than you can imagine".

He said no more. He stopped looking at me and turned His face away. The sun kissed his cheeks, filtering through the leaves of the olive trees that protected us. My son was beautiful. He was beautiful, in that hour of fullness, in that penultimate hour. I saw that a tear appeared in his eyes and that He looked away so that I would not notice. So I got up and, with a cloth that I always carry with me, I wiped it away. Then, standing before Him who was still sitting, I took his hands and said, looking into his sweet and sad eyes: "Son, I am your mother. If you had told me thirty-three years ago that it was going to end like this, I don't know what I would have done. Perhaps, in spite of that, I would have said yes to God. Yes, indeed, I would have said yes, because the price of that permission was to be your mother, to have been able to live with you for so long, to have loved you and to have felt loved by you. I have been lucky to be by your side and that is priceless. But now you tell me that the end has come. I want you to know that I will always be with you and that I will not let you down. If you ask me to be whole, I will be whole. If you ask me not to cry, you will not see a tear appear in my eyes. If you ask me to believe in what you have taught me, that God is Father and is love, I will believe it no matter what. You are my son, flesh of my flesh, I have to live up to you and not only in ordinary moments but also in circumstances like this. So, count on me. There are many things. I don't understand well, but we women are used, to believing without understanding, more so than men. Besides, after all, who can pretend to understand God, who is greater than the heavens. We women know very well that great things escape the most subtle reasoning, and that God, as you have so often said, has hidden His mysteries from the wise and learned and has revealed them to simple people. Come on, let me hug you and let's go back to town. I don't want to see you sad. Whatever has to happen must happen and both you and I have to face it accordingly. If it is time to die, let us die on our feet, with the dignity of knowing that we are doing what God asks of us and with peace in our souls".

I don't know how, dear John, I was able to tell Him that. It was an effort I would never have believed myself capable of. Because, logically, I was devastated inside. I wanted just to cry, to scream, to tell Him to get out of there quickly while there was still time. I was his mother and I wanted to defend Him at all costs, I wanted to defend my son as I had done when He was a child and Herod threatened Him, or as I had done so many other times against illness and the thousand dangers of life. Instead, He asked me to resist standing upright, whole, strong, like a pillar on which He could lean, He who was the support of all of us. He was asking me to make an enormous sacrifice: the sacrifice of my tears; the sacrifice of depriving myself of the consolation I had left, of giving free rein to my pain and letting myself be carried away by the enormous anguish that was tearing my soul apart.

Anyway, shattered on the inside and seemingly calm on the outside, I made Him stand up, ran my hand through his curly, beautiful black hair, slid my fingers through his wet eyelids and pushed Him back to the village. There I was, John, pushing my son, my own son, toward the cross, toward his destiny, toward his mission. It was I who was leading the lamb of God to the slaughter. Because He asked me to, of course, but also because I understood that this was God's will, that is, the will of my son. A terrible scene that I enacted as if I was deranged, as if a force greater than all my strength combined was carrying me on my wings to fulfill what the Father and my own son expected of me. I, holding my Creator who was at the same time my child. I, who had given life to Him, encouraging my redeemer to give his life for me and for all. I, who pushed my son into suffering, when I would have wanted Him to flee from there or to let me take his place. How was that heroic act possible? Where did I get the strength to act like that, to love with that measure, to support the one who supported us all when he could no longer stand? It came to me from God, obviously, and it came to me from the fact that I am a woman and a mother. Is there anything that a mother, with God's grace, is not capable of doing? Even that, even leading her son to the cross, because He has asked her to do so and because it is the best way to help Him, even that I was able to do, without knowing how, without knowing, almost, why.

When we arrived at Lazarus' house, everything had passed. Jesus had recovered and was once again the confident, firm, determined man. His moment of anguish had been buried in my arms and my heart had been like a desert that drinks a torrent of tears or like an oasis that quenches the thirst of great caravans. At the expense of leaving me dry inside. But that was the price I had to pay. It was my contribution to the redemption of the world, as I later learned, and I was determined to do my part well.

Moreover, I did not have time for many reflections. The house was lively because more people had arrived, among them my cousins, the mothers of James, Simon and Jude Thaddeus. I had a long-standing intimacy with Mary, and she had always been on my side during the hard times in Nazareth. Without anyone telling her, taking advantage of the fact that it was Passover and that many Galileans and Nazarenes were going up to Jerusalem, they also wanted to come to have the opportunity to see their sons. When they heard that we were in Bethany, they had come there, and their surprise was great when they found me in the house.

Soon the boys who had been sent to Jerusalem returned. They brought word that Joseph of Arimathea had agreed to lend the hall of his house for the Passover supper, although he was surprised that it was to be held the day before, as my son had indicated, and he was also surprised that Jesus would dare to go there knowing that they were seeking to kill Him. Yet He was willing to take all kinds of risks, for it was already known among the notables that he sympathized with Jesus and was among his followers. But in addition, the two disciples said that the city was crowded, as always when the feasts were celebrated, and that everyone was wondering whether or not Jesus would dare to go to the temple. There were many Galileans camped on the top of the Mount of Olives, where they often did, and among them were many who were very devoted to Jesus, from Capernaum and from other areas of our land. They were all excited, ready to demonstrate their fidelity to my son and to confront the Jews, whom they considered jealous that a prophet who performed remarkable miracles came from Galilee and not from Judea. The two disciples also told us that the Roman soldiers were on guard, stationed in the tower of Antonia, as always when crowds came to Jerusalem, ready to put down any riot. And finally, they said that among the pilgrims there were many groups of zealots and rioters who were spreading anti-Roman proclamations and encouraging the people to revolt against the oppressors.

In short, a most complicated situation, in which everything was mixed and in which it was difficult to act without provoking one or the other.

"Tomorrow we will go to Jerusalem", said my son. They all murmured, wavering between fear and amazement. Then He looked at me, and, speaking to all but looking at me, He added, "Do not worry; my hour has not yet come. But the Scriptures must be fulfilled, and the Son of man must enter Jerusalem as the prophets have foretold, "Fear not, O daughter of Zion; behold, your king is coming on a donkey's colt".

"Do you want to enter Jerusalem on a colt?" Judas Iscariot then asked him. Are you crazy? Don't you realize that the dignity of the Messiah demands that He should at least enter on a horse or in a chariot?

"My dear boy", answered my son, looking at him with gentleness, for he loved him very much, "you still do not understand, and you have little left. Remember that I have often told you that we must not act as others do. Among them, those who are in charge make themselves be served and always seek the first places; among us, we should all aspire to serve others and we should try to occupy ourselves with the humblest things. Besides, a colt is not such a bad mount, especially when it is borrowed, for I do not propose to you, Judas, to buy one. It would be a shame to deprive the poor of that money".

Judas kept silent, because he understood that Jesus was referring to his protest about the waste of the perfume poured by Mary on the feet of Christ the night before. No one dared to say anything and so we all went to bed, each one with their troubles and I with mine, I do not know if they were greater than those of my son, but they were certainly different. I prayed almost all night, although I stayed in bed, without getting up, so as not to disturb. And I asked God, again and again, if possible, to let me suffer for Him. I understood that what He had to do I could not do, because he was God and I was not, because He was the Messiah, and I was a simple village woman. But I was his mother, and no one could take that title away from me. With that title in my hand, I was daring to appear before the Almighty, to litigate with Him and to claim relief for the fruit of my womb even at the cost of the burden that should fall on his shoulders falling on mine. "If someone has to pay, as my son has told me", I said to the Lord, "let me pay a little too. Have mercy on me and let me suffer for Him. Relieve Him and burden me, for in this way you will help me more than if He bears all the burden. Let the sword of sorrow come upon me, which Simeon announced to me and which I have always feared. Let it pierce me, but let it not sink into Him. May he not suffer alone, for it would be unworthy of me to be well when I see Him suffering so much". John, that was my prayer that night and the following nights until everything was fulfilled. And the fact is that when someone loves, as you and I loved Him, life, happiness, illusion, in short, everything resides in the fact that the loved one lives, while death is that He suffers or dies. You prefer a thousand times to suffer yourself than for Him to suffer. When you love, you prefer a thousand times to serve than to be served, to cry than to be cried for, to help than to be helped. And I have to tell you that in those sleepless nights, the Lord granted me what I asked for.

Not only did He greatly console me using those ways that are unique to Him, but he assured me that I would not cease to suffer with Him and that my suffering would alleviate his. He assured me, and later I confirmed it myself, that it would be my gaze that would sustain Him in the most difficult moment and that I would have the privilege of being the only one who could serve as his relief, as it has been so.

Early the next morning Jesus gathered you together and went to Jerusalem. It was the first day of the week. You were walking along, and all of you wondered where He would get the colt. Finally, it appeared near the city, as did the crowds of Galileans and other pilgrims who came to greet Jesus and welcome Him with shouts of:

> "Hosanna! Blessed is He who comes in the name of the Lord
> and King of Israel!"

My son, who in Galilee had refused the title of king when the enthusiastic crowds wanted to offer it to Him after the multiplication of the loaves and fishes, was now apparently delighted. He did nothing to excite the people, but He let them do what they wanted, and He seemed happy surrounded by those people who acclaimed Him and showed Him their affection. He knew that it was all the same now and that is why He did not care about anything. He rejected, however, the proposal of the leader of the zealots to lead a riot in the temple. "No violence", He said, "that is not the way my Father wants. He who kills with iron shall die with iron". That man, a certain John of Gischala, also a Galilean, who is still the leader of a band of guerrillas, told him that he was not getting anywhere like that and that he had heard that everything was in place for his arrest. He even warned Him that there were traitors among his people and gave Him an ultimatum: "Either you join us, or you won't be able to rely on us when you need to". My son replied, as He later told me: "My ways are not your ways. I have come to save what was lost, not to increase the destruction. You seek to establish a kingdom that is of this world and I stand for a kingdom that is not of this world. You believe in strength. I believe in love. You may think you will win, and you may even win a battle, but you will be defeated. I, on the other hand, am going to die soon, but I will soon live again, forever". John of Gischala left in a rage, and I believe that this irritation, of which the Pharisees soon found out, was decisive in what happened later, for they understood that my son no longer had any kind of support, despite the apparent popular fervor that surrounded him.

However, this support of the people, including some magistrates, allowed Him to remain in Jerusalem for a few days and forced his enemies to seek to trap Him secretly, without the people knowing about it until there was no longer any possibility of retreat.

He returned to Bethany two days before the Passover. I think He did it only for my sake, to bid me a last farewell and to receive, once again, my kisses and my consolation, of which He was so much in need in those dark hours. We spent the morning together. Again, He preferred that we walk along the paths that connect the orchards around the village. He wanted to get away from the hustle and bustle of the house and did not want witnesses for what He had to tell me. I saw Him agitated. Before the others, He always showed good spirits and a remarkable determination, pushing everyone to fulfill God's will and reminding them that what was going to happen was foreseen by the Most High, with me He unburdened; Himself and did not hide his anguish, his fear and even his doubts. Yes, John, his doubts. You know He had them. Now you all know it. You know what the hours of solitary prayer in the Garden of Olives were, while you slept. But you did not know it then, nor did you even suspect it. You were used to seeing Him always firm, standing, serene and powerful, you had forgotten that He was also a human being. But I, who had carried Him in my arms, could not forget that. That man capable of performing the greatest miracles was, nevertheless, a person and, as such, He had his moments of darkness, his anguish, his temptations. Also, precisely because He was truly a man and not a marble statue like those that pagans place in their temples, He needed to be consoled, to be helped, to be supported in his terrible internal struggles. You did not sense that, not even you, who were so close to his heart. Only a woman can grasp that, and that is why I believe that we were the ones who knew how to help Him the most in those difficult moments. But not even the others could reach where I was able to enter. That is why, because I was his mother and with me He had no need to pretend, to hide, or even to keep anything to Himself so as not to scandalize me by offering me the spectacle of an anguished man, that is why He came, like a lost and frightened child, to seek my support when He was just a little short of finishing his race and reaching the finish line.

In that conversation, contrary to what had happened a few days before, we spoke little. We just walked together for a while and then sat in silence. We exchanged phrases from time to time, without much content, while I noticed that it did Him a lot of good to be by my side. He did tell me about the triumphal entry into Jerusalem and the conversation with John of Gischala. At the end, when lunchtime was approaching and we had to return to the house where everyone was waiting for us, He looked me straight in the eye and repeated: "Whatever happens, do not doubt me or the love of God. God is love, don't forget that. Whatever you see, keep the faith.

Mother, I need your faith. There is a unique communication between you and me and I will know how you feel wherever you are. Therefore, I beg you to stand firm. I need your steadfastness, your faith and your hope. I need you to stand, because heed what I am telling you, you are going to be my only support, the only one that the Father has wanted me not to lack". I said nothing. I wanted so much to cry, to throw my arms around his neck and even, in a more powerful way than before, I wanted to ask him to leave everything and for us to return immediately to Galilee. But I realized that this was unbecoming of Him, of God and also of me. I realized, moreover, that it was just the opposite of what He was asking of me, so, silently and with my heart in my throat, I nodded. Any words would have ended in sobs and I could not allow that, because it would have only served to increase his sorrow. I nodded and kissed his forehead. Then, to shorten the difficult moment, I took Him by the hand and started walking towards Bethany. We had barely gone a few steps, when He tugged me and pulled me to Him. He gave me a long, eternal hug. He sank his head on my chest and began to cry. "What's wrong with me, mother, what's wrong with me? Why do I feel this terrible anguish? If I already knew that all this had to happen, why is it that now my heart is rebelling and my whole being is at war against my will and against the will of the Father? Why do my body and even my soul resist dying? What law is this that demands that I go on living even though my head tells me that the time has come to fulfill the mission for which I have come? Mother, I am frightened and afraid. I feel weak, almost incapable of going forward, tempted by cowardice more strongly than when the devil tried to seduce me in the desert. Mother, pray for me, ask God to shorten this bitter hour".

He stayed like that for a long time. In the meantime, I prayed, begging the Lord to grant Him relief and strength. My prayer had immediate effect. Jesus calmed down. He raised his head, and I was able, with a fold of my dress, to wipe his eyes. Then He smiled, kissed me again on the forehead and, now recovered, said: "I love you. I have told you so many times and still they seem insufficient. I love you very much, mother. I love and admire you. I am proud of you. What is going to happen is God's work, my work. But it is also your work. Ask the Father, as I have just begged you, to sustain me in this struggle. Your prayer is powerful, more powerful than you yourself can now understand. The one who loves you so much can deny you nothing. But ask God, now and always, that his will may be done and that I and all of us may always be ready to fulfill it. And now let us go, they are waiting for us in Bethany, in Jerusalem and even to the ends of the earth. Let us go with a light step, for there are many suffering, and we possess the medicine that will relieve them. And do not forget, on the third day I will rise again". That was all, John. The next day, the day the Romans dedicate in honor of their god Jupiter, after lunch, you left for Jerusalem. He had decided that that was the day on which you were to celebrate the Passover. We did not understand it well, but we thought it was because He wanted to celebrate a special feast with you. I imagined that He wanted to be alone with his friends, just as He had been with me under the olive trees. He hadn't told me anything about what was going to happen at the party or afterwards, although it didn't take me long to sense that the final moment had arrived.

He said goodbye to everyone in the house of Lazarus with a "see you soon". One by one He embraced them and kissed their foreheads, while He made over them that sign still mysterious to all and which I had seen Him make over his father and grandparents, the sign of the cross. When he reached me, the embrace was longer, but there was nothing more. Only at the end, when he was in the street, he turned to me and said, "You know. God is love. Always. See you in three days, mother. The others, who did not know that He would be gone that long, were surprised and, when he left, they asked me what He had meant. I, who sensed it, shrugged my shoulders and replied: "You know how He is. Maybe He is not coming tomorrow to celebrate Passover with us and, since the next day is Saturday, He thought he would come back the first day of the week".

I watched Him walk away down the path shaded by olive trees. The sun was still high, and it was hot. Soon He plunged into the group that you formed. A joyful group, because, like children who ignore the suffering of their parents, you were happy on your way to Jerusalem, with the honey still on your lips, after the success obtained a few days before, when His majestic entrance. Only at the end, just before a bend in the road took Him out of my sight, He turned and looked at me. We were far apart, but I knew he was suffering. He raised his hand and I raised mine. We both waved them in the air, as if we wanted to stop time and hold each other in an endless embrace. Then He disappeared from my sight. It was the last time I saw him healthy, strong, beautiful and joyful. I did not contemplate His sweet face again until I saw Him, disfigured, in the road of bitterness.

My strength had been drained. The effort I had made to be whole while He was by my side had left me completely exhausted. So, I excused myself and retired to my room. I had been praying to God, begging Him for that son we had in common. But I did it just as He had reminded me to do, in the end just as I had always done: "If it is possible, Father, let this cup pass from Him. But let your will be done. And do not forget that I am eager to share it with Him". I later learned that this had also been His prayer that night. Perhaps we were praying it at the same time, because what happened was this: after a long time of prayer, I felt myself collapsing and went to bed. It was still daylight, although it was beginning to get dark. Soon I fell asleep, and I must not have been asleep for long when I noticed something strange. I sat up in bed, as if something had come out of me again, as if a new birth had taken place. Only later did I know what it was: it was the moment when He was giving you his body and blood in bread and wine. It was a new birth of Him, and, in spite of the distance, I could feel it, and, like the first time, I rejoiced. I just didn't know what it was all about.

After a few moments of confusion, I got up and sat on the bed. Then I began to notice, one after another, all the sensations my son was feeling. It was something incredible, something that had never happened to me before, at least not with that intensity. At first, I did not realize what was happening to me, until I understood that we were united in an inexplicable way and my anguish and everything else was exactly what He was feeling. That is why I believe, John, that what you later told me about what happened that night I not only knew but had experienced. Deep down it is normal, for not only was God able to grant me the grace I had asked for so much, but the union between Him and me could hardly be severed. Besides, this was God's answer to my pleas. He had told me: "You will be my only support". And that was what it was all about, to feel with Him, to suffer with Him and, in this way, to share everything in order to share the burden and relieve Him.

Naturally, his passion was infinitely harder than mine. He was God and I was not. He was the lamb who bore the sin of the world and I was just a simple woman who had had the infinite good fortune to be his mother. But I was his mother and if there was a time to assert my privilege it was precisely that. I had not appealed to my motherhood during the moments of glory, when everyone flattered Him and fought to serve Him. Then He did not need me. Now, on the other hand, when even his closest colleagues doubted Him, I had the right to claim my role as a mother. Besides, He had asked me to do so, and I could not and would not do otherwise. Because the privilege consisted in being by his side, despite the distance, whith every passing moment. The privilege, for the one who loves, is to help the loved one; there is no greater reward than that. At no time that night or the following day was the communication between us interrupted. I do not know if He felt it. I will know when I join Him in heaven, which I sense will be soon. What I do know is that, from a certain moment on, I was aware that my spirit was united to his and that this was a grace that God had given me to relieve Him, even if he did not realize it.

That is why I fell to my knees and prayed in anguish and terror. I felt the loneliness that overwhelmed Him, and I felt his blood run down his forehead, without even staining mine, although I would have wished for it. With Him, while He prayed in the Garden of Olives, I begged God to pass the chalice without being rushed; but I also told Him that, above all, His will be done. I could almost hear the cries of those who came armed with sticks and spears. I clearly felt a miserable kiss, the kiss of the traitor, on his cheek and on mine, and I shuddered as I had never shuddered before, because for the first time I felt the breath of the Evil One near my face. And then all the rest, which you already know, and which constituted his dreadful passion. Yes, I also knew of your betrayal and that of Peter and that of your brother and that of his cousin. That is why, when several of you, including you, arrived at Bethany at midnight, I was not asleep, but on my feet and ready to leave for Jerusalem. I knew everything. I had suffered everything. And, dear John, I had already forgiven everything. I don't know if I did it out of love for God and to fulfill His will or because of a sixth sense that warned me that the moment was so decisive that only the most absolute holiness on my part could sustain my son in his terrible struggle. If I failed, He could collapse. If I won, he would have in me an ally against the forces of evil that had received permission to harass Him and, if they could, bring Him down. The fight was to death. It was a full-scale war, the last battle between good and evil. Skirmishes had been waged for centuries, ever since that first day when our father Adam had been seduced by the serpent. Now the final moment had come. The serpent raised its powerful head again, but this time without concealment, without hidden seductions, openly. It wanted to devour the rest of the good that had remained on earth. It wanted to wipe out those who had struggled to be faithful to their Creator. And there was my son, alone, on his way to the mountain of the Skull, on his way to the throne of the Evil One, to be immolated. What the astute seducer did not know was that next to that harassed man there was a woman and that woman was his mother. And against a mother's love not even a snake can fight. The first man did not have a woman by his side to push him on the path of good, but quite the opposite. Now it was the other way around. If sin had entered the world through a woman, a woman had to be the one to support the man in the fight against sin. And this chosen woman was me.

Yes, John, that night I knew what was happening, the great battle between good and evil. And that night I knew that my foot stepped on the head of the snake while it, desperate because of the defeat, bit me uselessly on the heel. My strength, the strength that only a woman who is a mother knows, helped my son to defeat the serpent, the Evil One. The victory was his, of course, for he was God, and it was He who died on the cross bearing the sin of the world. My meekness, similar to that of the Canaanite woman who had accepted to be compared to a dog in order to obtain from Jesus the salvation of her child, contributed to the prince of pride being brought down from his throne. I was aware of all that and I knew that I could not allow myself even a slight flirtation with any feeling that was far from God, from love, from the acceptance of His will. That night I fought with my son against evil. I supported Him while he staggered, so that He could overcome and definitively put an end to the power of the lord of darkness. That is why I forgave. That is why I also prayed for Judas and for all those who killed Him, as my son did from the cross. That is why I did not scold you or the others.

That is why I accepted to be your mother and the mother of all, even of those who had done and continue to do so much harm to my son. That is why, because only good can be used to defeat evil, and because evil begins to gain ground when good decides to use weapons other than those of forgiveness and mercy.

But this is anticipating events, John. Other things happened before.

You, with Philip, Thomas, James and Judas Thaddaeus, my nephews, arrived in Bethany and woke up everyone in the house and told them the bad news. Lazarus, immediately recovered from the surprise, thought of organizing the defense. It was urgent to warn the friends of Jesus, Nicodemus and Joseph of Arimathea above all, so that they could mediate with the Sanhedrin and prevent his death. Peter, with your brother James and some others, had remained in Jerusalem, hanging around the place where Jesus had been led. The others had fled, except for the traitor, Judas Iscariot, who had left with his accomplices. When you stood before me, remember, you fell on your knees and asked my forgiveness for being there, alive, instead of having died in the Garden of Olives defending Him. How much you loved Him, and He loved you! I picked you up and, already your mother before He asked me, I had to console you and assure you that God's forgiveness was granted because Jesus was earning it for us with what was happening.

Lazarus, his sisters and in general all of you insisted that I do not move from Bethany. I understood that it was the best thing to do, for I could not physically approach my son, while from the solitude of my room I could be in constant communication with him. So, you left in haste to return to Jerusalem, and we women were left alone at home. My nephews went to look for their respective mothers, who were in the city celebrating the Passover, and a few hours later they were with us.

I did not hesitate. I organized the true defense first with Martha and Mary and then with my cousins and with the other women who accompanied and loved Jesus so much. While you were running around, at night and at dawn, looking for lawyers and, at the same time, committing acts of betrayals like that painful triple refusal of Peter in the house of Caiaphas, we knew what we had to do: pray. Each one who arrived joined our group and knelt down in the great main room of Lazarus' house. After the first moments of surprise, screaming and crying, I managed to calm them down. It's time for us to behave like women", I told them. It's not about crying and mourning now. We are not paid mourners. My son is still alive, and He needs us. But He does not need our cries or our despair, but our prayer and our strength. So, no wailing. We have to be faithful to Him and that means that we have to believe, right now, in what He has taught us, that good is stronger than evil and that love is stronger than hate. Let us pray. Let us beg the Almighty to sustain Him in the fight and to give Him victory. And, come what may, let us keep our faith that, as Jesus has taught us, God is infinite love".

Dawn found us praying. We had been on our knees for hours. Sometimes we remained silent and at other times someone would recite aloud some old psalm or express a supplication to the Most High, whom we now almost always called Father. At one point I realized that the worst was over. That special grace which had been granted to me and which allowed me to be in communion with Him, had made me experience not only the anguish of the garden, but also the fear he felt while He was in that prison which was like a well.

Now I felt that He was terribly exhausted. And I noticed very clearly that He was calling me: "Mother, come, come to me. I need you".

I stood up. They all looked at me. They understood that God had communicated something to me. My hair was in disarray and my eyes were red, but I had not yet shed a tear. They did, and I don't blame them. I told them, "Let's go to Jerusalem. My son is calling me. The end is near, and He needs us by his side".

Without thinking twice, we all set off. We were in a hurry, accelerating our steps because I knew that there was little left. Despite my age and exhaustion, I was running more than walking. On the way, I felt, one after the other, the thirty-nine blows given to Him at the Litostrotos. I also noticed the frightful bite of the thorns on his innocent head. I even fell to the ground on more than one occasion, exhausted by that terrible beating. But before my companions could lift me up, I was already on my feet again, running, without even noticing that my hands were bleeding and that my knees were, like his, wounded. We arrived in Jerusalem and saw that the city was buzzing. We did not need to ask anyone. The news had spread by word of mouth and many were heading for the mountain of the Skull to contemplate the spectacle that was being announced. Jesus had already been condemned. The governor Pilate had already passed sentence and washed his hands. The time was near for the prisoner to be taken out of the Antonia Tower and led to the place of torture. We were a group of women lost in the crowd; we did not know where to go or what to do. At the same time, we could not stop listening to the comments of the people; some said that they were looking for all his followers and that the priests had arranged patrols throughout the city to arrest those who had stood out in his wake; others regretted what had happened, because, they said that, Jesus was a good man who had great power to perform miracles even if He had exceeded his powers and had challenged too many powerful people;

for others, the question was whether something spectacular would happen at the last moment, whether Jesus, nailed even to the cross, would not perform some extraordinary action that would manifest Him as the promised Messiah. They all agreed that they were before the definitive test: if He was the Messiah, He could not die crucified; if He died crucified, He was an impostor and therefore the priests had done well to put a stop to his great delusions of grandeur. Stunned and not knowing what to do, we thought we would head towards the Antonia tower, but it was impossible to get close to it, because of the large number of Roman soldiers that were taking over the surrounding area. So, we let ourselves be guided by the people and went towards the mount of the Skull, outside the city walls. We had a hard time moving through the crowd. Suddenly, when we were close to the exit gate of the city, a loud uproar immobilized us. The street was very narrow, with small shops on both sides that had not closed their doors to take advantage of the crowd and try to do some business with the people passing by. There was hardly any room to move or to take shelter, but we managed to get into a corner, as did the others. Soon it was known what was happening: the retinue with the prisoner had already left the Antonia Tower and was on its way to the Calvary; they were going as fast as possible to shorten the process and avoid the dreaded counterattack of my son's supposed supporters. But there was no trace of those supporters. We seemed to be the only ones, confused among the people, without fear but with our hearts beating like a runaway horse. My cousin Mary was next to me and she was crying, thinking of my son but also of the fate of her son. On the other side was the other Mary, the one they call the Magdalene. Martha was also nearby, as was Mary of Clopas, mother of Simon and Judas Thaddaeus. And then you appeared. You can't imagine how happy I was to see you; you were frightened like a little dog that had lost its mother and was looking for a place to hide between the people's legs. When you saw us, you ran towards us, crossing the street even though the patrol of soldiers was already approaching, clearing the way and hitting one person or the other to make them clear the path. You threw yourself into my arms and burst into tears, once again. "Nothing could be done", you said. To add, "You shouldn't look. I've seen Him and He is not the same. You shouldn't look". I squeezed you tightly and I gritted my teeth even tighter. I raised my eyes to heaven and begged for help to make it to the end without fainting. If for a few hours that special communication I had had with Jesus had diminished, due to the hustle of the journey, now I felt it I felt it more powerfully than ever. He was approaching along that alley which was a real road of bitterness. He was approaching amidst the shouting and the silence of the people, but I could feel Him even closer. Inside me, in my heart, in my thoughts; with my eyes I could not see Him yet, but my soul knew how his was, and I knew, moreover, that the same thing was happening to Him. He was looking for me and He had found me; I noticed that He was asking for what He had warned me He would require from me: fidelity, faith, support. I felt Him whole, very whole in spite of being extraordinarily exhausted. I closed my eyes and began to pray. It was a strange prayer that I have never been able to abandon; I prayed to God and at the same time I prayed to Him. Yes, to Him who appeared to me with less and less veils to hide his divine identity; however, when I tried to pronounce his name and say: "Jesus", I could not do it; He was inside me and I had fully identified myself with Him.

And then I opened my eyes and saw Him almost beside me. My companions screamed, especially Magdalene, who loved Him so much. I did not. He was looking at me, and what a gaze that was. He was looking in my eyes for what He needed to find: faith, faith, faith, and hope. "It's his mother", one of the people shouted, and immediately several soldiers stepped between us as if we were a threat, while He was being pushed to pass quickly through that stretch of the street. We could not say anything to each other, only look at each other. That was enough. I saw his pain and He saw mine. He saw my faith, drank from it, was satiated by it, while I was aware that He leaned on me and I beared the weight of a whole God who needed the help of a human being, even if that God was also a man and that human being was his mother. I thought that the weight was crushing me, but I myself clung to the other God, to the same and only God, the one we call Father. While one held me, I held the other, as if it were a strange bridge, as if the divinity was in contact with itself through me, determined as I was to carry to the end that strange separation that was necessary for my son to drink from the chalice of bitterness.

He was soon taken away. I did not see Him fall, as I was later told had happened. I did see the woman who, full of pity, wiped his face with a cloth. She was behind the retinue, very close to the soldiers who closed the platoon. We stood there too, with you. She, Veronica was her name, upon learning that I was his mother, spoke to me and, after hugging me tightly, showed me what she was holding in her hands: "Look", she said. And there He was: his face drawn on the white cloth, his blood staining everything; his image, once so beautiful and now disfigured by torture, recognizable in that cloth. "I give it to you", she added, "It's yours. I don't know how it happened, but here He is". I took it and put my face between his, making an effort not to let myself be carried away by emotion, for I knew that if I burst into tears, I would no longer be able to contain myself, and my son did not need to see a desperate mother, but a strong woman to support Him in his despair. So, I gave it to you, who looked at it in surprise, and you kept it, as you have done until now. Soon we were at the foot of the rock called the Skull, where the evildoers were crucified. There were already two men nailed to their respective crosses, and in the center stood the vertical pole on which the other, the one that would carry my son, would have to be hoisted. We were stopped before we arrived, so I could not see anything, for no matter how hard I tried, we could not make our way to the first rows full of onlookers and enemies. I think it was God's gift to me, for I did not have to watch as they drove the nails into his hands, or as they stripped him of his clothes, of that tunic that I myself had carefully woven, without a single seam, and which so many marveled at.

I saw Him as they began to lift him up. First there was a mighty silence. Everyone, even those who hated Him, fell silent. Perhaps it was time for a miracle. If heaven had to intervene, it must intervene now, or it would never do so. I knew that nothing extraordinary was going to happen, because the extraordinary was already happening: God murdered by God's creatures, with God's permission to save the murderous creatures. That was the miracle. But the people were waiting for some gesture. The silence lasted a few minutes. Until they nailed Him definitively, after resting his feet on the step on the cross.

Then, suddenly, the shouting broke out: the insults were tremendous and the soldiers themselves had to intervene to drive away the most cruel and bitter of their enemies. Although I expected everything, could not believe what I saw and heard. I saw a normal woman, a housewife, utter barbarities and threaten with her fist. I saw one who had been paralyzed and whom He had healed, spit on Him and curse at him. I saw the priests and Pharisees embrace each other with joy and leap with delight because, at last, their enemy was hopelessly lost.

Then I collapsed. Not even you, who had stayed by my side all the time, could help it. It was the only moment, I don't say of despair or even of discouragement, but of exhaustion. Between all of you you lifted me up and someone put a sip of water to my lips. As soon as I came to my senses, I wanted to stand up again. The shouting continued, but I no longer cared about what people were saying. I only cared about one thing: how my son was doing. I cared about whether He had noticed that I was exhausted and whether my faintness had had an impact on his mood. So, exhausted as I was, my legs shaking and my head spinning, I begged you to help me get to the front rows.

When, at last, we were able to make it, what I saw struck me in body and soul as if all the blows He had received a short time before in the courtyard of the Antonia tower had been given to me all at once. But this time, even though I no longer had any strength left, I did not collapse. His gaze located me at once, and we both supported each other. I drew strength from his weakness to resist, from the awareness I felt that He needed me. And He, with a silent supplication, stretched out his nailed hands to me and sought, in an impossible embrace, the help that only a mother can give.

I do not know if He had said anything before this, for He had already been crucified for some time when we managed to get close to Him. Other witnesses say that He had spoken several times and that He had even cried out, asking the Father why He had abandoned him. Perhaps that terrible moment coincided with my fainting; perhaps that moment of loneliness in which I could not hold Him led Him to rush to the depths of suffering. But what you and I and the other women were able to hear in the moments we were under the cross we will never forget. His mouth opened with effort, He broke through the scabs of blood that were clusting over His lips, and He said clearly looking at you and looking at me, "Woman, behold your son". And then he added: "Behold your mother".

Why that reciprocal handover? It took me a long time to understand. And it wasn't that I didn't love you. You had been by my side since you began to be at his side. You were, of all his disciples, the one He loved the most and also the one I loved the most. On many occasions, you had been a messenger to convey to me words of hope and accurate information about what was happening. He had asked you several times to take care of me and all that had brought us very close. Without him having to say anything else, I already loved you like a true son. He knew that and He was certainly glad to see the two of us together. But there was something else in his words. As I say, it took me a long time to fully understand. At that moment I only felt a blow and also an emptiness. It was as if someone had the pretension of replacing Him in my heart. No, as much as I could love you, you could never take his place, I could never love you as I loved Him. No one could ever fill the hole He left, and I could find comfort in no one once He was no longer there to give it to me. It was a rebellion that lasted an instant. It was not a rebellion against Him, nor against his will, but against myself, against the motherly feelings that were still inside. It was, deep down, a kind of purification, and not of something bad, but of something good, of the feeling of motherhood. But quickly, accustomed as I was to dealing with God, I knew that the moment of total oblation had come and that, therefore, even the best of feelings had to be offered so that God alone, in an absolute way, would reign in my heart and soul. My work, my son, was dying and God, who gave Him to me, was taking Him away from me. He was taking Him away from me, depriving him of the life He gave him. He was taking Him away from me, begging me to accept another, others, in his place and to love those others, including my son's murderers, as I loved Him. Therefore, as He died, I also died; as He ceased to experience absolute union with the Father, I also lost everything, so that, from that moment on, I would no longer have anything else to say but "only God". Only God, without anything else. Stripped of everything. Only God, a God who had taken away even the legitimate feelings of the mother.

Sensitive as I was to maintain full communion with Him, noticing that anything affected Him, I told Him yes, that from that moment on you would be my son and that I would not stop loving you and taking care of you as I had done with Him. I told Him without words, but He understood immediately. He breathed more deeply, as if relieved. He had come to make you his brothers. He had already succeeded in getting you to call his Father "Father". But for the brotherhood to be complete, it was necessary that you also share the mother. And for that, just as the Father accepted you as sons, precisely through the voluntary sacrifice of his only son, the mother had to do the same. And it was the son, the adored son, who asked for it. For it was also the son who had interceded before the Father to obtain this grace. And if the Father, who was God, had agreed, forgiven and adopted, the mother, a woman, could not be less.

And it was then that He said, looking toward the soldiers, "I am thirsty". There was a jar full of vinegar there. One of them wet a sponge and stuck it on a stick or a spear, I don't remember, and put it to his lips. My son sipped it greedily and, despite the acidity, I know that this was his last physical comfort. Even later I understood what He was thirsty for, which is the source of the water that quenches all thirst. But then it was enough for Him to express that desire and to let everyone know that if He was there, it was because of that thirst, because of the need to drink, until He was dry, from the infamous river of sins that floods the hearts of men.

And there was no more. Very soon after, as soon as the soldier put down the sponge, He raised his eyes to heaven and then looked at me. "All is accomplished", He said to me. And dropping his head on his chest, He definitively placed his spirit in the hands of his Father.

I don't know how to explain to you what I felt, John, because I found myself surprised. It was not only as if a weight was lifted off my shoulders, a weight that I did not want to lose, because that weight was his life and without his life I could not go on living. However, I felt absolutely relieved of a burden. So, while you were collapsing and my companions, especially Mary Magdalene, were falling to the ground and screaming, wringing their hands in pain and tearing their hair out in despair, I was serene. So much so that it seemed inhuman to me to be so, because it is as if I loved Him less than the others and even less than you, who also wept heartbrokenly and hid your head in my arms.

I felt worried and I reproached myself for not being in despair, desperate. My son had just died, and I was sad, undoubtedly, but I could not feel despair, I could not. It was terrible for me to see Him there, hanging from the wood, a wreck, disfigured, tortured in a way that is unspeakable, with the wound of the spear still dripping blood and with his forehead and face soiled by the mud and clots that, in drips, fell from the wounds that the crown of thorns had made in his head. It was a spectacle capable of moving the most hardened person, and even more so me, who was his mother. That was the fruit of my womb and now I saw him like that, destroyed and, above all, already dead.

Moreover, I had been so intent on supporting Him with my soul and supporting Him in his terrible inner struggle so that He could reach the end without fainting. I acted as a channel so that God's strength would reach Him uncessantly. He would not lack what God Himself was denying Him, on the other hand; I had been so intent on this that now, once he was dead, I should have been able to surrender to my despair, to my pain, to my own bitterness, to the harm that had been done to me by taking my son away from me. And yet I could not. I was ashamed to see you so dejected and not share in your despair. And it was not that I did not suffer or feel, but I could not sink into the bottomless pit in which you were plunged.

At this point, surprised at myself and almost angry that I could not feel any other way, you gently pushed me away. You must have thought that I had gone mad, that the terrible spectacle had upset me. The fact is that you told me that Magdalene and the other women would be in charge of burying the body of my son and that I should leave so as not to be dragged away in despair. You went to fetch Joseph of Arimathea and left me in the care of my cousin Mary. The twilight hour was approaching and almost all his enemies, well satisfied with their work, had left. Beside the body of the executed, only the soldiers, a few curious onlookers and ourselves remained. I had already gone a few steps away, with Mary and Salome, when I realized that I could not leave in that way. Although I did not know what was happening to me, what kind of strange sensation I was feeling, I realized that the corpse still lying on the cross was that of my son and that I could not leave just like that, without saying goodbye to Him, without holding Him in my arms for the last time.

Despite the protests of my fellow women, I turned around. Almost crawling, without strength, exhausted by all that whirlwind of sensations and bitterness, I returned to stand before the tragic spectacle. The soldiers had already unnailed one of Jesus' companions in torture, a certain Dimas, of whom they say had died in peace. His body was there, on the ground bent in an unbelievable way, with no one to mourn him, since not even his relatives had come to take an interest in him. The other thief was being taken down just at that moment. When they had finished with him, they prepared to do the same with my son. Then Magdalene approached them and begged them to let us help, to allow us to take care of that body so that it would not be mistreated as waste, since a messenger had gone to ask Pilate's permission to give it a dignified burial. One of the soldiers, the one who had relieved his thirst with the sponge soaked in vinegar, convinced his companions; he himself volunteered to do the hardest part of the task with the utmost care, for they had lowered the others by tearing their hands.

That's how I held Him in my arms again. He was dead. He was disfigured. His heart was no longer beating. His eyes were no longer shining, they were still terribly open. The dreadful crown had fallen off and the open wounds on his head were visible. Some of the blood still flowed from some of them, and his whole body was a raw sore, with the blows of the scourging marked vividly on his shattered skin. I sat down on the rock and laid his torso on my legs, while the rest of his body lay on the ground. Magdalene and the others wept with unbounded bitterness, while they tried with great care to clean his feet from the mud and blood. In the meantime, I hugged his body and sweetly kissed his face, but I still could not cry. As best I could, I closed his eyes, those eyes that I myself had opened to life, and placed a kiss on each of his eyelids and another on his forehead. Then I remembered that He had made a strange sign over some of the dying members of his family and friends whom He had accompanied at the moment of death; I remembered that that sign was precisely that of a cross and I realized that He had just died on a cross. I did not understand any more, but I understood that there was a connection between that and this, so now it was I who made that sign on his forehead. And then I hugged Him, I clung to Him, unable to let go while his arms fell to his sides, rigid, lifeless.

Then you arrived, with Pilate's permission, which Joseph of Arimathea had already arranged while Jesus was still alive in his agony. Joseph himself gave us his new tomb, which was very close by, in the cemetery that surrounded that part of the city just a stone's throw away.

When you saw me like that, with my dead son in my arms, clinging to Him as a shipwrecked sailor clings to the last remaining timber of the sunken ship, you scolded the others for having let me return and, with that new authority that gave you the charge of taking care of me, you spoke to me as gently as firmly: "Let's go", you said. "Let them prepare the corpse. It's time to go home".

I did not protest. I had not yet shed a tear and I felt like I was floating on a cloud, without understanding what was happening to me, without being able to explain to myself what I was doing there, alive, while He, the meaning of my life, was dead. Maybe I was, that afternoon, verging on the edge of madness, but I think it wasn't that, because later I had the chance to understand what was happening to me. So, I kissed him for the last time, and I remember saying to Him, without knowing why: "Son, see you later. You are not alone. Don't worry. Everything is going to be all right. I love you very much. See you soon, my love, my son, I will see you soon".

When you heard me, everyone, including you, redoubled your cries. No doubt you thought I had gone mad, because nothing I was saying made sense to you. I didn't know what I was saying either, but it was my soul talking, not my head.

It was already too late to go to Bethany. There was little light, the Sabbath was beginning, and neither I had the strength to walk, nor was it convenient to set out on the road. That is why you took me to the house of Nicodemus, who had offered to give us accomodation until the Sabbath was over. He was afraid of what might happen, as were you all, fearing that having killed Jesus, they would now want to get rid of all his disciples, including himself, although he was not one of the most notorious. But he was very kind to me, as was his wife and the rest of his household. With great solicitude they escorted me to the room that had been set aside for me, and a maid helped me to undress and wash. Then I went to bed. They stayed to celebrate the Passover dinner, even though the atmosphere was one of mourning and not of celebration.

In bed, unable to sleep and unable to cry, I seemed to be floating, outside of myself, with so many things inside that I found it difficult to sort them out and explain them. The strangest thing was that I knew my son was dead, while I had the feeling that He was not. Of course, I did not maintain with Him the communion that had been established during the last hours, since He left Bethany to celebrate the Passover with his disciples. But, at the same time, I felt Him there, somehow. And this made me terribly uneasy. I wanted to pray, to talk to Him, and I could not. It was then that I turned to God and, for the first time in my life, I asked Him "why?", and I asked Him where my son was, what had happened to Him and what was going to happen to Him. I was not interested in anything that concerned you: whether or not He was the Messiah, whether his death meant that all his preaching was false, and that God was not with Him. I cared about my son as a person before anything else, before his message and before his mission, and not because I did not value these things. I loved Jesus, you loved the idea, what He represented, but not the person, or at least not that person in the first place. That is why you were in crisis, scandalized and frightened. I, on the other hand, was only interested in knowing what had become of Him and why I could not feel Him either as dead or alive.

I noticed that God was becoming present in me, little by little, tenderly. With the love of a husband, with the love of a father and even almost with the love of a mother, He reassured me and asked me for patience. "Everything is going well". I could feel Him telling me; "continue to have faith in what our son has told you; it won't be long now", He whispered in the ears of my heart. And then I remembered that my son had insisted to me that He was going to be resurrected, so, therefore, He was still alive in some place that I was unaware of and that made it difficult for me to experience Him close to me as before; but He was alive, somehow, He was still alive, because I did not notice that He had died. That was the reason why, in spite of all that I had seen, I could not have plunged into the abyss of pain and despair that had gripped you. I could not do it, no matter how much I wanted and even needed it to be able to unburden myself and release the enormous tension. I couldn't because something inside me was lifting me up and telling me that reality was different from what appearances showed.

This, the certainty that my son was alive and that He was going to be resurrected, calmed me enormously, to the point that my heart began to beat stronger, almost with joy. And that was when exhaustion finally took hold of me and I fell asleep.

I slept most of the Sabbath. Those of Nicodemus let me rest and watched over my sleep. It was already the sixth hour when I awoke. The house was quiet. Our friend's wife, Rachel was her name, smiled at me when she saw me appear in the living room of the house. Her maids immediately attended to me. I wanted to leave to find out what had happened to my son, but they made me understand that since it was still the Sabbath, and a very special one at that, since the night before Passover had been celebrated, it was not convenient for me to leave the house. I might run into some fanatic who would not respect my age or my condition as a woman. They also told me that the others had done the same and that now they were all resting; in the end no one but me had come to that house, perhaps for fear that a raid would catch them all together. But the women had agreed to go to the tomb as soon as dawn broke on the following day, the first of the week, to complete the burial of Jesus in a dignified manner, with aromas and ointments, for they had not been able to do more than what was necessary because of their haste. I was told that, by order of Pilate and at the request of the priests who feared that his disciples would steal Him, some soldiers were watching over the body, so that there was no risk that it might be mistreated by his enemies.

Rachel was very kind and affectionate with me. She was anxious herself about her husband's fate, but she made efforts not to comment anything to me or let her own worries show. With her accompanying me, I ate something and then asked her permission to retire back to my room, waiting for the hours to pass so that I too could go to the tomb as soon as dawn broke.

When I was able to be alone again, I knelt down and began to pray. My prayer, now more serene, could only be one, also a strange one, but one that I could not change. If the night before I had dared to ask God questions, now I only felt the need, imperious, to thank Him. "Thank you, Lord, because you let me have Him. Thank you for allowing me to be his mother and enjoy Him for so many years. Thank you for having been able to live by his side, receiving tenderness after tenderness from Him. Who am I and who was I to deserve this extraordinary gift? Thank you because He has taught me to call you Father. Thank you because I was able to sacrifice myself for Him, to fight for Him, to suffer for Him. Thank you because, even in the final moment, I have been able to be of help to Him and I have been able to support Him in this extraordinary struggle that I still do not understand well but that has been the purpose of his life and his mission. And thank you, finally and above all, because I know that He is alive. Even if He feels far away now. And because He will come back, because I know He will be resurrected. And because I will be with Him again. And because someday we'll be able to be together forever. Forgive me for not thanking you for so many other things, for Yourself, for everything else I've received from your love. But now I feel the need to tell you only this: thank you for Jesus, because He is my son, because I have been able to know Him, because I have been able to help Him and because He is not dead but alive". And, as I was telling God all this, I really cried. All the pent-up anguish began to come out from inside me, in a quiet way, like a rain that falls without causing damage in the fields.

Praying and crying, kneeling by the bed, I fell asleep again. My head and arms on the bed. I don't know how many hours I stayed like that. I only remember that, just like thirty-four years before, I suddenly noticed that someone was in the room and I woke up startled. It was already night and yet I had the feeling that an extraordinary light was shining around me even though everything was still dark.

Then I saw Him. I didn't need to ask who He was. I had not the slightest doubt. There He was and it was Him, waiting for me to wake up and watching over my sleep. "Son!" I cried out and threw myself into his arms. "Mother", He said, as He ran his hand through my tangled hair, "Calm down. It's all over now. I'm here again, with you", Then He kissed me. I assure you, John, that it was Him and that his arms, his kisses, his voice and his gaze were his. Don't ask me if He looked like Him or not, if He had the same features or if there was something different. I didn't even stop to think about it or to compare with what was in my memory. It was Him, without any doubt, but not as a ghost, but real, as real as I was hugging Him, and he was running his fingers across my wet face and kissing my eyes full of tears.

"We have won, Mother, we have won. At last, the Evil One has been defeated. At last death is conquered. The battle has been hard and agonizing, but the victory is ours and it is definitive. You too have had a part in it, even if only through the Father and through me and the Spirit. You do not know how much your strength helped me and how it consoled me to see you there, next to the cross, full of faith and hope. The Father, who wanted to hide Himself, although he never really left me alone, did not allow me to lack what no huma n being is denied: the consolation of the mother, the support of the one who gave Him life. For this reason, as well as for what happened in the beginning, all generations will call you blessed, and there will be many who will raise their eyes to you from their own bitterness, when they are nailed to their crosses, so that you may console, support, accompany and relieve them. That will be your task, your eternal task: to be mother of all, educator of all, consoler of all, mediator of all".

"Of all of them, son?" I remember asking Him, a bit puzzled.

"Yes, of all", He answered me, "because I have not come to save those who were already saved, but those who were lost. Of all, even of my worst enemies, of those who have killed me. You are the mother of all, beginning with those who are close to you, whom you will have to help so that they do not quarrel among themselves, as mothers who have large families do. But you will also be the mother of those who are far away, of those who do not know me, of those who despise me. I have died for all; I love all, and I redeem all. And you cannot exclude from your heart those whom I accept. In order that they may truly be my brothers and sisters, you must be their mother, just as God must be their Father. Only in this way, with the Father and the mother in common, will we be truly united in the same family. Moreover, Mother, I know that in your heart there can be no room for exclusion, resentment or hatred. You will care for everyone, especially those who bear the imprint of my cross on their body or soul, and therefore you will love even sinners, for there is no greater cross or disgrace than to be far from God, confronted by and at enmity with the source of happiness and life".

We were together for a long time, both of us sitting on the bed, sometimes hugging, sometimes holding hands. Silent at times and enjoying each other's company. And also talking.

Then, when it was beginning to dawn, He said goodbye to me, "I'm going to see Magdalene and the others", He told me, "It's time for everything to start all over again. Be calm, help them overcome their fear and don't stop praying, because nothing you ask of the Father will be denied to you", He added, and gave me a long and definitive hug and a last kiss.

He left, as He had come, without making a sound, without being noticed. A breath of soft, fresh air came in through the window. I was still there, sitting on the bed, for a long time. I felt dazed, strange, calm, full. I couldn't think, I couldn't draw conclusions, I could hardly even pray. I could only feel and remember. To feel and remember his words, his presence by my side, his embrace, his kisses. To remember that He was alive and to allow, slowly, tears run down my cheeks, tears of relief, of gratitude and also of triumph.

CHAPTER 14

The hour of my children

John, I was not alone for long in the comfortable room of that cozy house. Or at least it seemed that way to me. Soon the house was filled with noise, exclamations of surprise and even sobs. The door opened and Rachel entered, accompanied by Magdalene. The first one could not suppress her tears; the other, on the other hand, seemed as if she was lost. Rachel began to speak, preparing me for what she considered a terrible blow, perhaps the definitive one for me, since they believed I was almost on the border of madness, for she was one of those who thought that someone had stolen the body of Jesus and that Magdalene, on discovering her fault, had become deranged.

> "Mary", said Nicodemus' wife, "our sister Magdalene has some-
> thing to tell you, something she says happened this very morning".

Magdalene did not let her go on: "I have seen the Lord. He is alive. He is risen. He has spoken to me and I have been able to embrace his feet and kiss them and bathe them with my tears as I did a few days ago. He is alive. Mary, He is alive". As she said this, she had clung to me and was crying and screaming and laughing, all at once, as if seized by a feeling that had broken her reason and her sanity.

But as nervous as they both were, and as shocked as they were by the news, they were even more surprised by my attitude and my words. Naturally, I could not pretend that I did not know anything. So, I told them the truth: "My daughters" without knowing why I called them that, as if my son's mandate had already begun to work in me without me realizing it "do not be afraid. My son is alive. He has risen from the dead. But that shouldn't surprise you, hadn't He announced it like this?" I did not dare to reproach them, because I did not think it was the right time, nor did I think it was my mission. It was enough for me to tell them what had happened to me: "Besides, I tell you that he was here. For several hours he talked with me, in this very room, and he said goodbye to me, telling me that He was going to the side of the tomb to talk to you, Magdalene".

Magdalene then went down on her knees before me. Her eyes were still as if astray and her hands clung to my garment, as she asked me, "Have you seen him too? Tell everyone, tell Peter and the others, tell Rachel and Nicodemus. They will believe you. They don't want to believe me; they say I'm crazy. But He is alive. I have seen Him, and He was not a ghost. He was flesh and blood, and his voice was the same voice, the one with which, full of tenderness and mercy, called me by name and raised me up every time I heard it".

As for Rachel, I could tell she didn't know what to do, whether to believe both of us or to think that we had both caught the same madness.

So, Nicodemus came in the room, and you were with him. The owner of the house seemed to have lost his usual gravity. He, too, was excited, not quite believing what one or the other was telling him. He turned first to his wife: "Rachel, John has just arrived and says that it is true, that the body is gone. Is it possible that He has risen? That would change everything. That would mean that God was really with Him".

You cut short the beginning of that reflection, and turned to me, do you remember. Mary had sat up and moved to one side, so that I found myself, unintentionally, in the center of the room. Then, after kissing my hands, you said to me: "Mother, I believe". That was all it took. You threw yourself into my arms and burst into tears.

"I believe". That was the word of the moment. "I believe" and that was all that needed to be said. Everything fit in that and it was enough.

I immediately told you and Nicodemus what I had told the two women. Nicodemus marveled and was ready to give credit to what Magdalene and I referred to, while good old Rachel still doubted. Then it was decided that the chief priests and the Pharisees should be queshoned to see if they had stolen the corpse. I shrugged my shoulders, while Magdalene protested and reproached him for his little faith. It was agreed that a meeting would be held in the evening, at Joseph of Arimathea's house, in the same place where our last supper with Jesus had taken place, to exchange information and find out what was to be done.

The afternoon came soon. Mary Magdalene and I did not separate. She calmed down at once and, after she had tidied herself up a bit because she looked as if she were crazy, with her hair disheveled and her face full of tears and mud, we began to pray together with the other women who had been coming to the house of Nicodemus.

When the time came, you came looking for me to go to the meeting. Nicodemus protested. He said that only men should be admitted to it, for what was to be discussed were matters of the utmost importance and that the presence of women, with their facility for tears and shouting, could make the deliberation endless. I kept silent, determined to accept anything. But then you said: "Mary is his mother and no one can stop her from being where her son is being talked about. Besides, if she does not go, I will not go either. Without her among us I do not think it is worth our while to go on". Nicodemus, embarrassed, begged my pardon and readily agreed to let me attend the meeting. I then pleaded for Magdalene, but she answered at once, refusing to go. She said that, indeed, she was still very nervous and that it was better not to complicate things further, since most of the disciples did not believe in what she had seen, and her words could have more of a counterproductive effect than a witnessing effect.

That was how we gathered that afternoon in the large hall of Joseph of Arimathea's house. We arrived secretly, taking advantage of the sunset. We looked like bandits, camouflaging ourselves to strike a blow against some rich property. The three of us arrived together, but the others arrived separately or, at most, two by two. Joseph himself would greet us at the door and then close it, until the next one knocked gently on the wood. The only one missing was Thomas, the one called "Didymus", who was finding out what the soldiers who had been on guard at the tomb had to say about the disappearance of the corpse.

With the doors closed, you full of fear, I calm and even happy, we gathered that afternoon on the first day of the week. Immediately the discussion began. Peter, standing up, explained what was known: that the body was not there, that Magdalene claimed to have seen the Master and even some angels, that the Pharisees had not stolen the body and that they were circulating the rumor that it had been the disciples who had gotten rid of Him to spread the fable that He had risen. No one had told him about Jesus' visit to me, the first of all. I kept silent and let him speak. "I know", he added, "that none of us had anything to do with the disappearance of Jesus' body. Besides, he had said that he would rise again on the third day, so we cannot rule out that this is what really happened. John believes so, and so does my brother Andrew. I do not know what to say".

You got up and asked permission for me to speak and tell everyone about the appearance of my son on the same Saturday night, before dawn. It was very difficult for me to do so, but when I was about to begin to speak, you know what happened: the light that I had seen reappeared, this time in the midst of everyone. And in that light was Him, alive, risen. "Peace be with you", were his first words.

Then he showed us his hands and uncovered his torso so that we could see the wound on his side. Everyone was speechless, paralyzed by surprise. I, too, remained in my place without moving, as if floating with joy. I wanted to go to Him and embrace Him, as I had done the night before, but I understood that my presence there should go unnoticed, just as it had during his public life. Now it was for you that he appeared resurrected; He did not need to convince or console me.

He then, to the everyone´s astonishment, repeated again:

> "Peace be with you. As the Father has sent me, even so I send you". Then, slowly, turning around until he had come full circle so that He could reach all of us, he blew gently. At the end He said, "Receive the Holy Spirit. Whose sins you forgive, their sins are forgiven; whose sins you retain, their sins are retained".

When he finished, I'm sure you remember, the shouting broke out. The shouting, the laughter, the hugs, everything was mixed up. You all surrounded Him and all of you, one after the other, embraced Him. You were the first, even before Peter, because you did not go through the stupor or doubt, since you had believed me, and you had believed Magdalene. When everything calmed down, He left you and looked for me. He knew I was there. Tired, I had sat and waited, quiet and happy, as I watched the spectacle of the disciples gathered around their Master. He came to me, lifted me up, embraced me at length and kissed my cheeks and forehead. This time I no longer cried. I was happy, endlessly happy. I was happy because He was there, in my arms, alive, resurrected. I was happy because you all believed in Him again. I was happy because his resurrection, I understood it too, represented what Nicodemus had begun to say: that He had conquered death, that the Father supported indisputably not only his message but his very person, his claim to divinity.

Then the days went by, time that He used to appear again to some and others, until He convinced the whole group that he was truly alive, that He was not a suggestion or a ghost. And also to remind you of the essence of his message, as well as the urgent need to live it and spread it.

As for the final farewell, you know that I was not with you when He ascended into heaven. At that time, you and I were again residing at Lazarus' house in Bethany. The evening before his Ascension into heaven, while I was quietly alone at home, I tried to do what I had done often times before, to gather myself in prayer and enjoy that spiritual communion with Him that was never broken, I noticed that his closeness intensified and, opening my eyes, I saw Him again by my side. He was smiling, although I knew at once that He had some bad news to tell me. "The time has come for me to leave, mother", He said, "But do not be sad, we will see each other again soon. I would like to take you with me at once, but you have a mission to accomplish and for now you are still needed here on Earth".

I nodded, silently, because it never crossed my mind to discuss his plans, but I could not avoid a sharp pain in my motherly heart. He was leaving for good and those visits were over and, perhaps also, that intimate feeling that allowed me to almost touch Him inside me. The feeling of orphanhood and abandonment suddenly enveloped me, and I was almost on the verge of bursting into tears.

As He read my thoughts as well as my eyes, He took my hands and, smiling, assured me that this would be a short separation and that, in any case, it would never be complete. "I will always be by your side and you will know that this is so", He said, "and this, dear mother, not only because you need it, but because I need it too. I need to be with you, just as I need to be with my apostles. The love I have for you has made me weak and needy. This is precisely a part of your mission, to make them understand that love is not only about receiving, but also about giving. And that the Almighty God who sustains and supports is also a weak God, a God with the heart of a man, who needs to receive the affection of those whom he loves so much. Do you think that these and those who believe through them will ever understand that I am not just an idea or a message, that I am a person and that I cannot be treated as a thing that neither feels nor suffers? Mother, how difficult it is going to be for them to understand this. However, that is the key to everything, because if they only receive or seek me in order to receive, they will not value enough what they have, because in reality you only truly love that which costs you little, that which, in some way, is your own work".

That said, we embraced even longer than usual. Unable to help it, tears began to slip, meekly, from my eyes and, like at other times, my son wiped them away with a fold of his robe as He kissed me tenderly. Then

He stood before me and asked me to bless Him. Not even to that, which I found absurd, did I refuse. But I immediately knelt down before Him and, kissing his hands and looking into his eyes, I said to him: "My son and my God, bless me now, for I have been your disciple during these years, for I have learned more from you than you could have learned from me". Always smiling, He placed his hands on me and prayed silently; then He made the sign of the cross on my forehead and, as He lifted me up, He said to me: "Again I tell to you, Mother, what I told you in this very house when I went to Jerusalem to suffer and die. Fear nothing. Never doubt the love of God and never cease to transmit this certainty to others. Whatever happens and however far away you may think the Father, the Holy Spirit or even I myself may seem to be, I assure you that we are at your side, just as we are at the side of every man". We gave each other a last embrace, shorter this time, and, detaching Himself from me, He left as he had come, in the silence and in the night.

I don't need to tell you much more, dear John, for you know all about what happened to me from then on. You have not abandoned me a single day since then. He, before everyone, had again insisted that you take care of me and introduced me to everyone as your mother. I have not ceased, from that moment on, to receive affection and appreciation, even when things were not going well among you and you were at odds with each other over the question of the rites of our ancient religion and the admission of the gentiles.

That has been precisely my mission since then: to try to unite you. It was not difficult for me while we were in Jerusalem, all of us together. But when Stephen was killed four years after his resurrection, and you took me out of the city to protect me, I have had a harder time. That was ten years ago. Now, that extraordinary boy, Paul, who competes with you and Peter in your love for me, is beginning to open new paths for my son's message. I can only rejoice at the news that reaches us from one side or the other, although there is also pain in some of them, such as those that speak of threats and persecutions, especially in our beloved homeland.

But my greatest concerns are for the family, for the unity within this family of which I am the mother, who has children who do not always agree among themselves.

That is why, John, I also want to leave you a will, as my son did shortly before He died, after that last supper with you. I don't know when my time will come, but I sense it is near, although I have the strange feeling that my son wants to take me with Him, all of me. But, anyway, don't pay too much attention to me because I myself only sense things, without fully understanding them, as I did in the beginning. Besides, it seems to me that I am keeping you too much by my side and that you too are burning with the desire to travel, to bring the good news that God is love to all the ends of the earth. That you have to be here, to take care of me, is perhaps too much of a luxury. For this reason, and because I am eager to be with my son and my God forever, I ask the Almighty to hasten the hour of my departure and I believe that my prayers will soon be answered.

This is my will, John. Sit down and write, my son:

"To all my son's brothers, peace.

I am about to end my time on Earth. My time on Earth is about to end, and I do not want to go without saying goodbye to you and without giving you, as your mother, my last words of advice.

The first of them is that you should never forget that God exists, that God is love and that it was He who loved us first. Whatever happens, in your personal life, in the lives of your loved ones, in the world around us, never stop believing in God's love. I have noticed that some of you, influenced by this Greek and Roman world so rich in speculation and so fond of wisdom, are forgetting that faith, that faith which our elders possessed and of which my son spoke to you about, is not just an intellectual matter, as if it were about accepting ideas. Faith is that and much more. Faith is believing in God's love and believing it when things do not turn out as you expected and even as you had asked God for therm to turn out. Have this faith. And may hope be born in you from it continually. Without hope you will not be able to survive the anguish of the present.

Without the hope that there is something more after death and that my son has opened for us the gates of paradise, you will not be able to persevere in the trials because your horizon will be very narrow and death will seem like it is your end and your limit.

But I do not only want to recommend faith and hope. I also want to speak to you about love. I have noticed that, more and more often, you dispute among yourselves over concepts or disquisitions over some of my son´s words and their meaning. I want to tell you how much this saddens me and how much it saddens Him. I assure you that the best of all is love and that what is less perfect in unity is worth more than the most perfect in disunity. He Himself expressed it in this way when, shortly before his death, He asked the Father for the extraordinary grace of unity for you, a unity similar to that which the Father. He and the Spirit already possess in heaven.

If you are not united, you will not survive. You will tear each other apart and everything will become a valid excuse to hurt each other. In the end, the same doctrinal issues will be used as justification to spread personal differences, execute grudges and carry out revenge. I am an old woman and I know enough about the heart of man and the strength of the Evil One to know what I am saying. That is why I warn you, with a troubled heart: remain united. Unity, which is only possible by loving the other for who they are and not as who we would like them to be, is and will always be the best fortress in which you will withstand all the attacks of the enemy. Unity will also be the main attraction for others to come and participate in our life. How can you convince anyone that God is good if you are at odds with each other? How can you preach love if you are quarreling among yourselves? The example of unity that you give will be attractive in itself and people will come to you because they will see you and say, "See how they love each other".

But this is not all I have to tell you. I have been the mother of a man, not the mother of an idea, however valuable it may be. The son I carried in my womb was, is, because He is alive, God, true God as true God is the Father and true God is the Spirit. But my son was, I assure you, a true man. And this I have to tell you precisely because I was his mother. As a man, he was cold, hungry, in pain and in joy. As a man, not only could He help, which He did, but He also needed help. My son, who is God, is your strength. But at the same time, my son, who is a human being, needs you, He is not indifferent to your affection, your sin, your scorn. It is precisely because of how much He loves you that you have the chance to make Him happy or to make Him suffer. Perhaps not all of you understand this, but those who love or have loved will understand it. You will not be able to understand my Son, nor God Himself, if you do not know what love is.

I myself have taken a long time to understand all this that I am telling you. It has not been easy for me to get the idea that that little child that I cradled in my arms and saved from death at the hands of Herod, was the son of Almighty God. But it is so, and that is the mystery, which is not a mystery that can be fully understood with the mind, but which is much clearer when contemplated with the heart. Because the most important thing that my son has come to teach us is that God is love and that, out of love for mankind, especially sinners, he became man and accepted to die on a cross as a criminal.

I also want to talk to you about the value of pain. I have suffered a lot, even though I have done it in silence most of the time and without you noticing it. And I tell you that suffering is redemptive. It is not that God enjoys our suffering, as if He were a cruel being, one of those gods of the Greeks or the Romans. God enjoys our happiness. But, and that is another mystery, suffering not only purifies us but, in a way that is sometimes incomprehensible, there is a communion of men that makes it possible for some to help others by offering to accept their problems and sorrows, just as my son saved us all by offering Himself as a sacrifice on the cross.

But pain does not come only from sickness, hunger or economic problems. The main pain is that caused by sin, because the greatest good is God and through sin we deprive ourselves of being in communion with him. That is why conversion and penance are necessary, to put our house in order so that the disorder introduced by sin may disappear and God can live again, at ease, in our house which is his.

Pain also sometimes comes from living together. I want to say something about this, which I have meditated a lot on. On a certain occasion, my son said that his mother and his brothers are the ones who listen to the word of God and keep it. And at another time He told you that where there are two or three united in his name, He would always be there in the midst of them. I believe that this means that, in some way, the motherhood that I have possessed can be yours, if you wish. For that, it is necessary that the will of the Father be fulfilled, that is, that we live according to his commandments. And it is also necessary to be united with the other brothers, in his name, with reciprocal love, as He asked. Notice what a great gift is placed within your reach: that of being the mother of Jesus, the mother of God himself. And it is enough to love and to love the one who is by your side. Therefore, I exhort you to forget all quarrels and all resentment. Notice what a treasure you are losing through divisions, for He will never be in a group in which love is not the bond that unites everything. Perhaps you think that it is worth fighting for this or that idea, but it is possible that in that fight you may lose charity and unity, and, with it, you may lose the presence of my son, who is your Lord and your brother, but who also offers himself to be your son.

I think that is why He insisted so much that all of us, myself included, have a clear point of reference, which is Peter, who presides over us in love, even if there are others who are more intelligent than him, who preach better or who get more disciples. It is around Peter where we have to be united, otherwise, if one center disappears, thousands will appear, and each one will want to have the last word on anything and the inevitable consequence will be division, loss of unity, the absence of my son in a family that is in conflict.

Finally, never forget those words that Jesus once said to you: "Come, you blessed of my Father, for I was hungry and you gave me food, I was thirsty and you gave me drink, I was naked and you clothed me, I was in prison and you came to see me. What you have done to the least of these, you have done to me". Never forget this, for two reasons. First, because if you do not love you will not be loved, that is, you will not be able to enter the kingdom of heaven, which is reserved for those who love. And also, do not forget, because there, in everyone who suffers, is my son waiting for your love.

I am very concerned that you understand this well, for being close to departure, I realize that I am going to leave my son without a mother. Do not think that I have gone mad. It is just that during these years, since He ascended to heaven, I have noticed that He was here, on Earth, in addition of being in the divine Eucharist, in all those who need help. And now that I already feel his voice calling me from above and calling me to his side, I am afraid to go and leave Him, having a hard time and without a mother. I will be with Him there, but I will not be with Him on earth, even if I never cease to watch over the one who's here from heaven. In every weeping man is my son, nailed to the cross as he was on that terrible Friday. And I would like you to not forget Him, especially those of you who say you love me, because if you want do something for me, I would ask you to do it for this son of mine who is crucified. If you love me, let me take your place so that I, through you, may continue to be at the side of my suffering son. If you love Him, come to help Him, to assist him, and not only to dedicate beautiful prayers to Him, although praying is a way of loving Him that he also needs very much.

I have nothing more to tell you. This is my testament. My departure, I sense, is near. I assure you that I will continue to watch over you from heaven, together with my son, as I have done up until now since he went away and left me in your care. I repeat, if you want to please me in any way, remain united, around Peter, around my son, around the Father and the Spirit, and treat those who suffer as I treated Jesus when he needed me. Do not forget that He, who sustains you because He is God, also needs you, because He is man. He is a heart which is in love that needs to receive love because He only knows how to give love".

Epilogue

Here, ends the chapter, a little abruptly, of the *Itinerarium* of Egeria, as it was discovered among the files coming from the monastery of Obona. It has been transcribed in its entirety and it is now the task of specialists to discuss whether it is an apocryphal written in the Middle Ages or even later, or whether there is a possibility that it belongs to the work collected by the Spanish nun on her pilgrimage to the Holy Land.

In any case, and in my opinion, I believe that the fears of the monks who tore these pages out of the original book were unfounded. The image that emerges of Mary, the mother of the Lord, is perhaps not only the typical one to which we are accustomed —that of an intercessor— but it is not irreverent either. In this dialogue with St. John, who always remains silent, like that Friar Leo who took notes of what St. Francis said, she shows herself above all as a "mother" and as a mother who knew how to fulfill her duty of supporting her son and not to use her son. Perhaps it is surprising that she recounts so few miracles; it is possible that many more came from her hands and her intercession, but perhaps she did not consider it opportune to dwell on them so as not to distract the future reader from the essential. And the essential thing is that, for Mary, Christ will always be God as well as man. He will always be the one who gives everything, as well as the one who needs to receive something. This evokes her last words, those of her testament, perhaps the source of those others that St. John gathers in his letters: God is love, God loved us first but, for this reason, God needs to receive and is waiting, like a heart in love, for those whom He loves so much to decide to return part of how much He has received. In this age of ours, plagued by ideologies and theorizations, perhaps it would be useful and urgent to meditate on these concepts. God is not an idea, not an entity of reason, a fruit of our thinking. God is a living being, with an ardent and loving heart. We can do something for God, and we must do something for God: to love Love, to love God who is Love. For, in the things of men as in the things of God, "Love is repaid with love". The fact that God loved us first does not mean that this is all there is to it. God loved us first and thus He set in motion a revolution, a history, a movement: that of love. God loved us first and is now waiting for us, in response, to love Him, as we love, out of love for Him, that "crucified Christ" who is alive, beside us, perhaps in our own home. And all this within the consummate unity, around the Pope, to make it clear that he who does not gather with Christ, scatters.

Final remark

As the reader will no doubt have guessed, the content of this book is a literary composition, even though it draws from the sources of the tradition of the Church and is in harmony with the official Magisterium. The author has tried with perhaps excessive boldness to get into the skin of the character, in this case the Blessed Virgin, to try to express what she must have felt and how hard it must have been for her to love in the difficult journeys that God asked her to go through. In any case, the result —the author is also aware of this— is only approximate; if it is difficult to know what another person thinks, experiences or suffers, the mystery becomes unfathomable when we are dealing, no less, with the Immaculate Mary, the one who was conceived without sin and who never knew of the stain that disturbs us both in the soul and in the body. If the reading of this story has helped us to know Mary better, to love her more and to imitate her better, all those who have worked on this book are satisfied and highly rewarded. If not, as in ancient theatrical performances, we beg the reader's forgiveness and indulgence.

Completed in Madrid on June 14, 1996,
solemnity of the Sacred Heart of Jesus,
eve of the Immaculate Heart of Mary.